Black Authors and Illustrators of Books for Children and Young Adults

THIRD EDITION

A Biographical Dictionary

BY

BARBARA THRASH MURPHY

FOREWORD BY

E.J. JOSEY

GARLAND PUBLISHING, INC.
A member of the Taylor & Francis Group
New York and London
1999

Library of Congress Cataloging-in-Publication Data

Black authors and illustrators of books for children and young adults :
a biographical dictionary / by Barbara Thrash Murphy.
     p.   cm. — (Garland reference library of the humanities ; v. 2157)
    Rev. ed. of: Black authors and illustrators of children's books / Barbara
Rollock. 2nd ed. 1992.
    Includes bibliographical references (p.   ) and index.
    ISBN 0-8153-2004-3 (case : alk. paper)
    1. Children's literature—Black authors—Biography—Dictionaries.   2. Chil-
dren's literature—Bio-bibliography—Dictionaries.   3. Children's literature,
American—Afro-American authors—Biography—Dictionaries.   4. Children's
literature, American—Illustrations—Bio-bibliography—Dictionaries.   5. Afro-
American authors—Biography—Dictionaries.   6. Afro-American artists—Biography—
Dictionaries.   7. Authors, Black—Biography—Dictionaries.   8. Artists, Black—
Biography—Dictionaries.   9. Illustrators—Biography—Dictionaries.   10. Blacks
in literature—Bibliography.   I. Murphy, Barbara Thrash.   II. Rollock, Barbara.
Black authors and illustrators of children's books. III. Series.
Z1037.R63   1999
[PN1009.A1]
809'.89282'08996—dc21
[B]   98-42690
                                                CIP

Cover art: *Cane Carrier*, 1996. Oil on canvas, 9" x 12". Jonathan Green,
    Naples, Florida
Cover design: Karin Badger
Book design: Karin Badger, with very special thanks to Jennifer Brosious

Dedicated to my Mother,

Katharyn Thrash,

who inspired me in so many ways

by her example,

and

to the memory of my Father,

Andrew Thrash,

and my daughter

Donna Katharyn Murphy

1960–1976

Contents

Acknowledgments

BARBARA THRASH MURPHY

This book would not have been possible without the generous contributions and support of my brother Andrew Thrash. I thank him for providing the technical equipment, hardware, software, and training needed to prepare this manuscript. I am thankful for the advice, suggestions, and assistance of my brother Paul Thrash, who lent his professional experience to support this work. Most especially, I am indebted to my daughter Deborah Murphy, an avid reader, who constantly asked, "How can I help?" I am grateful for the encouragement of my sons, James and Paul Murphy, my grandson Raymon Givner, Mary Hicks, Jean Thrash, Joseph James, and Alan and Beverly James, who kept me motivated.

I have received assistance from a variety of people and organizations. Among them, recognition is given to University of Pittsburgh librarian Pearl Woolridge and library assistant Ann Kenderson for sharing their knowledge of African American literary resources and in particular to librarian Ammon Ripple for making me aware of, and making available, pertinent research materials and bibliographical software that greatly aided my research. At the onset of this project, Amy Kellman, coordinator of children's services at Carnegie Library of Pittsburgh, graciously let me examine publisher catalogs and review books. My thanks to librarian Andrea L. Jones. Appreciation is extended to librarians Lydia Scott, Janet Green, and Joyce Broadus, also of the Carnegie Library, who permitted me to join the Black Books Committee, which reviewed and evaluated new titles. They, too, identified Black authors not known to me.

My sincere appreciation to Ann Johnson of Open Hand Publishing, Cheryl Willis Hudson and Wade Hudson of Just Us Books, Toni Trent Parker of BLACK BOOKS GALORE!, a children's book service, and illustrator Cheryl Hanna for their interest and for sharing information about the Black literary community. Review books and literature were sent by Lerner Publications, Clarion Books, Boyds Mills Press and Ingram Distributing Company. A sincere thank you must be given to the many publishing houses that forwarded my questionnaires to their authors and illustrators.

My appreciation for the support of Arnold Rose and Doris Mace, who solved many computer problems. Teresa Y. Neely did an extraordinary job of editing and aiding with the research.

To the many talented artists and writers whose bio-bibliographies make up this volume, for taking the time to respond to my requests for information, phone calls, and inquiries to check for accuracy, I am deeply indebted.

I must mention Eunice Washington, with special thanks, for enduring many early morning phone calls with courtesy and caring. Thank you to Joan and Jay Anderson, Dorothea Richardson, Maxine Jackson, Louise Stewart, Bettye Bell, Mayme Bailey, The Pittsburgh Chapter of The Pierians, and all of my friends, who expressed their interest in this work with many inquiries about its progress . . . then patiently listened while I told them!

Last because it is most important, I gratefully acknowledge the ever present support of my mother, a prolific and skillful author, who listened, sympathized (when needed), offered advice, and encouraged me from the inception to the completion of this book.

PHOTOGRAPH CREDITS

Opal Palmer Adisa: *Kathy Sloane*; Herb Boyd: *Christopher Griffith*; Ashley Bryan: *Susan Valdina*; Jeannette Caines: *Al Certa*; Gail Gordon Carter: *Linda Dalal Sawaya*; Afua Cooper: *James Hodgins*; Donald Crews: *Nina Crews*; Alice Faye Duncan: *Morgan Murrell*; James Forman: *B. Cotell*; Chester D. Freeman: *Dale Duchesne*; Marilyn Kaye Fullen-Collins: *Courtesy of Open Hand Publishing*; Nikki Giovanni: *Courtesy of Wm. Morrow*; Eloise Greenfield: *Monica Greenfield*; Lessie Jones Little: *David Jones*; Nikki Grimes: *Joelle Petit Adkins*; Mahji Hall: *Lloyd's Photography*; Virginia Hamilton: *Jimmy Byrge*; Cheryl Hanna: *Allen Einhorn/Modern Images*; Joyce Hansen: *Austin Hansen, photographer*; Regina Hanson: *Donn Bruns, ©1994 Perfect Image*; Philip S. Hart and Ayanna Hart: *Stanley H. Murray*; Vy Higginsen: *James J. Kriegmann*; Raymond Holbert: *Susan DeMersseman*; Joanne Hyppolite: *Joel Abueg*; Dolores Johnson: *Elizabeth King*; Lynn Joseph: *Ed Scott*; Richardo Keens-Douglas: *Courtesy of Annick Press*; Julius Lester: *Milan Sabatini*; Sharon Bell Mathis: *Marcia C. Bell*; Margaree King Mitchell: *Dixie Knight*; Sundaira Morninghouse: *Lloyd H. Wright, photographer*; Walter Dean Myers: *Ken Petretti*; Ifeoma Onyefulu: *Mamta Kapoor*; Gloria Jean Pinkney: *Myles Pinkney*; A.P. Porter: *Keri Pickett*; Faith Ringgold: *Hyperion*; S. Pearl Sharp: *Calvin R. Hicks*; Alex Simmons: *Monika Graff*; Eleanora E. Tate: *Zack E. Hamlett III*; Anika D. Thomas: *Courtesy of the Danville News*; Glennette Tilley Turner: *Lynard M. Jones*; Brenda Wilkinson: *Archie Hamilton*; Johnniece Marshall Wilson: *Thomas Victor*; Jacqueline Woodson: *A. Grace*; Sharon Wyeth: *Scott Walters*.

Introduction to the First Edition

BARBARA ROLLOCK
May 1987

Prior to the 1960s the names of few Black authors and illustrators of books for children were to be found in popular biographical sources or library reference books. Since then more names have appeared, with emphasis on the few who have achieved some prominence because of the volume of their published work or the awards they have received. Earlier citations featured only the same few well-known authors: James Weldon Johnson, Paul Laurence Dunbar, Langston Hughes, or Arna Bontemps. The fact that many more Blacks in the United States and elsewhere have made contributions to children's literature was overlooked. Their works can provide an integral study of the Black creative presence in children's books.

The books produced by those indigenous to a certain culture represent an important guide and resource in understanding the aspirations, thoughts, and viewpoints of that people. When books are neglected, both adults and children who need positive role models or awareness of a view other than the stereotypical one given by the media are deprived of a valuable insight into the true identity of a given group.

The biographical sketches included in this book of authors and illustrators are presented to acquaint all children with some creators of children's books. Their works have been published in the United States, they may live and work in this country, Africa, Canada, or Great Britain, and they happen to be Black. Bibliographies are provided that include a selection of the author's or illustrator's works and may list some out-of-print titles by contemporary authors—many of these books have had short publication lives even though they may have represented a significant breakthrough at the time of their appearance. The works of authors or illustrators now deceased are also included if they lived in the twentieth century, and particularly if their work has had some historical impact on the literature.

A few of the authors and illustrators in this book are listed even when they chose not to write on Black themes or on the Black experience. The criteria for selection do not exclude, for example, an illustrator like Donald Crews, whose graphic art form appeals to a general audience and is within the common everyday experience of all children. The only exclusions are those authors known primarily for adult books who have written only one book for children: James Baldwin's *Little Man, Little Man: A Story of Childhood* (Dial, 1977); Owen Dodson's *Boy at the Window* (Farrar, Straus, 1951; Reprint, 1972): Pearl Bailey's *Duey's Tale* (Harcourt, 1975); and Katherine Dunham's *Kasamance: A Fantasy* (Third Press, 1974) come to mind. Bill Cosby's cartoon-like books about Fat Albert are also omitted in spite of their popularity.

On the other hand, those whose publications have not been widely popular are included because the writer or illustrator had some great impact on children's literature. Works with original subject matter and quality literary style that have been issued by trade publishers have been preferred for selection. Edited works of interest to children and textbook materials are often cited, as well as books for older children or young adults.

Some may argue that this dictionary isolates rather than integrates talented authors and illustrators. The intention is to provide those ill-informed or curious about the subject with a single reference volume in which the works of Black authors and artists are recognized in relation to their particular contributions to children's literature.

The dictionary is arranged alphabetically by the author's and illustrator's surname. A selected bibliography appears at the end of each biographical sketch. Titles known to be out of print are followed by the abbreviation "o.p." Photographs of many of the artists are included. I hope that this dictionary will heighten awareness of and perhaps foster an appreciation for those authors and illustrators little known to child readers.

The biographical sketches reveal a range and depth of competencies, backgrounds, and experiences these people have brought to their children's books. A total of 115 sketches are included. Though many more have written or produced books for children in this century, the task of personally contacting authors and artists or finding adequate material about them has limited the scope of the dictionary. At this point, however, the names selected and listed represent those Black authors who have made or are making literary history in the world of children's books.

Introduction to the Second Edition

BARBARA ROLLOCK

June 1991

In the three years since the appearance of the first volume of *Black Authors and Illustrators of Children's Books,* publication of books for children has enjoyed a phenomenal boom. Along with the growing interest in children's literature has come a new emphasis on multicultural literature, and here books about African Americans and those of African descent have fared *almost* as well in publication since 1987 as they did in the 1970s. Significantly, they have involved more indigenous authors and illustrators.

In 1986 Walter Dean Myers spoke of the Black community's need "to reinvest value in education and, specifically, in reading skills." If the proliferation of publishers, such as Just Us Books and Black Butterfly Press, and the bookstores specializing in materials on African Americans is any indication, this community is on its way to awareness of its cultural needs and the means for initiating and disseminating this information.

In three years, too, three authors and two artists whom we recognized in the first edition for their contribution to children's books died: artist Romare Bearden and illustrator John Steptoe; authors Oliver Austin Kirkpatrick [John Canoe], Lorenz Graham, and Birago Diop, African writer and statesman. In this second volume, we have tried to include those who have brought something new to the field in the presentation of the culture. It is significant that this time also, people in pursuits other than writing for children have turned to creating for children. We acknowledge in the introduction to the first edition famous people who wrote only one or two books for children—performers Pearl Bailey and Bill Cosby, dancer Katherine Dunham, and writers James Baldwin and Owen Dodson. Among that group should have been listed TV newsman Bob Teague.

This year the author of note who is not included is Metropolitan Opera diva Leontyne Price, whose text for *Aida* is beautifully embellished by the art work of Leo and Diane Dillon. Actress Ruby Dee joins her husband among the authors that we have included in this volume. His plays are listed in the early volume. Her two books contain folktales.

We have tried to expand the scope of this edition with additional features: appendixes of publishers (a selection), bookstores and distributors, publishers' series, and award-winning books in the area of Black experience. More than a third of the biographical sketches have been updated and more than 35 new authors/illustrators have been added, bringing the list of creators of children's books in this area to over 150. A title index lists approximately 500 titles. No attempt has been made to identify out-of-print titles this time since, happily, many have come back in print.

Some authors live in the Caribbean, Africa, England, or France, and for this reason little information was available from some of them. They seem to be a peripatetic lot. Within the last three years, African authors Chinua Achebe, Buchi Emecheta, and Efua Sutherland either have been lecturing or teaching in American colleges or have been doing their research here in the United States. Their American counterparts are equally busy traveling between bicoastal homes, teaching assignments, or changing personal commitments, all of which alter any permanent residence or surroundings. For this reason we have to rely on information about their movements from the publishers who produce their books.

With the onset of the economic downturn of 1991, book budgets may suffer, but this no doubt will be more than offset by the thrust to supply children with books about their own and other cultures, and the impact of the publication of these books within the past few years will be felt into the future.

Introduction to the Third Edition

BARBARA THRASH MURPHY
January 1999

The parenting editor of *Essence* magazine, Joy Duckett Cain, gave me an opportunity to write a "Children's Book Guide" for Black History Month in 1994. During the course of that pursuit, I discovered *Black Authors and Illustrators of Children's Books* by the late Barbara Rollock, coordinator of children's services at the New York Public Library. Mrs. Rollock envisioned an important guide and resource to aid in understanding the aspirations, thoughts, and viewpoints of authors and illustrators indigenous to the Black culture. This was achieved in two editions. It is my hope to continue her efforts in this volume.

This third edition contains the 153 biographical sketches from the second edition with updated information for the majority, and 121 new authors and illustrators, expanding the listings to 274. More than 120 photographs have been added. Every effort was made to ensure the accuracy of the information by checking the data against a number of reputable reference sources. The expertise of the reference department at the Schomburg Center for Research in Black Culture, especially Sharon Howard, was extremely helpful.

The Wendell Wray Collection in the library at Chatham College in Pittsburgh, Pennsylvania, provided many facts and information necessary to complete some of the biographies.

More than one hundred fifty listees were contacted personally either as a new entry or to update a biography from the second edition. In this regard, artist/illustrator Cheryl Hanna was most helpful by putting me in touch with various people in the publishing genre which initiated a networking process that greatly facilitated locating many elusive individuals. Authors who are well known for their adult and scholarly works—such as Alice Walker, Langston Hughes, Augusta Baker, Paul

Laurence Dunbar, Nikki Giovanni, and historian Benjamin Quarles—are included with only their children's and young-adult book titles listed.

The designation of Black is used throughout the book to identify the ethnicity of not only African Americans but also of those entries who are from other countries throughout the world. Inclusive in the listings are authors and illustrators native to the Bahamas, the Caribbean Islands, the British Virgin Islands, Cameroon, Ethiopia, France, Grenada, Haiti, Indonesia, Jamaica, Nairobi, Nigeria, Panama, Senegal, Sierre Leone, Tanzania, Trinidad, Uganda and the Upper Volta. The individuals profiled in this work are identified by their full names (when available) with the parts they don't use professionally in parentheses—illustrator Cal Massey's name appears in his entry title as Massey, Cal(vin Levi). Individuals who use pseudonyms or pen names professionally are listed that way, with their given names in smaller print directly beneath.

Many new talents are also included, especially emerging young artists like thirteen-year-old illustrator Martin K. Riley, Jr., and author Anika Dawn Thomas, who wrote and illustrated her first published book at the age of thirteen. In quite a few instances, both talents are found in one person who conceives and creates those literary images that Black children can easily accept with alacrity.

The selection process for new entries involved mailing more than 1,287 questionnaires to 183 publishers of books of particular interest to Black children, asking that they forward them to these authors and illustrators and identify any additional names. Approximately 425 responses were received, but some were not African American authors and illustrators and therefore not included in this work.

The questionnaire requested birth year, place of birth, educational background, military service, occupations, inspirational influences, approach to writing and/or illustrating, achievements, awards, memberships, gallery and art exhibits, personal family information, a bibliography of published children's and young adult book titles and a photograph which formed the basis of each entry.

All of the author and illustrator book titles are not necessarily included in their bibliographies. The discretion of the authors and illustrators determined the appropriateness of the titles included. In most instances, the date of original publication is cited.

The bibliographies include titles that span the entire spectrum of literature for children and young adults to include picture books, humor, folk and fairy tales, animal stories, mysteries and adventure, science fiction and fantasy, historical fiction, poetry, drama, biography, and other nonfiction. These titles reflect the contributions of ancestral forefathers and foremothers to contemporary generations, linking past to present. With the proliferation of African American bookstores (a partial national registry can be found in Appendix 3), more books that symbolize the cultural heritage and the contemporary lifestyles that unite Black people can be selectively acquired.

Books by, about, and for African Americans have increased in number over the past decade. However, most literature for children continues to exclude the African American culture. It is important to continue to write and illustrate books of quality that express this heritage and have them available not only to Black readers but for the edification of all readers.

Foreword

E.J. JOSEY

Professor Emeritus, University of Pittsburgh
Past President, American Library Association

This new and enlarged edition of *Black Authors and Illustrators of Books for Children and Young Adults* is a tribute to the painstaking work of Dr. Barbara Thrash Murphy, who has not only updated entries from the second edition but has also added many new Black authors and illustrators. The biographical sketches of the authors and illustrators have, in most instances, been written by the writers and artists themselves. Of great reference value are the bibliographical listing of the works of these individuals; the index of the titles of their work; the listings of Black bookstores and of award-winning books. Above all, the book contains important biographical data on writers and illustrators that are invaluable for book reviewers and writers, as well as those whose task is to prepare background material for people who are engaged in research and preparing for radio and television talk shows and exhibits.

My Foreword is in itself a tribute to the genius of Barbara Rollock, whose dedication to library service to children was significant. It was her belief that "library service to children can be a viable part of the total library program, equal to the challenges of change with each new generation it encounters. . . . A community's future, a nation's future, are the children and young people, and we shortchange or ignore library service to them at our peril."

Concomitantly, Rollock was concerned about "the all-White world of children's books" that Dr. Nancy Larrick described in her 1965 article in the *Saturday Review*. It was Rollock's belief that these works did not provide positive images for Black children. The Larrick article heightened the awareness of editors and publishers, and they began to look for African American and other minority writers.

In 1969, a school librarian from New Jersey, Glyndon Flynt Greer, invited many of her American Library Association (ALA) colleagues, including Rollock and myself, to help her establish the Coretta Scott King Award to honor the work of African American authors and illustrators whose artistic and literary work portrayed the philosophy and ideals of Dr. Martin Luther King, Jr., as well as the Black experience in books for children and young people. The award is now one of the American Library Association's prestigious awards, and Rollock played a leading role in the coming-of-age of the ALA Coretta Scott King Task Force, which catapulted this award to a place that it now attracts 2,000 people to its award breakfast at the annual American Library Association conferences. I am delighted that I had the opportunity to work with Rollock on the Coretta Scott King Task Force of ALA. It was her work with the task force that made her painfully aware of the critical need for a reference tool such as *Black Authors and Illustrators of Children's Books*. The award and its establishment did four things: first, it encouraged more African American authors and illustrators to write and illustrate books; second, in itself it provided evidence that the book was significant and had merit in the minds of Black youngsters; third, it prompted more publishers to develop an interest in Black authors, illustrators, and their work; and fourth, it has led to a larger representation of Black authors and illustrators in American libraries.

Those librarians and bibliophiles who will be using this tome for reference and documentation will be pleased to note that among the writers included are librarians who are writers of books for children and young people. These librarian/writers are Joyce Arkhurst, Augusta Baker, Arna Bontemps, Elizabeth Fitzgerald Howard, Alice Faye Duncan, Sharon Bell Mathis, Sundaira Morninghouse (Carletta Wilson), Vaunda Micheaux Nelson, and Charlemae Rollins.

This work is international in scope for it has Black authors from around the world; thus, it constitutes a rich mine of literary talents from the diaspora. The international aspect of the work should remind us that literature is universal and that regardless of the culture one comes from or is immersed in there is a nugget of truth that applies to all cultures.

Black Authors and Illustrators of Books for Children and Young Adults is more than a reference tool. Not only will it stimulate the young and the old to explore and discover for themselves a great literature for children and young people written and illustrated by Black authors and illustrators, but the exploration of this work may inspire others to write and illustrate their own works, for books have the inexhaustible potential for enrichment of life and the human spirit.

Bibliographical Sources and References

FIRST EDITION

Adams, Russell L. *Great Negroes Past and Present.* Illustrated by Eugene P. Ross, Jr. Third Edition. Chicago: Afro-American, 1981.

Colby, Vineta, ed. *World Authors, 1975–1980.* New York: Wilson, 1985.

Dictionary of Literary Biography: Afro-American Fiction Writers After 1955. Detroit: Gale, 1984.

Evory, Ann, ed. *Contemporary Authors: A Bio-Bibliographical Guide.* Detroit: Gale, 1982.

Herbeck, Donald E., ed. *Caribbean Writers: A Bio-Bibliographical-Critical Encyclopedia.* Washington, D.C.: Three Continents, 1977.

Kingman, Lee, Grace Allen Hogarth, and Harriet Quimby, eds. *Illustrators of Children's Books, 1967–1976.* Boston: Horn Book, 1978.

Kirkpatrick, D.L., ed. *Twentieth-Century Children's Writers.* Preface by Naomi Lewis. Second Edition. New York: St. Martin's, 1983.

Klein, Leonard S., et al., eds. *Encyclopedia of World Literature in the Twentieth Century.* First Revised Edition. New York: Ungar, 1985.

Logan, Rayford U., and Michael R. Winston, eds. *Dictionary of American Negro Biography.* New York: Norton, 1982.

Matney, William C., ed. *Who's Who Among Black Americans.* Fourth Edition. Lake Forest Educational Communications, 1985.

Meltzer, Milton, ed. *The Black Americans: A History in Their Own Words, 1619–1983.* New York: Crowell, 1984.

O'Brien, John, ed. *Interviews with Black Writers.* New York: Liveright, 1973.

Preiss, Byron, ed. *The Art of Leo and Diane Dillon.* New York: Ballantine, 1981.

Rush, Theresa Gunnels, ed. *Black American Writers Past and Present.* Metuchen: Scarecrow, 1975.

Schockley, Ann Allen, and Sue P. Chandler, eds. *Living Black American Authors: A Biographical Directory.* New York: Bowker, 1973.

Ward, Martha, and Dorothy A. Marquardt, eds. *Authors of Books for Young People.* Supplement to the Second Edition. Metuchen: Scarecrow, 1979.

Zell, Hans M., et al., eds. *A New Reader's Guide to African Literature.* New York: Africana, 1983.

SECOND EDITION

Dance, Daryl C., ed. *Fifty Caribbean Writers: A Bio-Bibliographical Critical Sourcebook*. Westport: Greenwood, 1986.

Evans, Mari, ed. *Black Women Writers, 1950–1980: A Critical Evaluation*. Garden City: Anchor/Doubleday, 1984.

Lloyd, Iris, and William C. Matney, Jr., eds. *Who's Who Among Black Americans, 1990–1991*. Sixth Edition. Foreword by Donovan J. Heith. Detroit: Gale, 1990.

Metzger, Linda, sr. ed., et al. *Black Writers: A Selection of Sketches from Contemporary Authors*. Detroit: Gale, 1989.

Mwalima, I., and L.C. Mwadilifu, eds. *Who's Who in African Heritage Book Publishing, 1989–1990*. Second Edition. Chesapeake: ECA Associates, 1989.

New York Public Library. Office of Children's Services. *The Black Experience in Children's Literature*. New York: New York Public Library, 1989.

New York Public Library. Office of Young Adult Services. *Celebrating the Dream*. New York: New York Public Library, 1990.

Page, James A., comp. *Selected Black American, African and Caribbean Authors: A Bio-Bibliography*. Littleton: Libraries Unlimited, 1985.

Ploski, Harry A., and James Williams, comps. and eds. *The Negro Almanac: A Reference Work on the African American*. Fifth Edition. Detroit: Gale, 1989.

Vernoff, Edward, and Rima Shore. *The International Dictionary of Twentieth Century Biography*. New York: New American Library, 1987.

THIRD EDITION

Combs, Richard E., and Nancy R. Owens, eds. *Authors: Critical and Biographical References*. Metuchen, N.J.: Scarecrow, 1993.

Commire, Anne, et al., eds. *Yesterday's Authors of Books for Children: Facts and Pictures About Authors and Illustrators of Books for Young People, from Early Times to 1960*. Detroit: Gale, 1977–78.

Contemporary Black Biography. Volumes 1–15. Detroit: Gale, 1992.

Hawkins, Walter L. *African American Biographies: Profiles of 558 Current Men and Women*. Jefferson, N.C.: McFarland, 1992.

Herdeck, Donald E. *Caribbean Writers: A Bio-Bibliographical-Critical Encyclopedia*. Washington: Three Continents, 1979.

Hine, Darlene Clark, et al., eds. *Black Women in American History: the Twentieth Century*. Brooklyn, N.Y.: Carlson, 1990.

Hine, Darlene Clark, et al., eds. *Black Women in America: An Historical Encyclopedia*. Brooklyn, N.Y.: Carlson, 1993.

Kenyon, Olga. *Writing Women: Contemporary Women Novelists*. London; Concord, Mass.: Pluto Press, 1991.

Kutenplon, Deborah. *Young Adult Fiction by African American Writers, 1968–1993*. New York: Garland, 1996.

La Beau, Dennis, et al., eds. *Biographical Dictionaries Master Index*. Detroit: Gale, 1975.

La Beau, Dennis, ed. *Children's Authors and Illustrators: An Index to Biographical Dictionaries*. Detroit: Gale, 1976.

Loertscher, David V. *Biographical Index to Children's and Young Adult Authors and Illustrators*. Castle Rock, Co.: Willow Research and Publishing, 1992.

Malinowski, Sharon, ed. *Black Writers: A Selection of Sketches from Contemporary Authors*. Detroit: Gale, 1994.

New York Public Library. Office of Children's Services. *The Black Experience in Children's Books*. New York Public Library, 1994.

Newby, James Edward. *Black Authors: A Selected Annotated Bibliography*. New York: Garland, 1991.

Showalter, Elaine, et al., eds. *Modern Women Writers*. New York: Macmillan, 1993.

Silvey, Anita, ed. *Children's Books and Their Creators*. Boston: Houghton Mifflin, 1995.

Smith, Henrietta M. ed. *The Coretta Scott King Awards Book: From Vision to Reality*. Chicago: American Library Association, 1994.

Smith, Jessie Carney, ed. *Epic Lives: One Hundred Black Women Who Made a Difference*. Detroit: Visible Ink, 1993.

Smith, Jessie Carney, ed. *Notable Black Women*. Detroit: Gale, 1992.

Smith, Jessie Carney, ed. *Notable Black Women: Book II*. Detroit: Gale, 1996.

Smith, Valerie, et al., eds. *African American Writers*. New York; C. Scribner's Sons, 1991.

Stevenson, Rosemary M., comp. *Index to Afro-American Reference Resources*. New York: Greenwood, 1988.

Williams, Helen Elizabeth. *Books by African-American Authors and Illustrators for Children and Young Adults*. Chicago: American Library Association, 1991.

Black Authors and Illustrators
of Books for Children and Young Adults

Abdul, Raoul

(1929–)

AUTHOR

The author/musician was born in Cleveland, Ohio. He attended the Vienna Academy of Music and Dramatic Arts in Austria and pursued additional studies at Harvard University in 1966. In addition to performing lieder (songs) recitals in Austria, Germany, Hungary, and the United States, he was a frequent guest on radio and television and appeared in operatic roles in the United States. He has lectured widely in the United States at the Performing Arts Center in Washington, D.C., the Lincoln Center for the Performing Arts in New York City, the University of Connecticut, Howard University, and Columbia University.

His many awards include the Harold Jackson Memorial Award in 1968, the Distinguished Service Award from the National Association of Negro Musicians in 1978, and a key to the city of Cleveland in 1972. He founded the Coffee Concert Series in Harlem and has served on the faculty of the Harlem School of the Arts. He was secretary and editorial assistant to the late Langston Hughes and is the music critic for the *Amsterdam News* in New York City. Abdul lectures and teaches master classes in German Lieder and continues his twenty-year writing career at the *Amsterdam News* in New York City where he lives.

BIBLIOGRAPHY

The Magic of Black Poetry. Illustrated by Dane Burr. Dodd, 1972.
Famous Black Entertainers of Today. Dodd, 1974.

Achebe, Chinua
Albert Chinualumogu

(1930–)

AUTHOR

Achebe was born in Ogidi, Nigeria. Albert Chinualumoga are the first and middle names of the author which he dropped or shortened. Most of the English-speaking schoolchildren of Africa are familiar with the works of this Nigerian author, whose novels are often adapted for publication in secondary-school texts. Best known in the United States for *How the Leopard Got His Claws,* he combines folk tale themes and traditional African proverbs in his narratives, which provide glimpses of the cultural traditions unique to the Igbo people of Nigeria.

Achebe has held a variety of positions, including teacher, editor, and university professor, in both Nigeria and the United States. His publishing experience dates back to 1962 when he was founding editor of the Heinemann African Writers Series.

His awards include a Rockefeller fellowship in 1960, a Nigerian Merit Award in 1979 and honorary doctorates in literature from Dartmouth College in 1972, the University of Nigeria in 1981, and the University of Kent in 1982. He was made an honorary member of the American Academy and Institute of Arts and Letters in 1982.

Achebe has been the director of the Okike Arts Center, Nsukka, and he is the founder and publisher of *Uwa Ndi Igbo,* a bilingual journal of Igbo information and arts. Achebe has received twenty-six honorary doctorates from U.K., Nigeria, and the United States, including a D.Litt in 1996 from Harvard University.

He is a professor of Literature at Bard College in Annandale-on-Hudson, New York.

He is married and lives in Annandale, New York.

BIBLIOGRAPHY

Chike and the River. Cambridge, 1966.

How the Leopard Got His Claws. With John Iroaganachi. Illustrated by Per Christiansen. Third Press, 1973.

The Drum. Illustrated by Anne Nwokoye. Fourth Dimension, 1977.

The Flute. Fourth Dimension, 1977.

Adedjouma, Davida

(1956–)

AUTHOR

Adedjouma, an only child, was born in Chicago, Illinois. Through eighth grade she attended Howalton Day School, an all-Black private school on the city's South Side, then attended Francis W. Parker High School on the North Side, where her love of artistic expression continued to blossom. In 1974, she moved to St. Paul, Minnesota, to attend Macalester College and later the University of Minnesota.

Adedjouma has been publishing both fiction and creative nonfiction since 1985. Her commentaries, book reviews, and creative nonfiction have appeared in such publications as the *Minnesota Women's Press, City Pages,* and the *Journal of Justice.*

Her collection of short stories, *Last Summer,* won the 1987 Minnesota Voices Project Competition. Work from that collection has been anthologized in the United States and France and broadcast on National Public Radio. Her children's play, *Sweet Freedom: The Story of Harriet Tubman,* was produced at the Stepping Stone Theatre in February 1997.

Adedjouma teaches creative writing throughout the state of Minnesota as a rostered artist with the COMPAS Writers-in-the Schools Program, Stepping Stone Theatre, and at Hamline University in the Master of Fine Arts in Writing Program. While living in France from 1989 to 1991, she founded, directed, and produced a reading/jazz series at W.H. Smith Bookstore. She is also the owner of Creative Consultations, a writing/media relations agency that uses creative brainstorming as a tool for broadening awareness, appreciation, and celebration of cultural diversity, community empowerment, and artistic development.

Adedjouma has received numerous awards and fellowships, including a Bush Foundation Individual Artist Fellowship, two Dayton

Hudson, General Mills, and Jerome Foundation travel-and-study grants for extended research in France and Australia, a Minnesota State Arts Board career-opportunity grant, and the Loft's Minnesota Writers Career Initiative Award. In 1994, the *Minnesota Women's Press* chose Adedjouma as one of the state's outstanding women writers.

Her anthology of children's poetry, *The Palm of My Heart: Poetry by African American Children,* is the culmination of writing workshops she conducted with children age five through eleven at two community centers in Minnesota, and is an exploration of each child's definition of his or her own Blackness. Reviews of *The Palm of My Heart* appear in *Publishers Weekly* and the *Kirkus Reviews.* The book was named a 1997 Coretta Scott King Honor Book for illustration.

Adedjouma lives in Roseville, Minnesota.

BIBLIOGRAPHY

The Palm of My Heart: Poetry by African American Children. Illustrated by Gregory R. Christie. Lee & Low, 1996.
Sweet Freedom: The Story of Harriet Tubman (play). Stepping Stone Theatre, 1997.

See also Christie, Gregory R.

Adisa, Opal Palmer

(1954–)

AUTHOR

Adisa was born in Kingston, Jamaica, the second of two girls. What she remembers fondly, and attributes to her development as a writer, are the stories she heard as a child. Adisa wrote poetry as a young girl, and had her first poem published when she was thirteen-years-old student at Wolmer's High School for Girls in Jamaica. It was not until Adisa moved to New York City in 1970, where she attended Hunter College, that she seriously considered writing as a career and began to tell stories professionally. When she returned to Jamaica in 1976 with a bachelor's degree in communications from Hunter College, she worked at the Educational Broadcasting Corporation as an Education Officer/Director.

She has taught in numerous elementary and high schools, has anthologized more than thirty books of children's poetry, and is cofounder of Watoto Wa Kuumba, a children's theater group in Oakland, California. For her storytelling performances, she was named master folk artist in 1991–1992 by the California Arts Council. *Tamarind and Mango Women* won the 1992 PEN Oakland Josephine Miles Literary Award. In 1994 she taught playwriting and performance skills at Castlemont High School in Oakland, California, was poet-in-residence at Huckleberry House in San Francisco, California, and conducted poetry workshops at Brete Harte Middle School in Oakland, California.

She holds two master of arts degrees, in English and drama, from San Francisco State University and a doctorate in ethnic studies from the University of California, Berkeley. She is the chair of the Ethnic Studies/Cultural Diversity Program at California College of Arts and Crafts, where she is an associate professor.

Adisa lives in Oakland, California, and has three children.

BIBLIOGRAPHY

Pina, the Many-Eyed Fruit. Illustrated by Jimi Evans. Julian Richardson, 1985.

Bake-Face and Other Guava Stories. Kelsey Street, 1986.

traveling women. With Deborah Major. Jukebox, 1989.

Tamarind and Mango Women. Sister Vision, 1992.

Adrine-Robinson, Kenyette

(1951–)

AUTHOR

"I write because I have to. Something inside of me makes me respond to what I feel through my senses."

Adrine-Robinson was born in Cleveland, Ohio. After high school in 1969, she joined the Women's Army Corps, then attended Kent State University. She received a bachelor of arts degree in journalism-news-photography, with a minor in African American affairs, in 1976. In 1980, she earned a master of education degree in student personnel administration and in special education, and in 1985 she was awarded a master's degree in special education with an emphasis in developmental handicaps, learning disabilities, and behavior disorders. She began her professional career in 1986 teaching in the Cleveland city school system and in 1991 was a consultant at the Northeast Prerelease Center for Women in Cleveland. She is working on a new collection of poetry and is an associate professor and writer-in-residence at Kent State University.

Her professional memberships include the Poetry League of Greater Cleveland, International Black Writers and Artists, the Academy of American Poets, the Poetry Society of America, and the Verse Writers Guild of Ohio, and she is a past president and treasurer of the Urban Literary Arts Workshop in Cleveland.

Adrine-Robinson has one son, Jua, and lives in Euclid, Ohio.

BIBLIOGRAPHY

Be My Shoo-Gar. Edited by Adrine-Robinson. Kenyette Productions, 1988.

Black Image Makers. Illustrated by Ray Belanger. Edited by Adrine-Robinson. New Day, 1988.

Love Is a Child. Illustrated by Gayle Audrell Sanders. New Day, 1992.

Agard, John

(1930–)

AUTHOR

Agard—an actor, journalist, short-story writer, and poet—was born in Guyana, South America. He and his wife contributed to the art scene of Guyana, and his poetry has appeared in *Expression,* edited by Janice Lowe; *Plexus,* edited by R.C. McAndrew; and the *Sunday Chronicle.* Many of his short stories have been broadcast.

Besides works for adults, he has published five children's books. Agard lives in England.

BIBLIOGRAPHY

The Calypso Alphabet. Illustrated by Jennifer Bent. Holt, 1989.

Lend Me Your Wings. Illustrated by Adrienne Kennaway. Little, 1989.

Life Doesn't Frighten Me at All. Holt, 1990.

A Caribbean Dozen: Poems from Caribbean Poets. With Grace Nichols. Illustrated by Cathie Felstead. Candlewick, 1994.

No Hickory No Dickory No Dock: Caribbean Nursery Rhymes. With Grace Nichols. Illustrated by Cynthia Jabar. Candlewick, 1994.

See also Bent, Jennifer; Charles, Faustin O(lorun)

Arkhurst, Joyce (Cooper)

(1921–)

AUTHOR

"Spider stories (or Anansi *stories) are told up and down the coast of West Africa. They are told in many languages, but somehow the same plots occur. When I went to Liberia, I wanted to capture their wit, and I hoped to put them down in a form American children would enjoy. Also, I wanted to create another chance for these funny, wise stories to cross the ocean, as they had done centuries ago when Africans coming to the New World brought them here. Then they changed magically and became the* Anansi *stories of the Caribbean and the Br'er Rabbit tales of the American South. Now children can recognize this heritage of past and present and enjoy it all."*

Born in Seattle, Washington, Arkhurst graduated from the University of Washington and earned a master's degree from Columbia University's School of Library Service. She has worked as a children's librarian in the New York Public Library and as a school librarian in the New Lincoln School, New York City's public and private elementary schools. Arkhurst was a community coordinator in the Chicago, Illinois Public Library developing programs at the Children's Neighborhood Library Center during a two year stay in that city with her family.

As the wife of diplomat Frederick Arkhurst, former Ghana ambassador to the United Nations, she traveled to Ethiopia, France, Ghana, and Liberia, where she collected many folk tales. Although a retired librarian, she works with organizations on behalf of minority and women's issues.

Arkhurst lives in New York City with her husband. They have one adult daughter.

BIBLIOGRAPHY

The Adventures of Spider: West African Folk Tales. Illustrated by Jerry Pinkney. Little, Brown, 1964.

More Adventures of Spider. Illustrated by Jerry Pinkney. Scholastic, 1971.

Have You Seen a Comet? Children's Art and Writing from Around the World. John Day, 1971.

See also Pinkney, Jerry

Avery, Charles E.

(1938–)

AUTHOR, PHOTOGRAPHER

"My family has been first to inspire me in my pursuit of a career in writing and photography. Secondly, I would venture to say, inspiration came from the artist colony of all those brave civil-rights leaders who vigorously challenge the system. It is my opinion that literature for Black children should be directed at creating positive role models. We need to start to focus on a value system that is mentally and spiritually correct. I approach my photographic and writing work with a tremendous amount of vigorous energy, that energy being mental, physical, and spiritual. We need to teach children how to be proud and to respect one another."

Avery was born in Atlanta, Georgia. He served in the United States Army from 1956 to 1958 and has worked as a freelance photographer and writer.

Listed in the 1994 edition of *Who's Who in Black America,* Avery has published literary reviews in *Publishers Weekly, Elliot Bay Booknotes, Small Press,* and *Essence* magazine. Between 1973 and 1993, Avery's art show, titled *Camera and the City,* was exhibited in the Newark Museum. His art won second- and third-place awards in 1993 at a Chamber of Commerce exhibition in Plainfield, New Jersey.

He has new works in progress and is a full time artist.

Avery has two daughters and lives in Plainfield, New Jersey.

BIBLIOGRAPHY

Black Traces. Carlton Press, 1980.
Everybody Has Feelings. Open Hand, 1992.

Baker, Augusta (Braxston)

(1914–1998)

AUTHOR

"John Kennedy said, 'Children are the world's most valuable resource and its best hope for the future.' It is my hope that the public library will recognize this statement and will give its best service to the children and will support the librarians who are giving their best to tomorrow's library users."

These words identify Baker's principal interest. Well known for her storytelling skills, Baker, a librarian, was born in Sommerfield, Florida, and educated at the State University of New York in Albany, where she received her bachelor of arts and bachelor of science degrees in library science. She began her library career in the New York Public Library in 1937. While working as a children's librarian in the 135th Street branch, she began the James Weldon Johnson Memorial Collection of Children's Books About Negro Life and its accompanying bibliography. The bibliography was published in 1971 as *The Black Experience in Children's Books.*

Although she spent thirty-seven years in the New York Public Library as a librarian—rising to coordinator of children's services—Baker was also a popular lecturer and adjunct faculty member at Columbia University, Rutgers University, and the University of Southern Nevada, as well as a library consultant and organizer in Trinidad. Upon her retirement from the New York Public Library in 1980, she became storyteller-in-residence at the University of South Carolina in Columbia.

She has received many awards and honors, including the first Dutton-Macrae Award, in 1953, for advanced study in work with children; the Parents Magazine Medal in 1966 for outstanding service to the nation's children; the American Library Association's Grolier Award in 1968 for outstanding achievement in guiding and stimulating children's reading; the Clarence Day Award in 1974; a distinguished Alumni Award from the State University of New York at Albany in 1975; a Constance Lindsay Skinner Award in 1981 from the Women's National Book Association; and the Regina Medal in 1981 from the Catholic Library Association. She received an honorary doctorate in 1980 from St. John's University. Baker was retired from the School of Library Science at the University of South Carolina.

Every April, the University of South Carolina in Columbia observed "A Baker's Dozen," an occasion to celebrate storytelling and honor Augusta Baker at the same time.

Baker died in South Carolina in 1998.

BIBLIOGRAPHY

The Young Years: Anthology of Children's Literature. Edited by Augusta Baker. Parents, 1950.

The Talking Tree. Edited by Augusta Baker. Illustrated by Johannes Troyer. Lippincott, 1955.

The Golden Lynx. Lippincott, 1960.

Christmas Gif': An Anthology of Christmas Poems, Songs and Stories. Compiled with Charlemae Rollins. Follet, 1963. Morrow (Illustrated by Ashley Bryan), 1993.

The Black Experience in Children's Books. New York Public Library, 1971.

On Our Way: Poems of Pride and Love. With Lee B. Hopkins. Illustrated by David Parks. Knopf, 1974.

See also Bryan, Ashley; Johnson, James Weldon; Rollins, Charlemae (Hill); Hughes, (James) Langston

Barboza, Steven

(1952–)

AUTHOR

Barboza was born in New Bedford, Massachusetts, the fourth of eight sons. In the early years of the twentieth century, his maternal and paternal grandparents had immigrated to the United States from the Cape Verde Islands off West Africa. He was educated at Boston University, where he received a bachelor of arts degree in fine arts in 1976, and at the Columbia University Graduate School of Journalism, where he earned a master of science degree in journalism in 1979.

In 1986, he wrote an article for the *Washington Post* titled "Senegal's Gorée Island"; the following year, "Ivory Coast: West African Oasis" was published in the *Philadelphia Inquirer*. In 1988, Barboza wrote "Living for the Weekend," which appeared in *Essence* magazine. His articles have also appeared in the *New York Times, USA Today,* and *New York Newsday* newpapers and in *Emerge, American Visions, Essence,* and *Smithsonian* magazines. He has also written several chapters in a book series entitled African Americans: Voices of Triumph for Time-Life Books.

Barboza is married and lives in New York City.

BIBLIOGRAPHY

I Feel Like Dancing. Illustrated By Carolyn G. D'Amboise. Crown, 1992.
Door of No Return: The Legend of Gorée Island. Cobblehill, 1994.
The African American Book of Values. Doubleday, 1997.
Sugar Hill. Hyperion, 1998.

Barnett, Moneta

(1922–1976)

Barnett lived in Brooklyn, New York, and attended Cooper Union and the Brooklyn Museum Art School. The daughter of a tailor, Barnett illustrated many children's books. She was also a designer, a painter, and a photographer.

BIBLIOGRAPHY

Let's Go to Colonial Williamsburg. By Mary Jo Borreson. Putnam, 1962.

Time of Trial, Time of Hope: The Negro in America, 1919–1941. By Mitton Meltzer and August Meier. Doubleday, 1966.

A Mongo Homecoming. By Mary Elting and Robin McKown. M. Evans, 1969.

City Spreads Its Wings. By Lee B. Hopkins. Watts, 1970.

Fly Jimmy Fly! By Walter Dean Myers. Putnam, 1974.

Sister. By Eloise Greenfield. Crowell, 1974.

Me and Neesie. By Eloise Greenfield. Crowell, 1975.

My Brother Fine with Me. By Lucille Clifton. Holt, 1975.

Eliza's Daddy. By Ianthe Thomas. Harcourt, 1976.

First Pink Light. By Eloise Greenfield. Crowell, 1976.

See also Clifton, (Thelma) Lucille (Sayles); Greenfield, Eloise (Glynn Little); Myers, Walter Dean; Thomas, Ianthe

Battle-Lavert, Gwendolyn

(1 9 5 1-)

AUTHOR

Battle-Lavert was born in Paris, Texas, the first of four children. When she was a young child, storytelling, church, and music were important parts of family life. Battle-Lavert credits this training for her love of books and the motivation to become a writer.

While in elementary school and throughout her college years, she listened to stories as well as wrote them. She graduated from East Texas State University with a bachelor of elementary education degree in 1974 and earned a master's degree in reading in 1976. She taught elementary school for thirteen years, and for five years she was a reading/writing coordinator for the Texarkana Independent School District. Her interest in multicultural education has led her to conduct reading and writing workshops in schools throughout the country.

She is a member of the International Reading Association, the Society of Children's Book Writers and Illustrators, the Texas State Reading Association, and the Association for Supervision and Curriculum Developement.

A wife and mother of a son and a daughter, Battle-Lavert is a consultant for a publishing company. She lives in Texarkana, Texas.

BIBLIOGRAPHY

The Barber's Cutting Edge. Illustrated by Raymond Holbert. Children's Press, 1994.
Off to School. Illustrated by Gershom Griffith. Holiday House, 1995.

See also Griffith, Gershom; Holbert, Raymond

Bearden, Romare H(oward)

(1911–1988)

ILLUSTRATOR

Bearden was born in Charlotte, North Carolina, and grew up in New York City and Pittsburgh, Pennsylvania. The distinguished painter exhibited no interest in drawing until high school. He earned his bachelor's degree in mathematics at New York University and later studied at the Art Students League, New York City, under teacher George Grosz. Bearden went to Paris to continue to study painting and in the 1960s began his collages on Black themes. In 1977, the Museum of Modern Art in New York City held a major exhibition of his work.

He was art director of the Harlem Cultural Council and a co-founder with N. Lewis and Ernest Crichlow of Cinque Gallery in New York City for beginning Black artists.

BIBLIOGRAPHY

Six Black Masters of American Art. With Harry Brinton Henderson. Doubleday/Zenith, 1972.

Poems from Africa. Selected by Samuel Allen. Crowell, 1973.

A Visit to the Country. By Herschel Johnson. Harper, 1989.

I Live in Music. By Ntozake Shange. Stewart, Tabori & Chang, 1994.

The Block. By Langston Hughes. Selected by Lowery S. Sims. Viking, 1995.

See also Crichlow, Ernest; Johnson, Herschel (Lee); Hughes, (James) Langston.

Bennett, Lerone

(1928–)

AUTHOR

Bennett was born in Clarksdale, Mississippi, the son of Lerone Bennett Sr., and Alma Reed Bennett, and attended public school in Jackson. He graduated from Morehouse College in 1949 with a bachelor of arts degree and was awarded honorary doctorate of humane letters from Morehouse College in 1966, the University of Illinois in 1980, Lincoln College in 1980, Morgan State University in 1981 and Winston–Salem State University in 1989. He has received an honorary doctor of laws degree from Dillard University in 1980, an honorary doctor of humanities degree from Wilberforce University in 1977, and an honorary doctor of literature degree from Marquette University in 1979 and Tuskegee University in 1989.

Bennett started his career in journalism in 1949 as a reporter on the *Atlanta Daily World*. In 1952, he became the city editor of that newspaper. He became associate editor of *Jet* magazine in 1953; a year later, associate editor of *Ebony* magazine. He continued in that position through 1957, and in 1958 he became senior editor of *Ebony*. In 1987 he was named executive editor of *Ebony*, the position he still holds.

He was visiting professor of history at Northwestern University in 1968–1969 and senior fellow at the Institute of the Black World in 1969.

In addition to his honorary degrees, Bennett was honored by the Windy City Press Club for outstanding magazine writing in 1965 and received the Capitol Press Club's Journalism Achievement Award in 1963; the Patron Saints Award in 1964; the Society of Midland Authors Award for *What Manner of Man* in 1964; and the Literature Award of the American Academy of Arts and Letters in 1978.

Bennett serves on the boards of trustees at Morehouse College in Atlanta, Georgia and Columbia College in Chicago, Illinois, and is a board member of the Chicago Historical Society. He has also served on the National Advisory Commission on Civil Disorders, and he was a delegate to the Second World Festival of Black and African Art in Nigeria in 1977.

In 1978 he received the Literature Award from the American Academy of Arts and Letters; the Lifetime Achievement Award from the National Association of Black Journalists; and was honored as the 1991 Humanitarian of the Year by Amoco service station dealers and the Amoco Oil Company.

Bennett's books and short stories have been translated into French, German, Japanese, Swedish, Russian, and Arabic. He has traveled widely in Europe and Africa, and is on the Advisory Board of Who's Who among African Americans. He is executive editor of *Ebony* magazine and lives in Chicago, Illinois.

BIBLIOGRAPHY

What Manner of Man: A Biography of Martin Luther King, Jr. Johnson, 1964.

Before the Mayflower: A History of the Negro in America, 1619–1966. Revised Edition. Johnson, 1966.

Black Power, U.S.A.: The Human Side of Reconstruction, 1867–1877. Johnson, 1967.

Pioneers in Protest. Johnson, 1968.

Shaping of Black America. Johnson, 1975.

Wade in the Water. Johnson, 1979.

Great Moments in Black American History. Johnson, 1989.

Succeeding Against the Odds. With John Johnson. Warner, 1989. Amistad, 1993.

Bent, Jennifer

ILLUSTRATOR

Bent was encouraged by her schoolmaster to study bookkeeping, but she soon discovered that her abilities and certainly her preference lay in art. She is especially interested in portraying traditional Caribbean folklore themes, and her work reflects her Jamaican roots. Even though her parents returned to Jamaica, she decided to stay in England because she felt more at home there.

In 1985, she finished Harrow Art College in England with a degree in illustration. She worked as a freelance artist prior to her work in children's-book illustration. Her first book, *My Caribbean Home,* was published in England by Macdonalds and Company. She is, she has said, aware of a "lack of Black artists" and hopes to add to the small number who might be in the field, even though, in her words, "I've never really encountered much prejudice."

Bent lives in Watford, England.

BIBLIOGRAPHY

The Calypso Alphabet. By John Agard. Holt, 1989.
Tower to Heaven. By Ruby Dee. Holt, 1991.

See also Agard, John; Dee, Ruby (Ruby Ann Wallace)

Berry, James

(1 9 2 4 –)

AUTHOR

Berry has had a distinguished career as a poet and writer since leaving his coastal village birthplace in Jamaica, West Indies. He has lived in England for more than thirty years, involving himself in the social and cultural interests of the Black community.

His interest in multicultural education has led him to conduct writers' workshops in schools, and in 1977–1978 he was writer in residence at Vauxhall Manor Comprehensive School in London. His publications include poems, short stories, magazine articles, and anthologies that have appeared in the United States, England, and the Caribbean nations.

He was awarded a C. Day Lewis Fellowship in 1977–1978; *A Thief in the Village* . . . was named a Coretta Scott King Honor Book in 1989; and *Azeemah and His Son* won the Boston Globe-Horn Book Award for fiction in 1993.

BIBLIOGRAPHY

A Thief in the Village and Other Stories of Jamaica. Orchard, 1988.

Spiderman Anancy. Illustrated by Joseph Olubo. Holt, 1989.

When I Dance. Edited by Bonnie V. Ingber. Illustrated by Karen Barbour. Harcourt, 1991.

Ajeemah and His Son. HarperCollins, 1992.

The Future-Telling Lady. HarperCollins, 1993.

Classic Poems to Read Aloud. Illustrated by James Mayhew. Kingfisher, 1995.

Don't Leave an Elephant to Go and Chase a Bird. Illustrated By Ann Grifalconi. Simon & Schuster, 1996.

Rough Sketch Beginning. Illustrated by Robert Florczak. Harcourt, 1996.

Everywhere Faces Everywhere. Illustrated by Reynold Ruffins. Simon & Schuster, 1997.

See also Ruffins, Reynold

Bible, Charles

(1937–)

AUTHOR, ILLUSTRATOR

The artist was born in Waco, Texas, and attended San Francisco State College in 1966–1967, Pratt Institute in 1969–1970, and later Queens College of the City University of New York, where he earned his bachelor's degree in 1976. He has worked for various printing and publishing concerns and was art director for the Jamerson Printing Company in San Francisco from 1952 to 1954, holding the same position in San Mateo, California, at the Amistad Litho Company from 1963 to 1969. He has had exhibitions in universities, galleries, and museums in New York and California, including the New Muse Community Museum in Brooklyn, New York.

Bible served in the United States Navy from 1954 to 1956. His memberships include the National Conference of Artists, for which he was a regional director in 1975–1976; the College Art Association; the American Institute for Graphic Arts; the Council on Interracial Books for Children; and the Queens College of the City University of New York Veteran's Association.

BIBLIOGRAPHY

Black Means. . . . By Barney Grossman with Gladys Groom and the pupils of P.S. 150, the Bronx, New York. Hill & Wang, 1970.
Brooklyn Story. By Sharon Bell Mathis. Hill & Wang, 1970.
Spin a Soft Black Song: Poems for Children. By Nikki Giovanni. Hill & Wang, 1971.
Hamdaani: A Traditional Tale from Zanzibar. Holt, 1977.
Jennifer's New Chair. Holt, 1978.

See also Giovanni, Nikki (Yolanda Cornelia); Mathis, Sharon Bell

Blair, Culverson

(1947–)

ILLUSTRATOR

Blair was born in Austin, Texas, and graduated from the University of Texas with a bachelor of fine arts degree in advertising art. His career has taken him from freelance illustration and design consultation for the American Cancer Society, *Black Enterprise* magazine, *House and Garden, Men's Wear* magazine, the *Village Voice, Ms.* magazine, and New Jersey Bell to special projects with the Nestle Company, the Macmillan Company, and other various publishers.

In 1973–1974, Blair was a lecturer in art at the University of Illinois, Urbana-Champaign, where he taught basic graphic design and letter form. His work and illustrations have been published in many outstanding magazines, but his first work with children's books has been the Afro-Bets series.

Blair lives in Austin, Texas, and does freelance illustration.

BIBLIOGRAPHY

Afro-Bets 123 Book. By Cheryl Willis Hudson. Just Us Books, 1987.
Afro-Bets ABC Book. By Cheryl Willis Hudson. Just Us Books, 1987.
Afro-Bets: Book of Colors. By Margery Wheeler Brown. Just Us Books, 1991.
Afro-Bets: Book of Shapes. By Margery Wheeler Brown. Just Us Books, 1991.
Afro-Bets Kids: I'm Gonna Be! By Wade Hudson. Just Us Books, 1992.

See also Brown, Margery Wheeler; Hudson, Cheryl Willis; Hudson, Wade

Bolden, Tonya

(1959–)

AUTHOR

*"I think we need more fantasy, stories upon which our young can spin dreams
and stretch their imaginations. Also, our children need more stories about Black
children from other parts of the world. And with regard to books set in sub-
Saharan African nations, must the overwhelming majority of them be folk tales
or stories set in the village, long ago and far away? While this aspect of the
Black African history/culture is precious and must be passed on, without stories set in the cities, in contemporary times, young readers will have an un-
balanced flat concept of the Motherland. In the realm of nonfiction, I think
we need more books that do not merely give information, but which also challenge readers to think. This can be accomplished with writing that doesn't talk
down to the young, that includes concepts and language that might be a bit
difficult.*

In my work, I seek to teach and touch."

Bolden was born in New York City and grew up in East Harlem and
the Bronx, New York. She graduated magna cum laude from Princeton
University in 1981 with a bachelor of arts degree in Slavic languages and
literatures (majoring in Russian) and received a master of arts degree
in the same discipline from Columbia University in 1985, along with a
certificate of advanced studies of the Soviet Union. Before coming to
writing, she worked in the garment center in New York City and later
for the novelist and screenwriter James Goldman.

Bolden has written many literary reviews and other articles for
Essence, Black Enterprise, Small Press, the *New York Times Book Review,* and the 1989 and 1990 *Black Arts Annual,* among other periodicals. Since its inception in 1991, she has been the book columnist for
Young Sisters and Brothers magazine. Also, from the March 1994 issue

through the June 1995 issue, she served as editor of the *Quarterly Black Review of Books*.

In addition to her books for the young, Bolden has written several books for adults.

She lives in the Bronx, New York.

BIBLIOGRAPHY

Mama, I Want To Sing. With Vy Higginsen. Scholastic, 1992.

Rites of Passage: Stories About Growing Up by Black Writers from Around the World. Editor. Hyperion, 1994.

Just Family. Cobblehill, 1996.

And Not Afraid to Dare. Scholastic, 1998.

Through Loona's Door: A Tammy and Owen Adventure with Carter G. Woodson. Illustrated by Luther Knox. The Corporation for Cultural Literacy, 1997.

See also Higginsen, Vy

Bond, Higgins (Barbara)

(1 9 5 1 –)

ILLUSTRATOR

A native of Little Rock, Arkansas, Bond is the second of five children. She attended Phillips University in Enid, Oklahoma, and transferred to Memphis College of Arts in Tennessee, where she earned a bachelor of fine arts degree in advertising design. She has worked as a freelance illustrator designing books, magazine posters, and similar projects for such clients as the publisher Houghton Mifflin, RCA, NBC Television, *Essence* magazine, *Black Enterprise* magazine, Avon Books, and numerous advertising firms. Over a twenty-year career, she has designed collectors' plates and commercial posters, too.

Bond has also gained national exposure through her designs of three commemorative stamps for the United States Postal Service's Black Heritage Series of W.E.B. Du Bois, educator and author, inventor Jan Matzeliger, and chemist Percy L. Julian. At the unveiling in 1992, in Atlanta, Georgia, she received a standing ovation, and she considers this accomplishment one of her most gratifying projects. In 1979, she was awarded the CEBA Award of Merit for her work in *Black Enterprise* magazine.

Her poster designs for the Anheuser-Busch's Great Rulers of Africa Series, including pictures of a king of Mali (Mansa Kankan Mussi) and Queen Nefertiti of Egypt, were featured in the company's television commercial for *Roots: The Second Generation*. While Bond has painted other Black historical figures, she does not consider herself principally a Black artist. Rather, she sees herself simply as an illustrator trying to work as much as possible, preferring to paint nature scenes.

She and her husband have one son, Benjamin, and live in Teaneck, New Jersey.

BIBLIOGRAPHY

1999 Facts About Blacks. By Raymond M. Cohn. Beckham House, 1986.

Ancient Rome. By Daniel Cohen. Doubleday, 1992.

When I Was Little. By Toyomi Igus. Just Us Books, 1992.

Time for Sleep. By Claire Chapelle. Macmillan/McGraw-Hill, 1993.

Young Martin's Promise. By Walter Dean Myers. Steck-Vaughn, 1993.

Susie King Taylor: Destined to Be Free. By Denise M. Jordon. Just Us Books, 1994.

Thurgood Marshall: Supreme Court Justice. By Garnet Nelson Jackson. Modern Curriculum, 1994.

Toni Morrison: Author. By Garnet Nelson Jackson. Modern Curriculum, 1995.

See also Jackson, Garnet Nelson; Myers, Walter Dean

Bond, Jean Carey

AUTHOR

Born in New York City, Bond lived in Ghana in the 1960s. After graduating from Sarah Lawrence College, she worked for the National Association for the Advancement of colored People (NAACP) legal defense and education fund, among other organizations.

She was an editor and contributor to *Freedomways* magazine. Bond was also the Arts and Entertainment editor of the New York *Amsterdam News* and coordinator of the *Bulletin* of the Council on Interracial Books for Children.

BIBLIOGRAPHY

A Is for Africa. Watts, 1969.
Brown Is a Beautiful Color. Illustrated By Barbara Zuber. Watts, 1969.

Bontemps, Arna (Wendell)

(1902–1973)

AUTHOR

Bontemps is considered one of the initiators of the Harlem Renaissance movement of the 1920s and 1930s. He was born in Alexandria, Louisiana, but his family moved while he was still very young to the west coast, where he attended Los Angeles public schools. He studied at the University of Southern California and graduated with honors from Pacific Union College of California in 1923. He won the Crisis Magazine Prize in 1926, the Alexander Pushkin Prize in 1926–1927, and a Rosenwald fellowship and a Guggenheim fellowship for creative writing in 1949–1950.

His career spanned three decades. He was head librarian and publicity director at Fisk University, a member of the University of Illinois Chicago Circle Campus's Social Service Division in 1966, and served on the faculties of the University of Illinois and Yale University.

Bontemps was a close friend of Langston Hughes, his coeditor of the well-known anthology *Poetry of the Negro 1949–1970.*

BIBLIOGRAPHY

Golden Slippers. Illustrated by Henrietta Bruce Sharon. Harper, 1941.

The Story of George Washington Carver. Illustrated by Harper Johnson. Grosset, 1954.

100 Years of Negro Freedom. Dodd, 1961. Greenwood, 1980 (Revised Edition).

Lonesome Boy. Illustrated by Feliks Topolski. Houghton, 1955.

Frederick Douglass: Slave, Fighter, Freeman. Illustrated by Harper Johnson. Knopf, 1962.

American Negro Poetry. Edited by Arna Bontemps. Hill & Wang, 1963.

Hold Fast to Dreams: Poems Old and New. Selected by Arna Bontemps. Follett, 1969.

Mr. Kelso's Lion. Illustrated by Len Ebert. Lippincott, 1970.

See also Hughes, Langston (James)

Boyd, Candy (Marguerite) Dawson

(1 9 4 6 –)

AUTHOR

"I never wanted to be a writer of anything, except love letters to boyfriends or notes to friends. I loved to run my mouth. I spent more time writing, 'Marguerite Dawson will pay attention in class,' over and over again than learning. I daydreamed. I envisioned Black knights on black horses sweeping me up in their arms and taking me to paradise. I heard myself singing like the Divine Sarah Vaughn in a tight, pink, long satin dress in a crowded jazz club. Light-skinned, skinny, near-sighted, strange Black child that I was—I dreamed. Out of that tumultuous world came the stuff of stories."

Boyd was born in Chicago, Illinois. In the 1960s she worked with Dr. Martin Luther King, Jr. as a field staff worker for the Southern Christian Leadership Conference.

She earned her bachelor's degree at Northeastern and Illinois State Universities, her master's degree at the University of California, Berkeley, in 1978, and her doctorate in education at Berkeley in 1982. Among her awards is an honorable mention for *Circle of Gold* given by the Coretta Scott King Award Committee in 1985.

She is a professor in the School of Education at Saint Mary's College in Moraga, California. Boyd was honored in 1981 as the first tenured African American professor and received the school's first Professor of the Year award in 1991.

Boyd is a member of the national editorial board for *Scholastic* magazine and of the author team of the Macmillan/McGraw-Hill Middle School Reading/Language Arts Literature Program.

She lives in San Pablo, California.

BIBLIOGRAPHY

Circle of Gold. Illustrated by Charles Lilly. Scholastic, 1984.

Forever Friends (formerly *Breadsticks and Blessing Places*). Illustrated by Jerry Pinkney. Macmillan, 1985. Puffin, 1986.

Charlie Pippin. Illustrated by Cornelius Van Wright. Macmillan, 1987. Viking, 1988.

Chevrolet Saturdays. Illustrated by Todd Doney. Macmillan, 1993.

Fall Secrets. Illustrated by Jim Carroll. Puffin, 1994.

Daddy, Daddy, Be There. Illustrated by Floyd Cooper. Philomel, 1995.

A Different Beat. Illustrated by Dominick Finelle. Puffin, 1996.

See also Cooper, Floyd (Donald); Lilly, Charles; Pinkney, Jerry

Boyd, Herb

(1938–)

AUTHOR

Boyd was born in Birmingham, Alabama, and reared in Detroit, Michigan. His mother, a domestic worker, taught him to read before he attended school and introduced him to the world of literature.

His earliest inclination to write occurred when he was a teenager and began to cram notebooks with poetry, lyrics, limericks, and jokes. He graduated from Northwestern High School in 1956, worked in warehouses as a shipping and receiving clerk and stock boy, and spent two years in the United States Army. Except for an occasional article in the Army newspaper, Boyd continued to write but not for publication.

He entered Wayne State University (formerly Monteith College) in 1965 and graduated with a bachelor's degree in philosophy from Monteith College in 1969. In 1967, he was among the university's campus leaders who demanded courses in Black studies, and he joined other students and faculty in the development of the new program. His classroom scholarship as an undergraduate and graduate student in anthropology, his student activism, and his general maturity made him an ideal candidate to teach the experimental courses. Within two years he became a member of the founding team for the Center of Black Studies and for the next ten years he was an instructor of Black Studies at Wayne State University. Simultaneously with this tenure at Wayne State, there were several brief teaching stints at Oberlin College in Ohio, Marygrove College, and the Center for Creative Studies in Detroit.

During these years, Boyd's writing aspirations expanded, and his articles appeared regularly in the campus newspaper, the *Michigan Chronicle*, and several local community magazines. From 1970 to 1972, he was the Detroit correspondent for *Down Beat*, a jazz magazine, and the editor of several newsletters, and he subsequently was a freelancer for numerous periodicals, including *Black World,* the *Black Scholar, Crisis* magazine, *Emerge, Essence,* and *Black Enterprise.*

Boyd's byline appears frequently in the *Amsterdam News* and the *City Sun* newspapers in New York City, where he has lived since 1985, pursuing his writing career.

That same year, Boyd secured a teaching position in African American history at the College of New Rochelle, where he continues to teach.

BIBLIOGRAPHY

Roots: Students' Perspectives in Black History and Culture. Wayne State University Press, 1977.

Jazz Space Detroit. With Barbara Weinberg. Jazz Research Institute, 1980.

The Former Portuguese Colonies in Africa. Watts, 1981.

Who's Who in Detroit Jazz. With Leni Sinclair. Jazz Research Institute, 1984.

African History for Beginners. Writers & Readers, 1990.

Black Panthers for Beginners. Writers & Readers, 1995.

Down the Glory Road. Avon, 1995.

Brotherman: The Odyssey of Black Men in America–An Anthology. With Robert Allen. One World/Ballantine, 1995.

Encyclopedia of Black Intellectuals. Facts on File, 1996.

Martin Luther King, Jr.: A Biography. Waldman, 1996.

Brady, April

(1957-)

AUTHOR

Brady was born in Chicago, Illinois. As a child, she was extremely shy. This inability to connect with children forced her into reading and creating imaginary characters in stories. Her active imagination, and her need to escape, are what motivated her to write.

She studied journalism in high school while continuing to write. Her studies in college focused on art history and writing. Throughout her schooling, she was influenced by English teachers to pursue writing as a craft, using her experiences as an African American as the central focus. Brady pursued a career in the corporate environment, but it failed to satisfy her creative instincts. After fourteen years, she decided to use her writing skills to create children's stories. She writes stories to educate children and help them recognize the beauty of who they are and where they come from.

Her first book, *Kwanzaa Karamu*, covers the history of Kwanzaa, an African American holiday, and includes recipes from the African American culture, Africa, and the Caribbean. Recipes from *Kwanzaa Karamu* were included in the December/January 1995 issue of *American Visions* magazine.

Brady is single and lives in St. Louis Park, Minnesota.

BIBLIOGRAPHY

Kwanzaa Karamu: Cooking and Crafts for a Kwanzaa Feast. Illustrated by Barbara Knutson. Carolrhoda, 1994.
The Day Lizzy Felt the Ocean. Shamrock, 1996.

Brawley, Benjamin

(1882–1939)

AUTHOR

Brawley was born in Columbia, South Carolina, where his father, Edward McKnight Brawley, was pastor of a local Baptist church and a teacher at Benedict College. Benjamin Brawley attended schools in Nashville, Tennessee, and Petersburg, Virginia. He later attended Morehouse College, where he received his first bachelor's degree. In 1907, he received a second bachelor's degree, from the University of Chicago, and the following year a master's degree from Harvard University.

In 1913, he published *A Short History of the American Negro;* throughout 1916, he published books on English literature. His biography of poet Paul Laurence Dunbar is outstanding, and his book *A Social History of the American Negro* is still highly acclaimed. In 1927, he declined the Harmon Foundation's second-place award for excellence in education.

Brawley was married to Hilda Damaris Prowd; he died on February 1, 1939.

BIBLIOGRAPHY

Paul Laurence Dunbar: Poet of His People. University of North Carolina Press, 1936.
Negro Builders and Heroes. University of North Carolina Press, 1937, 1965.

See also Dunbar, Paul Laurence

Breinburg, Petronella

(1 9 3 7 –)

AUTHOR

Breinburg was born in Paramaribo, Suriname, South America. In 1965, she received a diploma in English from the City of London College. She attended Avery Mill Teachers College from 1969 to 1972 and Goldsmith College in London from 1972 to 1974. In Paramaribo, she taught school but was also a factory worker, a postal clerk, and a nurses' aide. She worked as a volunteer for the Red Cross and Girls' Life Brigade in Suriname, lectured in creative writing, and was an outdoor storyteller in London. For about two years, starting in 1972, she taught English part time.

Her memberships include the Royal Society of Health, the Greenwich Playwright Circle, and the Poetry Circle. In 1962, she received an award from the Royal Society of Health and in 1972 was given an Honorary Place Award from the Suriname Linguistic Bureau for her book *The Legend of Suriname.* Her picture book *My Brother Sean,* illustrated by Errol Lloyd, was a runner-up for the Library Association of London Kate Greenaway Medal in 1974.

BIBLIOGRAPHY

My Brother Sean. Illustrated by Errol Lloyd. Bodley Head, 1973.
Shawn Goes to School. Illustrated by Errol Lloyd. HarperCollins, 1974.
Tiger, Tinker and Me. Macmillan, 1974.
Doctor Shawn (formerly *Doctor Sean.* Bodley Head, 1973). Illustrated by Errol Lloyd. Harper/Collins, 1975.
Shawn's Red Bike. Illustrated by Errol Lloyd. Crowell, 1976.
Tiger, Paleface and Me. Macmillan, 1976.

Sally-Ann in the Snow. Bodley Head, 1977. Random House, 1989.
Sally-Ann's Skateboard. Bodley Head, 1979.

See also Lloyd, Errol

Brooks, Gwendolyn

(1917–)

AUTHOR

Pulitzer Prize–winner Gwendolyn Brooks was born in Topeka, Kansas, and began writing verses at the age of seven. Her inspiration comes from poets James Weldon Johnson and Langston Hughes, whom she met in Chicago, Illinois, where she spent all of her childhood. Her first poem, "Eventide," was published in *American Childhood,* a magazine for young people, when she was only thirteen years old. She started her own neighborhood newspaper and, by age seventeen, she was a regular contributor to the *Chicago Defender,* where more than seventy-five of her poems and other writings appeared in its "Lights and Shadows" column.

In 1943 and 1944, Brooks won first prize for poetry from the Mid-West Writers' Conference and again in August 1945 for her book of verse, *A Street in Bronzeville.* She won the Pulitzer Prize in 1950, the first Black to be so honored, for her second book, *Annie Allen,* and was named poet laureate of Illinois in 1968. She has lectured widely and taught at several colleges.

The poet became the twenty-ninth appointment as consultant in poetry to the Library of Congress in 1985. She is a member of the American Academy and Institute of Arts and Letters. She was presented the Lincoln Laureate Award in Springfield, Illinois, in 1997 and the Gwendolyn Brooks Park was dedicated to her in her birthplace city, Topeka, Kansas. Brooks recently celebrated her 80th birthday in Chicago, Illinois, where the city council approved a resolution to recognize the day. The occasion was called "Eighty Gifts," a reading tribute for each of her years. Brooks lives in Chicago, Illinois.

Brooks married the author of *Windy Place,* Henry Blakely, who died in 1996. She has two children, a son and a daughter.

BIBLIOGRAPHY

Bronzeville Boys and Girls. Illustrated by Ronni Solbert. HarperCollins, 1967.

Family Pictures. Broadside, 1970.

Aloneness. Broadside, 1971.

Report from Part One: An Autobiography. Broadside, 1972.

The Tiger Who Wore White Gloves. Illustrated by Timothy Jones. Third World, 1974.

Beckonings. Broadside, 1975.

Very Young Poets. Third World, 1991.

Winnie. Third World, 1991.

See also Hughes, Langston (James); Johnson, James Weldon

Brown, Kay

(1932–)

AUTHOR

"My book is geared for middle-group, pre-adolescents. This is a critical age (eleven, twelve, and thirteen), yet most books published are either for young children or older teenagers. Few books in this category speak to the particular problems of young people in this age category; even less for this group as it relates to African American children.

Specifically regarding Willy's Summer Dream, *I try to tell the narrative from his point of view of the world. The reader feels Willy's anguish and frustration at being labeled and the social isolation at being "different." Young people could identify with awkwardness and trauma of passing through such a period and would share the joy of Willy's small successes. It helps to point direction and offers hope."*

Brown was born and reared in New York City. She graduated from the City College of New York, receiving her bachelor of arts degree in 1968, and from Howard University in Washington, D.C., where she earned a master of fine arts. In 1968, Brown became a member of the Weusi Artists, and four years later she cofounded Where We At/Black Women Artists, serving as the organization's executive director for nine years. She is also a member of the Afro-American Writers Guild in Washington, D.C., and the National Conference of Artists, and has been a professor at Medgar Evers College in Brooklyn, New York. She is known primarily as an artist and printmaker. Her first novel for young adults *Willy's Summer Dream*, has received critical acclaim.

In 1983, Brown was awarded the Fanny Lou Hamer Award for Artistic Contribution to the Community in Brooklyn, New York. She has two children.

BIBLIOGRAPHY

Willy's Summer Dream. Gulliver/Harcourt, 1989.

Brown, Margery Wheeler

AUTHOR, ILLUSTRATOR

Brown was born in Durham, North Carolina, the third and youngest child. While she was still an infant, the family moved to Atlanta, Georgia, where she received her education. After graduating from Spelman College in 1932, she continued art studies at Ohio State University. Upon completion of her studies, she became an art instructor from 1943 to 1946 at Spelman College and later in the public schools of Durham, North Carolina, Atlanta, Georgia, and Newark, New Jersey, where she taught for twenty-six years, retiring in 1974.

Growing up in a family where heavy emphasis was placed on reading, Brown always had a great interest in books. As an inner-city teacher, she directed her interest in writing to subjects about and for inner-city children. For most of her books, she has been her own illustrator.

In 1936, she married Richard Earle Brown, now deceased, and they had one daughter, Janice.

Brown lives in East Orange, New Jersey.

BIBLIOGRAPHY

Old Crackfoot. By Gordon Allred. Astor-Honor, 1965.
Dori the Mallard. By Gordon Allred. Astor-Honor, 1968.
That Ruby. Reilly & Lee, 1969.
Animals Made by Me. Putnam, 1970.
I'm Glad I'm Me—Steve. By Elberta H. Stone. Putnam, 1971.
The Second Stone. Putnam, 1976.
Yesterday I Climbed a Mountain. Putnam, 1976.
No Jon, No Jon, No! Houghton, 1981.
Afro-Bets: Book of Colors. Illustrated by Culverson Blair. Just Us Books, 1991.

Afro-Bets: Book of Shapes. Illustrated by Culverson Blair. Just Us Books, 1991.
Baby Jesus, Like My Brother. Illustrated by George Ford. Just Us Books, 1995.

See also Blair, Culverson; Ford, George (Cephas)

Brown (Suggs), Virginia

(1924–)

AUTHOR

Brown spent most of her professional life as an elementary school teacher in the St. Louis public schools. She was supervisor of the Banneker Reading Clinic in the St. Louis, Missouri, public schools; an in-service teacher of remedial-reading techniques at Harris Teachers College in St. Louis; a television teacher of reading for adults; a consultant in the Reading Institute at the College of the Virgin Islands, St. Thomas and St. Croix; and executive editor of the Webster Division, McGraw-Hill Book Company, from which she retired in 1989.

Among other professional affiliations, Brown has been a member of the International Reading Association; the Association for Childhood Education, International; and the National Association for the Education of Young Children.

She received the 1966 National Council of Jewish Woman's Hannah G. Solomon Award for Outstanding Service to Young Children. Brown is a freelance author/editor/consultant for "Green Pages," a professional magazine for teachers. She was listed in the 4th edition of Who's Who in American Education in 1994–1995.

She is married to Charles F. Brown and lives in St. Louis, Missouri.

BIBLIOGRAPHY

Hidden Lookout. Skyline Series. Illustrated by Tom Lavelle. McGraw-Hill, 1965.

Watch Out for C. Skyline Series. Illustrated by Jack Smith and Tom Lavelle. McGraw-Hill, 1965.

Who Cares? Skyline Series. McGraw-Hill, 1965.

Out Jumped Abraham. Skyline Series. Illustrated by Don Kueker. McGraw-Hill, 1967.

Bryan, Ashley

(1 9 2 3 –)

AUTHOR, ILLUSTRATOR

"I cannot remember a time when I have not been drawing and painting. In elementary school, I began to make books. My first books, made in kindergarten, were illustrated ABC and counting books. At that time, the entire book production was in my hands. I was author, illustrator, binder, and distributor. These one-of-a-kind 'limited editions' drew rave reviews from family and friends and were given as gifts on all occasions. That feeling, for the handmade book, is at the heart of my bookmaking today, even though my original is now printed in the thousands. I grew up in New York City, in the Bronx, the second of six children. My parents sent all of the children to the free Works Progress Administration (WPA) art and music classes. We all drew and painted and learned to play an instrument."

After high school graduation, Bryan attended the Cooper Union art school. There he began a project illustrating African tales. He knew of the profound influence of African art on Western art and decided to use the abundant African art resources in New York City museums and libraries for this project.

Walk Together Children: Black American Spirituals was an American Library Association Notable Book in 1974, as was *Beat the Story-Drum, Pum Pum* in 1980. The latter also won the 1981 Coretta Scott King Award for the illustrations. Bryan has received Coretta Scott King Book Awards Honors for his writings and illustrations for *I'm Going to Sing: Black American Spirituals* in 1983, *Lion and the Ostrich Chicks and Other African Folk Tales* in 1987, *What a Morning! The Christmas Story in Black Spirituals* in 1988, and *All Night, All Day: A Child's First Book of African-American Spirituals* in 1992. In 1993, he was the first recipient of the Lee Bennett Hopkins Poetry Award, and he was chosen as the 1990 Arbuthnot Lecturer. At the Twenty-Seventh Annual Children's Book Festival in 1994, Bryan was awarded the University of Southern Mississippi Medallion, presented annually for outstanding contributions in the field of children's literature. He holds honorary doctorates from the Massachusetts College of Art, awarded in 1989, and Framingham State College, awarded in 1995.

Alvin Singleton composed a work from Bryan's collection of poems in *Sing to the Sun: Poems and Pictures* to be performed with chamber orchestra and with children's voices, with narration by Bryan. The piece was commissioned by a consortium of five major music festivals for the 1995–1996 season.

Bryan won a 1998 Coretta Scott King Honor Book Illustrator Award for *Ashley Bryan's ABC of African American Poetry*.

Bryan lives on a small island off the coast of Maine.

BIBLIOGRAPHY

Christmas Gif': An Anthology of Christmas Poems, Songs and Stories. Compiled by Charlemae Rollins and Augusta Baker. Follet, 1963; Morrow, 1993.

Moon, for What Do You Wait? Poems by Sir Rabindranath Tagore. Edited by Richard Lewis. Atheneum, 1967.

The Ox of the Wonderful Horns and Other African Folktales. Atheneum, 1971.

Walk Together Children: Black American Spirituals. Volume One. Atheneum, 1974.

The Adventures of Aku. Atheneum, 1976.

The Dancing Granny. Atheneum, 1977.

I Greet the Dawn: Poems by Paul Laurence Dunbar. Atheneum, 1978.

Jethro and the Jumbie. By Susan Cooper. Atheneum, 1979.

Jim Flying High. By Mari Evans. Doubleday, 1979.

Beat the Story-Drum, Pum-Pum. Atheneum, 1980.

I'm Going to Sing: Black American Spirituals. Volume Two. Atheneum, 1983.

The Cat's Purr. Atheneum, 1985.

Lion and the Ostrich Chicks and Other African Folk Tales. Atheneum, 1986.

What a Morning! The Christmas Story in Black Spirituals. Selected and edited by John Langstaff. McElderry, 1987.

Sh-ko and His Eight Wicked Brothers. Illustrations by Fumio Yoshimura. Atheneum, 1988.

Turtle Knows Your Name. Atheneum, 1989.

All Night, All Day: A Child's First Book of African-American Spirituals. Atheneum, 1991.

Climbing Jacob's Ladder: Heroes of the Bible in African American Spirituals. Selected and edited by John Langstaff. McElderry, 1991.

Sing to the Sun: Poems and Pictures. HarperCollins, 1992.

Story of Lightning and Thunder. Atheneum, 1993.

The Story of the Three Kingdoms. By Walter Dean Myers. HarperCollins, 1995.

What a Wonderful World. By George David Weiss and Bob Thiele. Atheneum, 1995.

The Sun Is So Quiet. By Nikki Giovanni. Holt, 1996.

Ashley Bryan's ABC of African American Poetry. Atheneum, 1997.

See also Baker, Augusta (Braxston); Evans, Mari; Giovanni, Nikki (Yolanda Cornelia); Myers, Walter Dean; Rollins, Charlemae (Hill)

Bryant, Michael

(1963–)

ILLUSTRATOR

Bryant was born in Newark, New Jersey, an unexpected twin. Drawing became his way of expressing himself. His mother was his greatest influence. Because of the encouragement of his family, after attending Clifford Scott High School, Bryant studied art and earned a bachelor's degree from Kean College in New Jersey and decided to pursue an art career. While in college, Bryant freelanced as a designer and layout artist. After college, he became an art director and illustrator for *Inview* magazine, a television guide.

In 1991, he won a Multicultural Mirror Competition, a fellowship given at the University of Wisconsin. In 1992, he signed a contract for his first picture book, *Our People,* and another soon followed for his second book, *Bein' with You This Way.* Both books have received widespread recognition and various awards, including the Jane Addams Peace Award, *Parenting* magazine's Reading Magic Award, the Parents Choice Award, and the Teacher's Choice Award. A review in the trade magazine *Publishers Weekly* describes Bryant as an "impressive accomplished artist."

Although he has studied the work of the masters, Bryant says his style has been mostly influenced by the American artists Norman Rockwell, Winslow Homer, and John Singer Sargent.

Bryant and his wife, Gina, live in Newark, New Jersey, with their two daughters.

BIBLIOGRAPHY

Family Celebrations. By Diane Patrick. Silver Moon, 1993
Bein' with You This Way. By W. Nikola-Lisa. Lee & Low, 1994.

Buffalo Soldiers: The Story of Emanuel Stance. Reflections of a Black Cowboy Series. By Robert H. Miller. Silver Burdett, 1994.

Good-Bye Hello. By Barbara S. Hazen. Atheneum, 1994.

Our People. By Angela Shelf Medearis. Atheneum, 1994.

The Story of Nat Love. By Robert H. Miller. Silver Burdett, 1994.

A Missing Portrait on Sugar Hill. By Diane Patrick. Silver Moon, 1995.

Skin Deep and Other Teenage Reflections. By Angela Shelf Medearis. Macmillan, 1995.

Treemonisha. By Angela Shelf Medearis. Holt, 1995.

Come Sunday. By Nikki Grimes. Eerdmanns, 1996.

I Love Saturdays and Domingos. By Alma F. Ada. Atheneum, 1996.

Ziggy and the Black Dinosaurs: Lost in the Tunnel of Time. By Sharon M. Draper. Just Us Books, 1996.

See also Draper, Sharon M(ills); Grimes, Nikki (Yolanda C.); Medearis, Angela Shelf; Miller, Robert H(enry)

Buchanan, Yvonne (Elizabeth)

(1 9 5 6 –)

ILLUSTRATOR

Buchanan was born in New York City, the oldest of four children. As a child of the 1960s, she grew up in front of the television and consequently developed her drawing skills by copying Bugs Bunny, Speed Racer, and other cartoons.

Her interest in animation was heightened when she attended the New York High School of Art and Design. At Parsons School of Design, majoring in illustration, she experimented with various styles until she found her best expressions with line and watercolor. After graduation in 1977, she pursued a freelance career, working for many companies including the *New York Times,* the *Washington Post,* and the *Wall Street Journal* newspapers.

In 1992, she illustrated the video of *Follow the Drinking Gourd,* the story of the Underground Railroad, which won, among others, a Showtime Award and the Chicago Children's Festival Gold Award in 1993, and it was published as a children's book in 1996. Her work has been exhibited at the Studio Museum in Harlem, the Cinque Gallery, the Art Directors Club, the University of Denver, Syracuse University, and the Society of Illustrators in 1993.

Buchanan is a professor in the Department of Illustrations at Syracuse University and lives in Brooklyn, New York.

BIBLIOGRAPHY

Juneteenth Jamboree. By Carole Boston Weatherford. Lee & Low, 1995.
Tingo, Tango, Mango Tree. By Marcia K. Vaughan. Silver Burdett, 1995.
Follow the Drinking Gourd. By Bernadine Connelly. Simon & Schuster, 1996.

See also Weatherford, Carole Boston

Bunin, Catherine A(nastasia)

(1969–)

AUTHOR

Born in Staten Island, New York, Bunin was adopted at the age of three months into an interracial family. This prompted her, at the age of six, to tell her Mom she was going to write a book about adoption. With the help of her mother, Bunin wrote the book *Is That Your Sister?*

Bunin now discusses issues of interracial adoption at the legal level. Bunin has a private law practice in Portland and Rockland, Maine. She is presently one of four minority attorneys in that state. She specifically handles parental termination rights and adoption issues.

Bunin is married and lives in Maine.

BIBLIOGRAPHY

Is That Your Sister? With Sherry Bunin. Illustrated by Sheila K. Welch. Pantheon, 1976.

Burns, Khephra (Keith)

(1 9 5 0 –)

AUTHOR

The author was born Keith Karlyle Burns in Los Angeles, California. Khephra is an acquired nickname, which he uses professionally. He attended schools in Compton and Watts with never a thought of one day becoming a writer. He enrolled at the University of California, Santa Barbara, and graduated in 1972 with a bachelor's degree in English. Over the next five years, Burns danced, painted, lectured part-time at Santa Barbara City College, drove a cab, moved to Oakland, California, played jazz, and sold insurance.

In 1978, Burns moved to New York City and sold his first work, *Marie Laveau,* a treatment for a screenplay, to Belafonte Enterprises. He was the writer and producer for a two-part series show, *Black Men in Dance.* Burns was also a writer on *Images and Realities, Part II: The African American Family* in February 1993; *Images and Realities, Part III: The African American Woman* in the fall of 1993; and *Images and Realities IV: African American Children* in October 1994. He was also the senior writer for *Triple Threat,* a Black Entertainment Television (BET) music game show in 1992.

Burns is the coauthor, with his wife Susan L. Taylor, editor-in-chief of *Essence* magazine, of *Confirmation: Wisdom of the Ages,* an adult anthology of inspirational writings from around the world, to be published by Doubleday. He has written articles for numerous publications, including *Essence, Swing Journal* (Japan), *Omni,* and *Art and Auction.* He was a contributing writer to *The Color of Fashion* published by Stewart, Tabori, and Chang, and *African Americans: Voices of Triumph,* a publication of Time-Life Books. Burns also edits the *Boulé Journal,* a quarterly publication of the Sigma Pi Phi fraternity. He has written album liner notes for such noted jazz artists as Nancy Wilson, Miles Davis (his Grammy Award–winning album, *Aura*), Arthur Blythe, Kirk Whalum, Jon Faddis, Marlon Jordan, and others, including a tribute album to John Coltrane.

Burns was the writer for William Miles's award-winning film documentaries *Black Champions* and *Black Stars in Orbit*; the latter he translated into a children's book.

He is a member of the Writers Guild of America, the Authors Guild, and 100 Black Men, and a 1981 recipient of the (CETA) Communications Excellence to Black Audiences Award for recruitment poster entitled "What Do You Do When Tough Ain't Enough."

He wrote a segment on New Orleans that was hosted by jazz musician Wynton Marsalis and the two segments of *Black Men in Dance* was a weekly, half-hour show produced by Essence Communications from 1983 to 1987.

Since 1992, Burns has written the Essence awards show which airs once a year as a two–hour prime-time television special.

He lives in New York City.

BIBLIOGRAPHY

Black Stars in Orbit: The Story of NASA's African American Astronauts. With William Miles. Harcourt, 1995.

Burroughs, Margaret Taylor (Goss)

(1917–)

AUTHOR

Burroughs was born in St. Rose, Louisiana, and educated at Chicago Teachers College (now Chicago State University) and the Art Institute of Chicago, Illinois, where she received her bachelor's and master's degrees in education. She taught at Kennedy King College, the Art Institute of Chicago, and Elmhurst College, and she is a founder of the National Conference of Artists and of the DuSable Museum of African American History in Chicago.

Burroughs was awarded an internship under a grant from the National Endowment for the Humanities in 1968 and was an American Forum for African Study fellow. She received the Senior Achievement Award in the Arts and the Women's Caucus for Art Award from the Houston Museum of Fine Art in 1988 and the Recognition Award from the African American Cultural Coalition in Joliet, Illinois, in 1992.

Still very active in the operation of the DuSable museum, Burroughs lives in Chicago, Illinois.

She is married to Charles Gordon Burroughs. They have two children and six grandchildren.

BIBLIOGRAPHY

Did You Feed My Cow? Illustrated by Joe E. DeVelasco. Follett, 1956, 1969.
Jasper the Drummin' Boy. Illustrated by Ted Lewin. Revised Edition. Follett, 1970.

Byard, Carole

(1942–)

ILLUSTRATOR

Byard was born in Atlantic City, New Jersey. She studied at Fleisher Art Memorial in Philadelphia, Pennsylvania, and graduated from the New York Phoenix School of Design. Her paintings are well known, and her exhibitions and one-woman shows have won prizes. She also has done illustrations for magazines, filmstrips, and advertisements and has taught at the New York League of Girls and Women and the New York Phoenix School of Design.

Working Cotton was selected as a 1993 Caldecott Honor Book and a 1993 Coretta Scott King Honor Book for its illustrations. Byard won the Coretta Scott King Award in 1980 for her illustration of *Cornrows* and an honorable mention in 1981 for *Grandmama's Joy*.

She lives in Kerhonson, New York.

BIBLIOGRAPHY

Willie. By Helen Hayes King. Doubleday, 1971.
Under Christopher's Hat. By Dorothy M. Callahan. Scribner, 1972.
Naomi and the Magic Fish: A Story from Africa. By Phulma. Doubleday, 1972.
The Sycamore Tree and Other African Tales. By Lee Po. Doubleday, 1974.
Africa Dream. By Eloise Greenfield. HarperCollins, 1977.
I Can Do It By Myself. By Lessie Jones Little and Eloise Greenfield. Crowell, 1978.
Cornrows. By Camile Yarbough. Coward, 1979.
Three African Tales. By Adjai Robinson. Putnam, 1979.
Grandmama's Joy. By Eloise Greenfield. Philomel, 1980.
The Black Snowman. By Phil Mendez. Scholastic, 1989.
Have a Happy. . . . By Mildred Pitts Walter. Lothrop, 1989.
Working Cotton. By Sherley Anne Williams. Harcourt, 1992.

See also Greenfield, Eloise (Glynn Little); Little, Lessie Jones; Mendez, Phil; Robinson, Adjai; Walter, Mildred Pitts; Williams, Sherley Anne; Yarbrough, Camille

Caines, Jeannette (Franklin)

(1 9 3 8 –)

AUTHOR

Caines grew up in Harlem, New York. She has been active in organizations such as the Salvation Army, for which she served on the board of directors. She also is a member of the Negro Business and Professional Women of Nassau County and a councilwoman of the Christ Lutheran Church, Nassau County.

Daddy was a 1977 Notable Children's Trade Book in Social Studies, and Just Us Women, illustrated by Pat Cummings, was a 1982 Coretta Scott King Award Honorable Mention book.

She lives in Charlottesville, Virginia, and has two children Alexander and Abby.

BIBLIOGRAPHY

Abby. Illustrated by Steven Kellogg. Harper, 1973.
Daddy. Illustrated by Ronald Himler. Harper, 1977.
Window Wishing. Illustrated by Kevin Brooks. Harper, 1980.
Just Us Women. Illustrated by Pat Cummings. Harper, 1982.
Chilly Stomach. Illustrated by Pat Cummings. Harper, 1986.
I Need a Lunch Box. Illustrated by Pat Cummings. Harper, 1988.

See also Cummings, Pat.

Campbell, Barbara

(1939–)

AUTHOR

Campbell was born in Reedland, Arkansas, and lived in St. Louis, Missouri, as a child. She earned her bachelor's degree at the University of California, Los Angeles.

She was a reporter for the *New York Times* city beat, the first Black hired for the reporter-trainee program, and was then promoted to the reporting staff. She worked at *Life* magazine for two years and at the *New York Times* for thirteen years. After leaving the *New York Times*, Campbell has been writing magazine articles on social issues, especially pertaining to African American Youth. Most of her articles have appeared in *New York* magazine.

In 1969, she was nominated for the Pulitzer Prize for articles on narcotics, civic issues, welfare conditions, civil rights, the poor, Blacks, children, and older citizens. In 1995 she won the Newswomen's Club of New York prize in best magazine feature writing. This was a special honor as she competed against writers from such magazines as *The New Yorker*.

Campbell lives in Greenwich Village, New York City, with her sons Jonathan and Zachary.

BIBLIOGRAPHY

A Girl Called Bob and a Horse Called Yoki. Dial, 1982.
Taking Care of Yoki. HarperCollins, 1986.

Carew, Jan (Rynveld)

(1920–)

AUTHOR

Carew was born in the village of Agricola, Rome, in Guyana. Most of this author's works are known for their theme: the search for roots. He did pre-university studies at the Berbice High School, Guyana, served four years in the British Army, attended Howard University, Washington D.C. and then attended Charles University, Prague, La Sorbonne, Paris. His studies were mostly in pure science, and he began writing and painting while at the university. After two successful exhibitions of his paintings, one in Cleveland and the other in London, he turned to writing mostly adult novels, some of which were translated into several languages, including German, Portuguese, Spanish, and Russian.

Between 1961 and 1965, Carew was under contract to write three television plays a year for Associated Television in London, England. In August 1997, the National Film Theater of Britain did a special screening of his first TV play, *The Big Pride,* billed as the first important piece of Black TV drama to appear in Britain and Europe. The second TV play, *The Day of the Fox,* starred Sammy Davis, Jr. Subsequently, while leaving Toronto, Canada, he wrote *Behind God's Back* for a 1969 special Canadian Broadcasting Corporation ninety-minute TV drama program called *Festival*, starring Cicely Tyson and the black English actor Earl Cameron.

He is Emeritus Professor, having retired from Northwestern in 1967. He was a senior Fellow in the Council for the Humanities and in the Department of Afro-American Studies at Princeton University. From 1966 to 1969 he lived in Toronto and edited *Cotopaxi*, a review of Third-World literature.

In 1969 he was awarded a fellowship from the Canada Arts Council. Carew was editor of a special Caribbean edition of *De Kim* in

Amsterdam, the *Kensington Post* in London, and the *African Review* in Ghana. In 1974 he won a certificate of excellence from the American Institute of Graphic Arts for *The Third Gift*.

His children's books, *The Third Gift* and *Children of the Sun* were both illustrated by Leo and Diane Dillon and both appeared in Japanese editions.

In 1975 he set up the Jan Carew Annual Lectureship at Princeton. That same year he won the Burton Annual Fellowship from Harvard University's Graduate School of Education. He was awarded the 1979–1980 Pushcart Prize for his essay "The Caribbean Writer & Exile."

Carew lives in West Chester, Pennsylvania, where he is painting full time and is writing a novel.

BIBLIOGRAPHY

The Third Gift. Illustrated by Leo and Diane Dillon. Little, Brown, 1974.
Children of the Sun. Illustrated by Leo and Diane Dillon. Little, Brown, 1978.

See also Dillon, Leo

Carter, Gail Gordon

(1 9 5 3 –)

ILLUSTRATOR

"I believe it is important to show the various shades of Black people in my work, both figuratively and literally. As a people, we come from many different backgrounds, mixes of races and cultures. I would love for young readers to see fictional characters whom they resemble living in and dealing with the multicultural world of today. Or, expose them to Black American subcultures, something real to which they may be able to relate and even experience."

Carter was born and grew up in Los Angeles, California. She earned a bachelor of arts degree in psychology from Pitzer College in Claremont, California, then attended the School of Social Welfare at the University of California, Los Angeles, where she obtained a master of social welfare degree.

Art took a back seat to a career in social work, which focused on outpatient psychiatric and adoptions work. Her pursuit of art as a career began in late 1990 after her marriage and relocation to Portland, Oregon. Illustrating picture books is her first really enjoyable work. She is a member of both the national and local chapters of the Society of Children's Book Writers and Illustrators.

Her first book, *Mac and Marie and the Train Toss Surprise*, was praised in *Horn Book*, which stated, "The illustrations are exquisite." It also was the most highly recommended book on *Smithsonian* magazine's Christmas list for 1993 and has appeared in national textbooks (third-grade readers) for 1996–1997. Her second book, *May'naise Sandwiches and Sunshine Tea*, made the list of Notable Trade Books compiled by the joint committees of the National Council of Social Studies and the Children's Book Council. Both books received good reviews from the *School Library Journal*. *The Glass Bottle*

Tree was included on The Bank Street College list of Children's Books for the year 1996.

Carter's artwork has been exhibited in several Portland-based galleries, and her artistic interpretation of Martin Luther King's renowned "I Have a Dream" speech hangs in the City Hall of Corvallis, Oregon. She has also painted a 6×6-foot panel for a traveling multicultural mural addressing 500 years of the Columbus legacy.

She and her husband have one daughter and live in Portland, Oregon.

BIBLIOGRAPHY

Mac and Marie and the Train Toss Surprise. By Elizabeth Fitzgerald Howard. Four Winds, 1993.
May'naise Sandwiches and Sunshine Tea. By Sandra Belton. Four Winds, 1994.
The Glass Bottle Tree. By Evelyn Coleman. Orchard, 1995.

See also Howard, Elizabeth Fitzgerald

Carter, Mary Kennedy

(1934-)

AUTHOR

Carter was born in Franklin, Ohio, and graduated from Ohio State University. She received a master's degree from Columbia University and also attended London University and Makerere University in Kampala, Uganda. She was an elementary school teacher in the Cleveland public school system, a tutor and supervisor of teachers for the Uganda Ministry of Education, a research assistant at Teachers College at Columbia University, and a teacher of Black studies in the Roosevelt, New York, school district. Other teaching assignments have included her work as professor at the United States Merchant Marine Academy in 1979; as a school consultant for the Baldwin, New York, schools; and as a curriculum writer in the Rockville Centre, New York, schools since 1983.

Carter's memberships include the National Council for Social Studies, the National Education Association, the Baldwin Educational Assembly (where she served as a board member until 1984), and the Jack and Jill Association of America. She was awarded the Afro-American Fellowship in 1963.

She is married to Donald Wesley Carter and lives in Freeport, New York.

BIBLIOGRAPHY

Count on Me. American Book, 1970.
On to Freedom. Illustrated by Joyce Owens. Hill & Wang, 1970.

Cartey, Wilfred

(1932–1992)

AUTHOR

Born in Port-of-Spain, Trinidad, Cartey earned his bachelor's degree from the University of the West Indies in Jamaica and his master's in fine arts and doctorate from Columbia University in 1956 and 1964. He subsequently received a Fulbright travel grant, a Bernard Van Ler Foundation fellowship, and a Columbia University travel-and-research grant.

Cartey was Distinguished Professor of Black Studies at City College in New York in 1973; professor of Afro-American studies at the University of California, Berkeley, in 1974; and resident professor in the Extramural Department, University of the West Indies.

He has been a consultant in African and African American studies and has held the Distinguished Professorship Martin Luther King Chair at City University of New York.

In 1985 and 1986, Cartey received a grant from the Research Foundation of the City University of New York. He has received numerous academic and professional honors, including the award of honor and citation of merit from the Middle States Council for Social Studies in 1973 for his book *Black Traces*. He was an authority on African, Caribbean, and Afro-American literature as well as an accomplished poet.

He was laid to rest in Trinidad.

BIBLIOGRAPHY

The West Indies: Islands in the Sun. Nelson, 1967.
Black Images. Teachers College Press, 1970.
Modern African Writings. Edited by Wilfred Cartey. Illustrated by Wendy Kindred. Lodestar, 1970.

Carty, Leo

(1931–)

ILLUSTRATOR

When Carty was eleven years old, he won a scholarship to the Museum of Modern Art School in New York City. He subsequently studied at Cooper Union, Pratt Institute, and the School of Visual Arts.

He lives in Brooklyn, New York. Carty has two children.

BIBLIOGRAPHY

Fifty Thousand Names for Jeff. By Anne Snyder. Holt, 1969.
Where Does the Day Go? By Walter Dean Myers. Parents, 1969.
Nat Turner. By Judith Berry Griffin. Coward, 1970.
The House on the Mountain. By Eleanor Clymer. Dutton, 1971.
I Love Gram. By Ruth A. Sonneborn. Viking, 1971.
Sidewalk Story. By Sharon Bell Mathis. Viking, 1971.
A Tree for Tompkins Park. By Dawn C. Thomas. McGraw-Hill, 1971.

See also Griffin, Judith Berry; Mathis, Sharon Bell; Myers, Walter Dean; Thomas, Dawn C.

Charles, Faustin O(lorun)

(1944–)

AUTHOR

Charles was born in Trinidad, in the Caribbean, the second of two children. As a child, he loved listening to stories told by his grandparents and reading books of folk tales. His maternal grandmother was his main influence in becoming a storyteller. At school, he began composing stories, and he published his first piece at the age of twenty-one in a national newspaper in Trinidad.

In 1962, he moved to England to pursue a literary career and began to publish poems in magazines and newspapers. From 1973 to 1977, Charles worked as a visiting speaker for the Commonwealth Institute in London, visiting schools and talking about the Caribbean and telling stories. From 1977 to 1980, he attended the University of Kent at Canterbury. He graduated with a bachelor of arts degree with honors.

His work has appeared in anthologies for children such as *Can You Hear? Can I Buy a Slice of Sky?, A Caribbean Dozen: Poems from Caribbean Poets,* by John Agard and Grace Nichols, and *Scary Stories;* and he has written a children's operetta that was staged by a primary school in London. He is a member of the Children's Writers and Illustrators Group of the Society of Authors in England, and he does freelance storytelling all over that country.

He is married, with two daughters, and lives in London, England.

BIBLIOGRAPHY

Tales from the West Indies. W.H. Allen, 1985.
Under the Storyteller's Spell. Edited by Faustin O. Charles. Viking, 1989.
The Kiskadee Queen. Edited by Faustin O. Charles. Blackie, 1991.
Uncle Charlie's Crick Crack Tales. Karia, 1994.

See also Agard, John

Chesnutt, Charles W(addell)

(1858–1932)

AUTHOR

Chesnutt was born in Cleveland, Ohio. His parents were freemen who met on their flight north from North Carolina. Young Chesnutt became proficient in reading German, Latin, and French and in law, mathematics, and legal stenography. These studies added to his competency when he became a teacher.

He was a teacher-administrator and was named principal of the State Normal High School in North Carolina when he was only twenty-two years old. He was also a stenographer, a journalist, a lawyer, and a short-story writer for the MacClure syndicate and other periodicals. His first published story appeared in a Fayetteville, North Carolina, newspaper. In 1899, his now famous *The Conjure Woman,* a work for adults, appeared.

In 1928, he received the Spingarn Medal from the National Association for the Advancement of Colored People (NAACP) for his "pioneer work as a literary artist depicting the life and struggles of the Americans of Negro descent, and for his long and useful career as scholar, worker, and freeman."

BIBLIOGRAPHY

Conjure Tales. Illustrated by John Ross and Romano Clair. Retold by Ray Anthony Shepard. Dutton, 1973.

Childress, Alice

(1920–1994)

AUTHOR

Childress was born in Charleston, South Carolina, but grew up and attended school in Harlem, New York, where she was reared by her grandmother. She was an actress and writer who put her theatrical experiences to good use in her books. Her plays for adults have won considerable acclaim; *Trouble in Mind* was awarded an Obie for the best Off-Broadway production in 1955–1956.

She was an actress and a director in New York's American Theatre and a member of the Harlem Writers Guild and New Dramatists. Many of her articles appeared in *Freedomways, Black World*, and *Essence* magazines. In 1966, she received a Harvard University appointment for independent study at the Radcliffe Institute.

Her book *Rainbow Jordan* was selected as one of the Best Books of the Year by *School Library Journal* in 1981. It was also a Notable Children's Trade Book in Social Studies and a Children's Book Council choice as well as a 1982 Coretta Scott King Honor Book Award winner.

Childress was married to film editor Nathan Woodard. She died in 1994.

BIBLIOGRAPHY

A Hero Ain't Nothin' but a Sandwich. Coward, 1973.
When the Rattlesnake Sounds: A Play About Harriet Tubman. Illustrated by Charles Lilly. Coward, 1975.
Let's Hear It for the Queen. Illustrated by Loring Eutemey. Coward, 1976.
Rainbow Jordan. Coward, 1981.
Those Other People. Putnam, 1988.

See also Lilly, Charles

Chocolate, Debbi

Deborah Mique Newton Chocolate

(1954–)

AUTHOR

"I grew up in Chicago, the youngest of five children. My grandparents were musicians and dancers in the theater. By the time I was seven, when I wasn't reading, painting, or drawing, I was busy re-creating my mother's childhood memories of the theater in my own stories. When I turned nine, my mother bought me an eight-millimeter film projector. On Saturday afternoons in late autumn and early winter, when the weather was too cold for my friends and I to play outside, I'd set up the folding chairs in my basement, pop popcorn, and sell tickets to my 'movie theater' to all the kids in the neighborhood. Later I turned to music and became quite an accomplished trumpet player.

I still get my ideas from movies, paintings, music, and the theater. My childhood friends, the children I meet, and my own two little boys often provide the foundation for an interesting character. As a children's book author, my purpose is always the same: I write to entertain and to share my vision of life's hope, its beauty, and its promise."

Chocolate was born in Chicago, Illinois. She is a graduate of Spelman College in Atlanta, Georgia, where she received her bachelor's degree in political science and journalism in 1976. She was awarded a fellowship in creative writing from Brown University in Providence, Rhode Island, where in 1978 she earned a master of arts degree in creative writing and English. In 1990 and 1991, she received grants from the city of Chicago Council on the Arts to complete two picture books.

A former editor of books for children, Chocolate is a member of the Children's Reading Roundtable, the Children's Literature Assembly, and the Society of Children's Book Authors and Illustrators.

In 1992, *My First Kwanzaa Book* was cited as a Book of the Month Club selection and an American Booksellers Association Pick of the List. In 1993, *Talk, Talk: An Ashanti Legend* won the Parents Choice Award. In 1994, *Imani in the Belly* was selected as an American Booksellers Association Pick of the List, and, in 1995, *On the Day I Was Born* was cited as a Book of the Month Club selection.

The author is married to Robert Chocolate and lives in Wheaton, Illinois, with their two sons Bobby and Allen Whitney.

BIBLIOGRAPHY

Kwanzaa. Illustrated by Melodye Rosales. Children's Press, 1990.
My First Kwanzaa Book. Illustrated by Cal Massey. Scholastic, 1992.
NEATE: To the Rescue. Just Us Books, 1992.
Spider and the Sky God. Illustrated by Dave Albers. Troll, 1993.
Talk, Talk: An Ashanti Legend. Illustrated by Dave Albers. Troll, 1993.
Elizabeth's Wish. Illustrated by Melodye Rosales. Just Us Books, 1994.
Imani in the Belly. Illustrated by Alex Boies. BridgeWater, 1994.
On the Day I Was Born. Illustrated by Melodye Rosales. Scholastic, 1995.
The Best Kwanzaa Ever. Scholastic, 1996.
Kente Colors! Illustrated by John Ward. Walker, 1996.
The Piano Man. Illustrated by Eric Yalesquez. Walker, 1998.

See also Massey, Cal(vin Levi); Rosales, Melodye (Benson); Ward, John (Clarence)

Christie, Gregory

(1971–)

ILLUSTRATOR

A native of Plainfield, New Jersey, Christie is the youngest of three children. He showed an interest in the arts at an early age and began to paint at the age of thirteen. Honing his skills at the School of Visual Arts in New York City, he simultaneously began working at the Solomon R. Guggenheim Museum. Upon graduating in May 1989 with a bachelor of fine arts degree, Christie traveled to Europe to discover other styles of art and cultures. This exposure led him to develop a new direction in his illustration, illustration with a fine-art edge.

Christie has illustrated for several companies, including Avon, MCA, Warner Brothers, various other record companies, and publications. He received a 1997 Coretta Scott King Illustrator Honor Award and the 1997 Firecracker Award for the *Palm of My Heart: Poetry by African American Children*. He is represented by Arts Counsel, New York City.

Christie lives in Brooklyn, New York, in the Fort Greene neighborhood.

BIBLIOGRAPHY

The Palm of My Heart: Poetry by African American Children. By Davida Adedjouma. Lee & Low, 1996.
Richard Wright and the Library Card. By William Miller. Lee & Low, 1997.

See also Adedjouma, Davida

Clay, Wil

(1938–)

ILLUSTRATOR

Clay was born in Bessemer, Alabama, and started his commercial art career at Macomber Vocational High School in Toledo, Ohio. Greatly encouraged by well-known Toledo artist Ernest Spring to pursue an art career, Clay received further training at the Vesper George School of Art in Boston, Massachusetts, in 1959–1960.

He moved to Houston, Texas, where he set up a graphic-design firm, remaining there until about 1975. By 1989, he was back in Toledo, where he works and teaches in his studio located at Common Space.

His collaboration with Constancia Gaffeney-Brown resulted in his winning the international competition sponsored by the Arts Commission of Greater Toledo to honor Dr. Martin Luther King, Jr. His sculpture *Radiance,* a six-foot bronze-and-stainless-steel work of King, features modeled heads of King on a polished steel sphere. The work was dedicated in downtown Toledo in September 1989.

In 1990, he visited Cameroon for six months. While in Africa, he worked with the Bamileke people and the Fulani, studying their art in beadwork, painting, woodworking, and the like in relation to their folkways and tribal lifestyles.

The illustrations for his first children's book, *Tailypo,* were inspired by childhood memories of visits to his two grandmothers, both of whom lived in rural Alabama. He won a 1993 Coretta Scott King Honor Book Award for *Little Eight John* by Jan Wahl.

Clay's art can be found in private collections not only in the United States but also in Canada, Sierra Leone, and Cameroon.

Clay is the father of two sons and four daughters. He lives in Toledo, Ohio.

BIBLIOGRAPHY

213 Valentines. By Barbara Cohen. Holt, 1991.

Tailypo. By Jan Wahl. Holt, 1991.

Little Eight John. By Jan Wahl. Lodestar, 1992.

The Real McCoy: The Life of an African American Inventor. By Wendy Towle.
     Scholastic, 1993.

Themba. By Margaret Saeks. Lodestar, 1992. Puffin, 1994.

The House in the Sky. By Robert D. San Souci. Dial, 1996.

I Am Rosa Parks. By Jim Haskins. Dial, 1997.

See also Haskins, James (Jim)

Clifton, (Thelma) Lucille (Sayles)

(1 9 3 6 –)

AUTHOR

Clifton was born in Depew, New York. When she was five years old, she moved to Buffalo, New York, where she later met a young novelist and poet named Ishmael Reed. He showed her poems to Langston Hughes, and some were published in the anthology he edited with Arna Bontemps, *Poetry of the Negro 1949–1970*. There Thelma Lucille Sayles also met her husband, Fred Clifton, a writer, artist, and philosophy teacher at the University of Buffalo. They married in 1958 and had six children.

Clifton received the Discovery Award from the Young Women's and Young Men's Hebrew Association Poetry Center in New York City in 1969. Her first book of poems for children was *Some of the Days of Everett Anderson*. She received grants from the National Endowment for the Arts in 1969 and 1972. From 1979 to 1985, she was poet laureate of Maryland and poet in residence at Coppin State College in Baltimore and a visiting writer at Columbia University School of the Arts.

She won the Coretta Scott King Award in 1984 for *Everett Anderson's Goodbye* and Coretta Scott King Honor Book Awards in 1974 and 1977.

After the death of her husband, she moved to Santa Cruz, California, and taught in the university there. She makes her home in Columbia, Maryland, where she continues her career with an active teaching and lecturing schedule. Clifton is Distinguished Professor of Humanities at St. Mary's college of Maryland.

BIBLIOGRAPHY

The Black BC's. Illustrated by Don Miller. Dutton, 1970.
Some of the Days of Everett Anderson. Illustrated by Evaline Ness. Holt , 1970, 1988.

All Us Come Cross the Water. Illustrated by John Steptoe. Holt, 1973.

The Boy Who Didn't Believe in Spring. Illustrated by Brinton Turkle. Dutton, 1973, 1988. Viking, 1992.

Don't You Remember? Illustrated by Evaline Ness. Holt, 1973. Dutton, 1985.

Good, Says Jerome. Illustrated by Stephanie Douglas. Dutton, 1973.

Everett Anderson's Year. Illustrated by Ann Grifalconi. Holt, 1974, 1992 (Revised Edition).

The Times They Used to Be. Illustrated by Susan Jeschke. Holt, 1974. Dell, 1976.

My Brother Fine with Me. Illustrated by Moneta Barnett. Holt, 1975.

Everett Anderson's Friend. Illustrated by Ann Grifalconi. Holt, 1976, 1992 (Revised Edition)

Amifika. Illustrated by Thomas DiGrazia. Dutton, 1977.

Everett Anderson's 1–2–3. Illustrated by Ann Grifalconi. Holt, 1977, 1992 (Revised Edition)

Everett Anderson's Nine Months Long. Illustrated by Ann Grifalconi. Holt, 1978.

The Lucky Stone. Illustrated by Dale Payson. Delacorte, 1979. Peter Smith, 1992.

My Friend Jacob. Illustrated by Thomas DiGrazia. Dutton, 1980.

Sonora Beautiful. Illustrated by Michael Garland. Dutton, 1981.

Everett Anderson's Goodbye. Illustrated by Ann Grifalconi. Holt, 1983, 1988.

Everett Anderson's Christmas Coming. Illustrated by Jan Spivey Gilchrist. Holt, 1991.

Three Wishes. Illustrated by Michael Hayes. Delacorte, 1992. Dell, 1994.

Dear Creator. Doubleday, 1996.

See also Barnett, Moneta; Gilchrist, Jan Spivey; Miller, Don; Steptoe, John (Lewis)

Coker, Deborah Connor

AUTHOR

Coker received a master's degree in early childhood education from Bank Street College in 1992 and a bachelor of science degree in public communication from Syracuse University.

For eight years, she was a project editor in the College Department at Random House publishing company, responsible for five to seven titles per year in various disciplines. She also has worked as a full-time lead teacher at the Family Academy School, New York City, teaching the primary grades for three years, and as codirector of the College Intern Program and full-time member of the executive council.

She is presently director of the Lower School at the Family Academy School handling administrative affairs and providing staff leadership, supervision, and curriculum creation and research.

Coker won the Little, Brown and Company New Voices/New World Multicultural Fiction Contest in Children's Literature.

The mother of two boys, she lives in New York City.

BIBLIOGRAPHY

I Like Me. Illustrated by Keaf Holliday. Western, 1995.
Aunt Mattie's Present. Illustrated by Brenda Joy Smith. Little, Brown, 1996.

Cooper, Afua

(1 9 5 7 –)

AUTHOR

Cooper is Jamaican born of African descent. As a young child, Cooper liked reading poetry and historical fiction and decided to write both when she grew up. *The Red Caterpillar on College Street* is her first book of children's poetry and has been widely acclaimed. The *Canadian Book Review Annual* said in 1989 that it is "a refreshing change from the almost adult-oriented and lavish picture books of more affluent publishers." Cooper is completing *Waiting for the Moon,* a collection of short stories, and a series of children's stories entitled *Fatima's Nightgown.*

Her poems have been published in anthologies in Britain, the United States, Canada, and the Caribbean. She also recorded her poetry on the album *Womantalk* (Heartbeat Records) in 1984.

Cooper has been writer-in-residence at two Ontario school boards and is a regular participant in the League of Canadian Poets' Poetry in the Schools series. She enjoys writing and performing her poetry to children and is a well-known figure on the Canadian children's poetry scene.

In addition to her literary works, Cooper is pursuing a doctorate in African-Canadian history at the University of Toronto, where she teaches a course in Canadian Black history. She serves on a number of juries for the Toronto, Ontario Arts and the Canada Council. She is publishing poetry and working on an adult manuscript.

Cooper is married and has a son and two daughters. She lives in Toronto, Ontario, Canada.

BIBLIOGRAPHY

The Red Caterpillar on College Street. Illustrated by Stephanie Martin. Sister Vision, 1989.

Cooper, Floyd (Donald)

(1956–)

ILLUSTRATOR, AUTHOR

Cooper was born in Tulsa, Oklahoma. A graduate of Tulsa Central High School, he earned a bachelor of fine arts degree from the University of Oklahoma, Norman. While at the university, he studied under Mark English, and after graduation he worked with a greeting card company in Missouri. Children's-book illustration initially was a way to complement his work in advertising.

Cooper hopes that his work will "produce books about Blacks for White kids. One of the more satisfying rewards for my work comes when I get the opportunity to do a book about the Black experience to broaden and enlighten someone who may not be aware."

After moving to the eastern part of the country, he discovered the diversity and creativity he sought in children's-book illustration in 1984. His first book, *Grandpa's Face,* was an American Library Association Notable Book. He has received recognition from the Society of Illustrators, exhibited at "The One Show," and received Coretta Scott King Honor Book Awards for his illustrations in 1994 and 1995.

Cooper lives in West Orange, New Jersey.

BIBLIOGRAPHY

Grandpa's Face. By Eloise Greenfield. Philomel, 1988.
Chita's Christmas Tree. By Elizabeth Fitzgerald Howard. Bradbury, 1989.
Laura Charlotte. By Kathryn O. Galbraith. Philomel, 1990, 1993.
Martin Luther King, Jr., and His Birthday. By Jacqueline Woodson. Silver Burdett, 1990.
Martin Luther King, Jr.: The Dream of Peaceful Revolution. By Della Rowland. Silver Burdett, 1990.
When Africa Was Home. By Karen Lynn Williams. Orchard, 1990.

The Girl Who Loved Caterpillars. By Jean Merrill. Putnam, 1992.

Be Good to Eddie Lee. By Virginia Fleming. Putnam, 1993.

Brown Honey in Broomwheat Tea. By Joyce Carol Thomas. HarperCollins, 1993, 1996.

From Miss Ida's Porch. By Sandra Belton. Four Winds, 1993.

Imani's Gift at Kwanzaa. By Denise Burden-Patton. Simon & Schuster, 1993.

Pass It On: African-American Poetry for Children. Compiled by Wade Hudson. Scholastic, 1993.

Coming Home: From the Life of Langston Hughes. Putnam, 1994.

Coyote Walks on Two Legs. Compiled by Gerald Hausman. Putnam, 1994.

Meet Danitra Brown. By Nikki Grimes. Lothrop, 1994.

Daddy, Daddy, Be There. By Candy Dawson Boyd. Philomel, 1995.

Gingerbread Days. By Joyce Carol Thomas. HarperCollins, 1995.

Gordy. By Anne Mazer. Hyperion, 1995.

How Sweet the Sound: African-American Songs for Children. Selected by Wade Hudson and Cheryl Willis Hudson. Scholastic, 1995.

Jaguarundi. By Virginia Hamilton. Scholastic, 1995.

King Sejong's Secret. By Carol Farley. Lothrop, 1995.

Papa Tells Chita a Story. By Elizabeth Fitzgerald Howard. Four Winds, 1995.

Pulling the Lion's Tail. By Jane Kurtz. Simon & Schuster, 1995.

Arabbin' Man. By Monalisa DeGross. Hyperion, 1996.

Faraway Drums. By Virginia Kroll. Little, Brown, 1996.

Mandela. Philomel, 1996.

Ma Dear's Apron. By Patricia C. McKissack. Knopf, 1997.

African Beginnings. By James Haskins and Kathleen Bensen. Lothrop, 1997.

See also Boyd, Candy (Marguerite) Dawson; DeGross, Monalisa; Greenfield, Eloise (Glynn Little); Grimes, Nikki; Hamilton, Virginia (Esther); Howard, Elizabeth Fitzgerald; Hudson, Cheryl Willis; Hudson, Wade; McKissack, Patricia C(arwell); Thomas, Joyce Carol; Woodson, Jacqueline

Cornish, Sam(uel James)

(1935–)

AUTHOR

The author grew up in Baltimore, Maryland, and attended Douglass High School, which he left after his first semester. He was in the Medical Corps of the United States Army from 1958 to 1960 and later attended Goddard College in Vermont. Cornish worked in various places, from an insurance company to bookstores, and later became a consultant on children's writing for the Educational Development Center, Newton, Massachusetts, in its Open Education Follow-Through Project.

Cornish is a professor of writing, literature and publishing at Emerson College in Boston, Massachusetts.

BIBLIOGRAPHY

Your Hand in Mine. Illustrated by Carl Owens. Harcourt, 1970.
Grandmother's Pictures. Illustrated by Jeanne Johns. Bradbury, 1974.
Walking the Streets with Mississippi John Hurt. Illustrated by James Calvin. Bradbury, 1978.

Crews, Donald

(1 9 3 8 –)

AUTHOR, ILLUSTRATOR

Crews was born in Newark, New Jersey, and attended Arts High School, where admission for music and art training is by competitive examination. He also attended Cooper Union in New York City. Crews served two years of military service in Germany, where he married Ann Jones, a fellow student from Cooper Union.

Freight Train and *Truck* were Caldecott Honor Books in 1979 and 1981, respectively. *Freight Train* was also an American Library Association Notable Book and a Junior Literary Guild choice, along with *Truck* and *Carousel*. In 1979, the American Institute of Graphic Arts Children's Book Show exhibited *Rain* and *Freight Train*. *Flying* was listed as one of the *New York Times* best illustrated books. The artist's work has also appeared in *Graphis* magazine.

Crews lives in upstate New York. He and his wife have two adult daughters, Nina and Amy.

BIBLIOGRAPHY

We Read: A to Z. Harper, 1967.
Ten Black Dots. Scribner, 1968.
Freight Train. Greenwillow, 1978.
Rain. By Robert Kalan. Greenwillow, 1978.
Truck. Greenwillow, 1980.
Light. Greenwillow, 1981.
Carousel. Greenwillow, 1982.
Harbor. Greenwillow, 1982.
Parade. Greenwillow, 1983.
School Bus. Greenwillow, 1984.
Bicycle Race. Greenwillow, 1985.

Flying. Greenwillow, 1986.

Eclipse: Darkness in Daytime. By Franklyn M. Branley. HarperCollins, 1988.

How Many Snails? A Counting Book. By Paul Giganti, Jr. Greenwillow, 1990.

Bigmama's. Greenwillow, 1991.

Shortcut. Greenwillow, 1992.

When This Box Is Full. By Patricia Lillie. Greenwillow, 1993.

Sail Away. Greenwillow, 1995.

Tomorrow's Alphabet. By George Shannon. Greenwillow, 1996.

More Than One. By Miriam Schlein. Greenwillow, 1996.

Crichlow, Ernest

(1914)

ILLUSTRATOR

Crichlow was born in New York City and remembers loving to draw since grade-school days, when he drew from models suggested by his teacher. After his graduation from Haaren High School (now defunct) in New York City, some of his art teachers arranged for his scholarship at the Commercial Illustration School of Art and raised money for his art supplies.

His collaboration with Lorraine and Jerrold Beim on *Two Is a Team,* an easy book about the interracial friendship of two little boys, was the beginning of a successful career in children's-book illustration, generally on Black themes. His artwork has been exhibited in many art shows. He has taught at Shaw University, the State University of New York at New Paltz, the City College of New York, and the Brooklyn Museum Art School.

In 1969, with Norman Lewis and Romare Bearden, he founded the Cinque Gallery in New York City for beginning Black artists, and codirected a group of Black artists at Saratoga, New York, under the aegis of the State Education Department of Arts and Humanities. Crichlow was also a member of the Black Academy of Arts and Letters. He received the first-ever medallion for lifetime achievement during the opening of the University of Pittsburgh's second annual "Images" Black Artist exhibition in 1987.

In 1990, Crichlow held a one–man show at the Cinque Gallery, at which actor Morgan Freeman bought three of his paintings. Crichlow taught art classes for thirty years in Trump Village, a middle-class development community in Brooklyn, New York. He paints full time and lives in Brooklyn, New York, with his son Tony.

BIBLIOGRAPHY

Two Is a Team. By Lorraine and Jerrold Beim. Harcourt, 1945.

Freedom Train: The Story of Harriet Tubman. By Dorothy Sterling. Doubleday, 1954.

Corrie and the Yankee. By Mimi Cooper Levy. Viking, 1959.

Mary Jane. By Dorothy Sterling. Doubleday, 1959.

William. By Anne Welsh Guy. Dial, 1961.

Forever Free. By Dorothy Sterling. Doubleday, 1963.

Galumph. By Brenda Lansdown. Houghton, 1963.

Lift Every Voice. By Dorothy Sterling and Benjamin Quarles. Doubleday, 1964.

Lincoln's Birthday. By Clyde R. Bulla. Harper/Collins, 1965.

Street Dog. By Richard E. Drdek. Singer, 1967.

African Folk Tales. Edited by Jessie Alford Nunn. Funk & Wagnalls, 1969.

The Magic Mirrors. By Judith Berry Griffin. Putnam, 1971.

See also Bearden, Romare; Griffin, Judith Berry; Quarles, Benjamin

Cullen, Countee (Porter)

(1903–1946)

AUTHOR

Cullen was born in New York City. The scholarly Cullen was among the most respected poets to emerge from the Harlem Renaissance of the 1920s and 1930s. He was adopted by the Reverend and Mrs. Frederick A. Cullen. Young Countee was an outstanding student at De Witt Clinton High School, at the time one of the best secondary schools in New York City. He was vice president of his graduating senior class, editor of the *Clinton News,* and chairman and editor of the senior edition of the school's literary magazine, the *Magpie.* He was also treasurer of the Inter-High School Poetry Society. Cullen was a member of the school's honor society and Arista, and he graduated with honors in at least five subjects: Latin, English, French, history, and mathematics.

Cullen began writing poetry as a child. In high school, he won a second prize for the poem "In Memory of Lincoln" and a contest prize for his well-known "I Have a Rendezvous with Life." He attended New York University, was elected to Phi Beta Kappa—one of a few to receive the honor in 1925 from that college—and in the same year won the Witter Bynner undergraduate poetry contest and second prize (Langston Hughes won the first) in a literary contest sponsored by *Opportunity: A Journal of Negro Life.*

His first collection of poems, *Color,* an adult work published in 1925, won the Harmon Foundation's Award for Literature, awarded by the National Association for the Advancement of Colored People (NAACP) for "distinguished achievement in literature by a Negro." He received his master's degree in English from Harvard University in 1926 and was assistant editor of *Opportunity,* for which he wrote a monthly column, "The Dark Tower."

BIBLIOGRAPHY

The Lost Zoo. With Christopher Cat. Follett, 1949. Silver Burdett (Illustrated by Brian Pinkney), 1991.

My Lives and How I Lost Them. With Christopher Cat. Harper, 1942. Silver Burdett (Illustrated by Nubia Owens), 1993.

See also Pinkney, Brian.

Cummings, Pat(ricia Marie)

(1950–)

ILLUSTRATOR, AUTHOR

Cummings was born in Chicago, Illinois. As part of an army family, she spent her childhood in many places in and out of the United States. She received her bachelor's degree from Pratt Institute in 1974 and became a freelance illustrator.

Cummings won Coretta Scott King Honor Book Awards for her illustrations in 1983, 1987, and 1989; her illustrations for *My Mama Needs Me* won the 1984 Coretta Scott King Award; and *Talking with Artists* won the 1992 Boston Globe-Horn Book Award for nonfiction. She also received the Communications Excellence to Black Audiences Award for an illustration advertising Con Edison and an honorable mention in 1978 for a poster for the United Nations Committee on Apartheid.

Cummings is a professor in the Illustration Department at Parsons School of Design in New York City and is a board member of the Center for Multicultural Children's Literature at HarperCollins publishing company. She is a member of the Graphic Artists Guild, the Society of Children's Book Writers and Illustrators, the Authors Guild, and the Writers Guild of America.

Cummings is married to Chuku Lee. They live in Brooklyn, New York.

BIBLIOGRAPHY

Good News. By Eloise Greenfield. Coward, 1977.
Beyond Dreamtime. By Trudie MacDougall. Coward, 1978.
The Secret of the Royal Mounds. By Cynthia Jameson. Coward, 1980.
Just Us Women. By Jeannette Caines. Harper, 1982.
My Mama Needs Me. By Mildred Pitts Walter. Lothrop, 1983.

Fred's First Day. By Cathy Warren. Lothrop, 1984.

Jimmy Lee Did It. Lothrop, 1985.

Chilly Stomach. By Jeannette Caines. Harper, 1986.

C.L.O.U.D.S. Lothrop, 1986.

Springtime Bears. By Cathy Warren. Lothrop, 1986.

I Need a Lunch Box. By Jeannette Caines. Harper, 1988.

Mariah Loves Rock. By Mildred Pitts Walker. Bradbury, 1988.

Storm in the Night. By Mary Stolz. Harper, 1988.

Willie's not the Hugging Kind. By Joyce Durham Barrett. Harper , 1989.

Mariah Keeps Cool. By Mildred Pitts Walter. Bradbury, 1990.

Two and Too Much. By Mildred Pitts Walter. Bradbury, 1990.

Clean Your Room, Harvey Moon! Bradbury, 1991.

Go Fish. By Mary Stolz. HarperCollins, 1991.

Petey Moroni's Camp Runamok Diary. Bradbury, 1992.

Talking with Artists. Bradbury, 1992.

Carousel. Bradbury, 1994.

C Is for City. By Nikki Grimes. Lothrop, 1995.

Talking with Artists: Volume Two. Simon & Schuster, 1995.

My Aunt Came Back. HarperCollins, 1997.

Pickin' Peas. By Margaret Read. HarperCollins, 1998.

Lulu's Birthday. By Elizabeth Fitzgerald Howard. Greenwillow, 1999.

See also Caines, Jeannette (Franklin); Greenfield, Eloise (Glynn Little); Grimes, Nikki; Howard, Elizabeth Fitzgerald; Walter, Mildred Pitts

Curtis, Christopher Paul

(1 9 5 4 –)

AUTHOR

Curtis was born in Flint, Michigan. He spent the first thirteen years after high school hanging doors on the assembly line at Flint's historic Fisher Body Plant No. 1.

Family members, particularly his wife, have been a great influence on Curtis's writing. He credits his heartfelt respect for the power of words to his grandfathers, one a Negro Baseball League pitcher and the other a band leader.

Curtis believes he is genetically predestined to entertain. He has won numerous awards for his essays and short stories, including a 1996 Newbery Honor Book Award and a 1996 Coretta Scott King Honor Book Award for *The Watsons Go to Birmingham–1963,* which is being translated into seven languages. He worked in Allen Park, Michigan.

The father of a son Steven and a daughter Cydney, Curtis lives in Southfield, Michigan, and is a full time writer.

BIBLIOGRAPHY

The Watsons Go to Birmingham–1963. Delacorte, 1995.
Bud, Not Buddy. Delacorte, 1998.

Davis, Ossie

(1 9 1 7 –)

AUTHOR

An actor, playwright, and director, Davis was born in Cogdell, Georgia, and has performed on stage, screen, and television. He and his actress wife, Ruby Dee, appeared on Howard University's WBBM-TV's *In Other Words . . . Ossie and Ruby,* and cohosted the *Ossie Davis and Ruby Dee Story Hour* on radio from 1974 to 1978 and the Public Broadcasting System (PBS) television series *With Ossie and Ruby* in 1981.

Davis prefers to be known foremost as a writer. His role as chairman of the board of the Institute of New Cinema Artists, which specialized in training young film and television production talent, is perhaps his proudest contribution to the industry.

Through their company, Emmalyn Enterprises, he and his wife produced, with PBS, some of their best work: *Martin Luther King: The Dream and the Drum*; *A Walk Through the 20th Century* with Bill Moyers; and the critically acclaimed series *With Ossie and Ruby.* Together they have received a number of honors, including the Frederick Douglass Award from the New York Urban League for their work in the play *Boseman and Lena*; the Drama Desk Award in 1974; and the Martin Luther King, Jr., Award from Operation PUSH in 1977. Davis' film performances have been in the movie *The Client,* the film production of John Grisham's bestselling novel and in the movie *Grumpy Old Men* with Jack Lemmon and Walter Matthau. He has worked with Spike Lee in *School Daze, Do The Right Thing, Jungle Fever,* and voice narration in the movie *Malcolm X.*

His *Escape to Freedom: A Play About Young Frederick Douglass* won the 1979 Coretta Scott King Award.

Davis and his wife have three grown children. They live in New Rochelle, New York.

BIBLIOGRAPHY

Escape to Freedom: A Play About Young Frederick Douglass. Viking, 1978.
Langston: A Play. Delacorte, 1982.
Just Like Martin. Simon & Schuster, 1992.

See also Dee, Ruby (Ruby Ann Wallace)

Dee, Ruby
Ruby Ann Wallace

(1923–)

AUTHOR

Dee was born Ruby Ann Wallace in Cleveland, Ohio, and is married to actor-playwright Ossie Davis, who has written plays for children as well as adults.

She is primarily known as an actress but has also published books. Dee wrote poetry before venturing into the children's book world, and she has said her purpose in writing is to "create exciting and challenging reading for children—to inform the senses and entertain."

Among her treasured experiences are working with her husband and their son Guy Davis in the storytelling, folklore, and music review *Two Hahs and a Homeboy.* Compiled by Dee, the program draws on her own works, along with the original writings of her husband and son, and of the late anthropologist/folklorist Zora Neale Hurston.

Dee received her bachelor of arts degree from Hunter College in New York City and in the 1950s attended actors' workshops at Fairfield University, Iona College, and Virginia State College. She has been active as an actress in films, an actress and writer in the American Negro Theater, and the cohost with her husband of the radio program *Ossie Davis and Ruby Dee Story Hour* from 1974 to 1978 and of the Public Broadcasting System's series *With Ossie and Ruby* in 1981.

She won an Emmy from the Academy of Television Arts and Sciences for a single performance in 1964 in *Express Stop from Lenox Avenue.* With Davis, she received the Frederick Douglass Award from the New York Urban League for their work in the play *Boseman and Lena*; the Martin Luther King, Jr., Award from Operation PUSH in 1977; and the Drama Desk Award in 1974. She is enrolled in the Hunter College Hall of Fame and received the college's President's Medal. She was inducted into the Theater Hall of Fame in 1988 and into the National

Association for the Advancement of Colored People (NAACP) Image Award Hall of Fame in 1989.

Dee and her husband have three grown children. They live in New Rochelle, New York.

BIBLIOGRAPHY

Glowchild and Other Poems. Edited by Ruby Dee. Third World Press, 1972.
Two Ways to Count to Ten. Illustrated by Susan Meddaugh. Holt, 1988.
Tower to Heaven. Illustrated by Jennifer Bent. Holt, 1991.

See also Bent, Jennifer; Davis, Ossie

DeGross, Monalisa

(1 9 5 0–)

AUTHOR

"I am from a large family and was surrounded by my grandparents, aunts, uncles, and many cousins. Not many of my older family members read well, but they told marvelous stories. So I was raised on a beginning, a middle, and an end."

DeGross was born in Baltimore, Maryland. Reading has been an integral part of the author's life. She has been involved in children's literature through her job as an assistant to the youth coordinator and school and student-service coordinator at the Enoch Pratt Free Library in Baltimore. DeGross started collecting children's picture books and ended up writing children's books. She received the 1996 Sunshine State Young Reader's Award for *Donavan's Word Jar.* Working at the library is a bonus to a reader and writer.

DeGross is married and has two children, Donavan and Nikki. She lives in Baltimore, Maryland.

BIBLIOGRAPHY

Donavan's Word Jar. Illustrated by Cheryl Hanna. HarperCollins, 1994.
Arabbin' Man. Illustrated by Floyd Cooper. Hyperion, 1996.

See also Cooper, Floyd (Donald); Hanna, Cheryl (Irene)

De Veaux, Alexis

(1 9 4 8 –)

AUTHOR

De Veaux, recognized as a poet, novelist, and playwright, was born and reared in Harlem, New York. She has taught creative writing; written a novel, *Spirits in the Street*; and written a biographical prose poem, *Don't Explain: A Song for Billie Holiday,* which was named a Coretta Scott King Honor Book in 1981. Her plays *Circles, Tapestry,* and *A Season to Unravel,* performed by the Negro Ensemble Company in New York City in 1979, displayed her interest in the theater.

An Enchanted Hair Tale won a Coretta Scott King Honor Book Award in 1988 and was a featured book on the Public Broadcasting System's highly acclaimed *Reading Rainbow.* DeVeaux received the Lorraine Hansberry Award for Excellence in African American Children's Literature presented in 1991 by the Drew Child Development Corporation, and the 1974 and 1975 Art Books for Children Awards from the Brooklyn Museum.

She holds both a master of arts and a doctorate in American studies from the State University of New York at Buffalo where she teaches.

De Veaux lives in Buffalo, New York.

BIBLIOGRAPHY

Na-ni. HarperCollins, 1973.
Don't Explain: A Song of Billie Holiday. Harper, 1980.
An Enchanted Hair Tale. Illustrated by Cheryl Hanna. Harper, 1987.

See also Hanna, Cheryl (Irene)

Dillon, Leo

(1 9 3 3 –)

ILLUSTRATOR

Born in Brooklyn, New York, Dillon attended the Parsons School of Design and the School of Visual Arts, both in New York City. He and his wife, Diane, work as a team, and all of the books listed below are illustrated by both of them. They met at Parsons, married shortly after graduating, and have illustrated book jackets, magazines such as *Ladies Home Journal,* posters, and children's books.

Their books have won many honors and awards, including their Caldecott-winning books *Why Mosquitoes Buzz in People's Ears* and *Ashanti to Zulu: African Traditions* and Coretta Scott King Honor Books *Aida* and *The People Could Fly: American Black Folktales.*

Leo and Diane Dillon have one son, Lee, and live in Brooklyn, New York.

BIBLIOGRAPHY

Behind the Back of the Mountain: Black Folktales from Southern Africa. By Verna Aardema. Dial, 1973.

Songs and Stories from Uganda. By William Moses Serwadda. Transcribed and edited by Hewitt Pantaleoni. Crowell, 1974.

The Third Gift. By Jan Carew. Little, Brown, 1974.

Song of the Boat. By Lorenz Graham. Crowell, 1975.

The Hundred Penny Box. By Sharon Bell Mathis. Viking, 1975.

Why Mosquitoes Buzz in People's Ears. By Verna Aardema. Dial, 1975.

Ashanti to Zulu: African Traditions. By Margaret Musgrove. Dial, 1976.

Children of the Sun. By Jan Carew. Little, Brown, 1978.

Honey, I Love. By Eloise Greenfield. Crowell, 1978.

Listen, Children: An Anthology of Black Literature. Edited by Dorothy S. Strickland. Bantam, 1982.

Brother to the Wind. By Mildred Pitts Walter. Lothrop, 1985.

The People Could Fly: American Black Folktales. By Virginia Hamilton. Knopf, 1985.

Moses' Ark: Stories from the Bible. By Alice Back and J. Cheryl Exum. Delacorte, 1989.

Aida. By Leontyne Price. Harcourt, 1990.

Alaskan Lullaby. By Nancy Carlson. Dial, 1990.

The Race of the Golden Apples. By Claire Martin. Dial, 1990.

The Tale of the Mandarin Ducks. By Katherine Paterson. Lodestar, 1990.

Pish, Posh, Said Hieronymus Bosch. By Nancy Willard. Dial, 1991.

Many Thousand Gone: African Americans from Slavery to Freedom. By Virginia Hamilton. Knopf, 1993.

Her Stories: African American Folktales, Fairy Tales and True Tales. By Virginia Hamilton. Scholastic, 1995.

See also Carew, Jan (Rynveld); Graham, Lorenz; Greenfield, Eloise (Glynn Little); Hamilton, Virginia (Esther); Mathis, Sharon Bell; Musgrove, Margaret (Wynkoop); Serwadda, William Moses; Strickland, Dorothy S(alley); Walter, Mildred Pitts

Diop, Birago (Ismael)

(1906–1989)

AUTHOR

This son of a Wolof father was born in Ouakam, a suburb of Dakar, Senegal. He went to school in Rue Thiong, Dakar, and later won a scholarship to Lycee Faidherbe in Saint-Louis, Senegal. He worked as a nurse in a military hospital in Saint-Louis and obtained a scholarship to study veterinary medicine. He left Senegal to study at the University of Toulouse in France, where he received his degree as a veterinary surgeon. While studying in Paris, he met Leopold Senghor, the first president of Senegal and noted African poet, who later appointed Diop the Senegalese ambassador to Tunisia.

Speaking about Diop's *Tales of Amadou Koumba* as told by the griots (traditional West African storytellers), Senghor said Diop's work "restores the fables and ancient tales, in their spirit and in their style."

Among his books translated from the original French are *Tales of Amadou Koumba* and the children's book *Mother Crocodile = Maman–Caiman,* which was translated and adapted by Rosa Guy and illustrated by John Steptoe and won a 1982 Coretta Scott King Illustrator Award.

Diop won the French African Grand Prix in Literature in 1964. He died in Dakar, Senegal, in 1989 at the age of 83.

BIBLIOGRAPHY

Jojo. Third Press, 1970.

Mother Crocodile = Maman–Caiman. Translated and adapted by Rosa Guy. Illustrated by John Steptoe. Delacorte, 1981.

Tales of Amadou Koumba. Translated by Dorothy S. Blair. Delacorte, 1981.

See also Guy, Rosa (Cuthbert); Steptoe, John (Lewis)

Draper, Sharon M(ills)

(1952–)

AUTHOR

Draper was born in Cleveland, Ohio. She has spent twenty-five years teaching junior high and high school students how to appreciate the beauty of literature and how to communicate their ideas effectively. As a challenge from one of her students, she entered and won first prize in the 1991 *Ebony* magazine literary contest, for which she was awarded $5,000 and the publication of her short story, "One Small Torch." She has published numerous poems and short stories in a variety of literary magazines.

    Tears of a Tiger was honored with the 1995 American Library Association/Coretta Scott King Genesis Award for Outstanding New Book. It also was selected as a Notable Children's Trade Book in the Field of Social Studies for 1955 by the National Council for Social Studies and the Children's Book Council and was named one of the 1994 Children's Books of the Year by the Children's Book Committee of Bank Street College.

    Draper is an active member of the National Council of Teachers of English, the Ohio Council of Teachers of English Language Arts, the Conference on English Leadership, and the American Federation of Teachers. She is also a member of Delta Kappa Gamma, the honor society for women educators, and Phi Delta Kappa, education honor society. Additionally, she was selected as Outstanding High School English Language Arts Educator for 1995.

    Draper has been a strong, active supporter of, and participant in, the activities, goals, and ideals of the National Board for Professional Teaching Standards. She was one of the first teachers in the nation to achieve national board certification in English/language arts. Her essay, "The Touch of a Teacher," was selected by the National Governor's

Association to be included in its Goals 2000 book, *Governors and Education*. She was named 1997 National Teacher of the Year at the White House by President Clinton. Her book *Forged by Fire* won the 1998 Coretta Scott King Author Award.

Draper lives in Cincinnati, Ohio.

BIBLIOGRAPHY

Tears of a Tiger. Simon & Schuster, 1994.

Ziggy and the Black Dinosaurs. Illustrated by James Ransome. Just Us Books, 1994.

Ziggy and the Black Dinosaurs: Lost in the Tunnel of Time. Illustrated by Michael Bryant. Just Us Books, 1996.

Ziggy and the Black Dinosaurs: Shadows of Ceasar's Creek. Illustrated by James Ransome. Just Us Books, 1997.

Forged by Fire. Atheneum, 1997.

See also Bryant, Michael; Ransome, James (Earl)

Dunbar, Paul Laurence

(1872–1906)

POET

"Little brown baby wif' spa'klin' eyes,
Who's pappy's darlin' an' who is pappy's chile? . . ."

Although he preferred writing in standard English, Paul Laurence Dunbar was best known for his poetry in dialect. He was born in Dayton, Ohio, on June 27, 1872. His widowed mother, an ex-slave, married Joshua Dunbar, who died when Paul was twelve years old. His mother could read and write and encouraged young Paul with his writing. He attended Dayton public schools. At Central High School, he had great success with his peers and teachers. He was a member of the school's literary society and wrote for the school paper, editing the paper in his senior year.

Dunbar worked as an elevator operator and a courthouse messenger, and, while working at the Chicago World's Fair in 1893, he met Frederick Douglass, then commissioner of the Haitian exhibit, who hired him as a clerical assistant.

With the help of many White friends and the "Introduction" written by the leading literary critic William Dean Howells to his third collection of poems, *Lyrics of Lowly Life,* Dunbar achieved wide recognition. Tuskegee University's song was among his many works. In spite of his personal evaluation of his work, his dialect poetry is considered his best.

The poet married schoolteacher Alice Ruth Moore in 1898; the marriage ended in separation in 1902.

The Dunbar House at 219 North Summit Street in Dayton, Ohio, which the poet shared with his mother in his last days, has been maintained as a state memorial by the Ohio Historical Society.

BIBLIOGRAPHY

Complete Poems of Paul Laurence Dunbar. With an introduction to *Lyrics of Lowly Life* by W.D. Howells. Dodd, 1914.

Little Brown Baby. Illustrated by E. Berry. Edited by Bertha Rogers. Dodd, 1940.

Duncan, Alice Faye

(1 9 6 7 –)

AUTHOR

Duncan, an only child, was born, reared, and still lives in Memphis, Tennessee. Visiting museums and watching movies are her favorite pastimes. Music, art, and books provide her with the inspiration to write. While in the tenth grade, Duncan discovered playwright Lorraine Hansberry's memoirs and short stories by author Toni Cade Bambara. She was so taken with Bambara's characters and Hansberry's passion for life that she tried her hand at creating tales. Her poetry, essays, and plays won several local and state student contests.

Duncan attended the University of Memphis, and, with encouragement and instruction from several of her professors, she began writing profile stories and record reviews for the *Memphis Star,* a music magazine.

In 1992, Duncan enrolled in a children's literature class to help her with her new job as a children's librarian. This new world of literature captured her attention, and she soon wrote a children's book, *Willie Jerome,* a tribute to kids who know to follow their own dreams. Duncan serves as a school librarian and a motivational "entertainer" for youth and adults.

BIBLIOGRAPHY

The National Civil Rights Museum Celebrates: Everyday People. Illustrated by J. Gerald Smith. BridgeWater, 1994.
Willie Jerome. Illustrated by Tyrone Geter. Macmillan, 1995.
Miss Viola and Uncle Ed Lee. Illustrated by Monica Stewart. Simon & Schuster, 1998.

See also Geter, Tyrone

Dyson, Kymberli Michelle

(1 9 6 9 –)

AUTHOR

"I understand there is a prominent void in the genre of Black literature and conscientiously write with this in mind."

Dyson was born in Los Angeles, California, and reared in Pasadena, California. She attended Marshall Fundamental High School, where she participated in various clubs and held several class offices. At the University of California, Berkeley, she majored in economics and drama. While there she wrote her first children's story in the Christian Children's series. She then entered the University of Southern California's bachelor of fine arts theater program.

Dyson has always taken to acting, writing, and communicating in a creative fashion. At the age of twenty-four, she started her own company, this little light publishing. Her first children's book, *Clyde, the Cloud Who Always Cried,* is the first of a fourteen-book children's series.

Dyson no longer teaches but continues to work to be a positive role model for children. She works for a battered women's shelter and for Kaiser Permanente's Educational Theatre programs which educate school children about health issues.

She lives in Pasadena, California.

BIBLIOGRAPHY

Clyde, the Cloud Who Always Cried. Illustrated by Patricia Suzanne Murray. this little light, 1994.
Clyde and Seymour, the Sea Who Wouldn't Share. Illustrated by Patricia Suzanne Murray. this little light, 1995.
Clyde and Susanna, the Sun Who Always Loved Her Shine. Illustrated by Patricia Suzanne Murray. this little light, 1995.

Edwards, Audrey

(1 9 4 7 –)

AUTHOR

Born in Tacoma, Washington, Edwards earned her bachelor's degree at the University of Washington and her master's degree from Columbia University. She has been a freelance writer, contributing articles to the *Daily News* and the *New York Times* newspapers in New York City and *Black Enterprise* and *Redbook* magazines; a senior editor of *Family Circle* magazine; a reporter for Fairchild Publications; and city editor of Community News Service, a Black and Puerto Rican news service. She has also taught at New York University and the New School for Social Research.

Edwards was an associate editor of *Black Enterprise* from 1977 to 1978, a regional director of the National Association of Black Journalists from 1981 to 1983, and a member of the New York Association of Black Journalists since 1983. She was the editor of *Essence* magazine from 1981 to 1986 and wrote an adult book *Children of the Dream* published by Doubleday in 1992. She received the Coretta Scott King Fellowship from the American Association of University Women in 1969 and the Unity Award from Lincoln University in 1985.

Edwards lives in Brooklyn, New York, and is a real estate broker.

BIBLIOGRAPHY

The Picture Life of Bobby Orr. With Gary Wohl. Watts, 1976.
The Picture Life of Muhammad Ali. With Gary Wohl. Watts, 1976.
Muhammad Ali: The People's Champ. With Gary Wohl. Little, 1977.
The Picture Life of Stevie Wonder. With Gary Wohl. Watts, 1977.

Egypt, Ophelia Settle

(1903–1984)

AUTHOR

Egypt was born in Clarksville, Texas. She worked as an educator, a so-cial-service administrator, and a writer. She will be remembered prima-rily for her work as director of a home for Black unwed mothers and as founder in 1981 of one of Washington, D.C.'s first birth-counseling clinics, the Parklands Egypt Clinic.

Educated at Howard University, the University of Pennsylvania, and Columbia University, Egypt was a consultant to governmental and social-service organizations and a member of many associations in the social-service field. She was an instructor at Fisk University and an as-sistant professor and fieldwork supervisor at Howard University Medical School.

Her *Unwritten History of Slavery* was a collection of interviews conducted with former slaves during her travels in Kentucky and Ten-nessee from 1929 to 1931. She received the Iota Phi Lambda sorority's Woman of the Year Award in 1963, the International Women's Year Award, and the Club Twenty Award in 1975. At the time of her death in Washington, D.C., she was preparing a children's edition of her slave interviews.

BIBLIOGRAPHY

James Weldon Johnson. HarperCollins, 1974.

Ellis, Veronica F.

(1950–)

AUTHOR

"I always stress that teachers include multicultural children's books in the literature they present to students. American society is a mosaic of different cultures. Children must learn to understand the differences in people. The knowledge they gain from reading quality multicultural literature will ensure that understanding."

Ellis is a native of Liberia, West Africa. She received a bachelor of arts degree in English from Boston University in 1972 and a master's degree in education from Northeastern University in 1974. She has taught African culture and English from junior high school to the college level. For ten years, she was a reading-textbook editor with the Houghton Mifflin publishing company in Boston, Massachusetts.

She teaches writing at Boston University and multicultural children's literature at Wheelock College, also in Boston. She was a consultant/instructor for the Children's Literature In-Service Program from 1990 to 1992, sponsored by the University of Massachusetts Davis Foundation and the Foundation for Children's Books in Massachusetts. Ellis has written several theme books to accompany the Macmillan Reading Series and the Houghton Mifflin Readers.

Ellis is a board member of the Massachusetts Youth Teenage Unemployment Reduction Network (MY TURN), Inc. In 1990, she was recognized as a Distinguished Role Model in Brockton, Massachusetts, where she lives with her husband and two children.

BIBLIOGRAPHY

Afro-Bets First Book About Africa. Illustrated by George Ford. Just Us Books, 1990.

Book of Black Heroes: Great Women in the Struggle. Volume 2. With Toyomi
  Igus and Valerie Wilson Wesley. Just Us Books, 1991.
Land of the Four Winds. Illustrated by Sylvia Walker. Just Us Books, 1993.
Wynton Marsalis. Raintree Steck–Vaughn, 1997.

See also Ford, George (Cephas)

Emecheta, Buchi (Florence Onye)

(1944–)

AUTHOR

The author was born in Lagos, Nigeria. Emecheta displayed advanced intellectual ability at an early age and attended Methodist Girls' High School from age ten. After winning a scholarship to study in England, she followed her husband, by an arranged marriage, to London, and they later separated. Emecheta was left to support their five children. She eventually earned an honor's degree in sociology from London University. Her persistence in writing and submitting manuscripts resulted in the publication of a number of her articles in the *New Statesman*.

In 1978, the year she was recognized as the best Black British writer, Emecheta won the Jock Campbell New Statesman Award for Literature. In 1983, she was cited among the best young British writers. Since 1979, she has been a member of the Home Secretary's Advisory Council, and in 1982–1983 she served in the Arts Council of Great Britain.

Emecheta lives in Crouch End, London, England, where she works as a sociologist and a writer of historical novels.

BIBLIOGRAPHY

Titch the Cat. Illustrated by Thomas Joseph. Allison & Busby, 1979.
Nowhere to Play. Illustrated by Peter Archer. Schocken, 1980.
The Moonlight Bride. Braziller, 1983.
The Wrestling Match. Braziller, 1983.

Epanya, Christian A(rthur Kingue)

(1956–)

ILLUSTRATOR

Epanya was born in Bonadoumbe-Douala, Cameroon, the second of six children. His family placed a strong value on reading, and his love of books influenced his desire to become an illustrator.

Epanya graduated from the Lycee du Manengouba at Nkongsamba with a baccalaureat Serie D in 1977, and in 1978 he attended the Universite de Yaounde, where he studied chemistry and biology. He traveled to France, where he attended the Ecole Emile Cohl art school from 1990 to 1992 and graduated with distinction. That same year, his work was selected at the Montreuil Children's Book Fair, and in 1993 his illustrations were selected at the Bologna Children's Book Fair, where he received the UNICEF (United Nations Children's Fund) Illustrator of the Year Award.

His artwork was exhibited at the Ninth District Library of Lyon, France, the Social Center and the Cultural Center of Venissieux, a suburb of Lyon, in 1994. In December 1994, UNICEF issued a greeting card with his illustration titled "The Sorcerer's Dance."

Epanya is the father of two daughters and lives in Lyon, France, where he works as a freelance illustrator.

BIBLIOGRAPHY

Ganekwane and the Green Dragon. By Corlia Fourie. Whitman, 1994.
Why the Chameleon Never Hurries. By Christina Fessler. Boyds Mills, 1995.
Konte Chameleon Fine, Fine, Fine! By Christina Kessler. Boyds Mills, 1997.

Eskridge, Anne E(lizabeth)

(1949–)

AUTHOR

The author, born and reared in Chicago, Illinois, believes that writing has always been an integral part of her life. Observing the way teenagers behaved, talked, and thought provided her with many hours of material for stories. Growing up, she wanted to write stories about Black youth that reflected their personalities and, at the same time, to add a mystical/magical quality to her stories. Eskridge began taking writing seriously as a professional option when she started teaching writing for mass media at a vocational school in Detroit, Michigan. She has won numerous writing grants and has participated in a variety of writing workshops.

One of Eskridge's works, "Brother Future," was produced as a Wonderworks Family movie that aired in 1991 on the Public Broadcasting System (PBS). The movie's director won the Directors Guild of America Award, and the work won Eskridge the Communications Excellence to Black Audiences Award of Distinction from the World Institute of Black Communicators.

The Sanctuary, a children's book, was written during Eskridge's teaching experience and received excellent reviews in *Publishers Weekly* and *School Library Journal.*

Eskridge lives in Detroit, Michigan.

BIBLIOGRAPHY

The Sanctuary. Cobblehill, 1994.

Evans, Mari

Evans was born in Toledo, Ohio, and attended the University of Toledo. She later moved to Indianapolis, Indiana. Evans, well known for her talent as a musician, educator, and writer, was an associate professor in the African Studies and Research Center at Cornell University, as well as writer-in-residence at many other colleges and universities. She also was an ethnic-studies consultant for a publishing firm and a television writer and director of *The Black Experience* program at WTTV in Indianapolis, Indiana. In addition to her political writings, she has written three volumes of poetry and four children's books.

Evans was a visiting associate professor in the Department of Afro-American Studies at the State University of New York at Albany and has taught Afro-American literature at Indiana, Northwestern, and Purdue Universities. She received the first annual Black Academy of Arts and Letters Poetry Award, was awarded a Copeland Fellowship from Amherst College in 1980, received the Black Arts Celebration Poetry Award in a National Endowment for the Arts Creative Writing in 1981, and in 1984, was a Yaddo Writers Colony Fellow.

Some of her poetry has been choreographed (reinterpreted as dance) and used in other media. Evans lives in Indianapolis, Indiana.

BIBLIOGRAPHY

J.D. Illustrated by Jerry Pinkney. Doubleday, 1973.
I Look at Me. Illustrated by Mike Davis. Third World, 1974.
Singing Black. Illustrated by Ramon Price. Reid Visuals, 1978.
Jim Flying High. Illustrated by Ashley Bryan. Doubleday, 1979.

See also Bryan, Ashley; Pinkney, Jerry

Fauset, Jessie (Redmon)

(1884–1961)

AUTHOR

Fauset was born in Snow Hill, New Jersey, the daughter of a minister. A writer of poetry, short stories, novels, and essays, she is best remembered as the first Black woman to graduate from Cornell University. She was a French teacher and the literary editor of *Crisis* magazine.

She was instrumental in establishing the literary foundation of the Harlem Renaissance of the 1920s and 1930s by encouraging and publishing works of the Harlem Renaissance literary greats, notably, Langston Hughes, Jean Toomer, and Countee Cullen, when she served as editor of *Crisis* and as editor and primary writer for the *Brownies Book*, a magazine for Black children published by the National Association for the Advancement of Colored People (NAACP).

She died in Philadelphia, Pennsylvania, on April 30, 1961.

BIBLIOGRAPHY

Brownies Book. Edited by Jessie Fauset. Dubois & Dill, 1920–1921.

See also Cullen, Countee (Porter); Hughes, Langston (James)

Fax, Elton C(lay)

(1909–1993)

AUTHOR, ILLUSTRATOR

The artist was born in Baltimore, Maryland, and received his bachelor's degree from Syracuse University in 1931. Through the years, he gave "Chalk Talks" lectures to groups in high schools and elementary schools in which he gave workshops. During these lectures, Fax drew and sketched in chalk on the board and did portraits in crayon and pencil of the children for them to keep. He also worked as a U.S. Department of State specialist in South America and the Caribbean, represented the American Society of African Culture on tour in Nigeria in 1963, and participated in international educational exchanges.

He taught at A&T College in Greensboro, North Carolina, Claflin College in Orangeburg, South Carolina, and at the Harlem Art Center in New York City. Fax has held memberships in the American Society of African Culture and the International Platform Association. He won the Coretta Scott King Award in 1972 for *Seventeen Black Artists*. Shortly before he died, Fax received an honorary Doctor of Letters degree from Syracuse University in New York.

BIBLIOGRAPHY

Dr. George Washington Carver: Scientist. By Shirley Graham. Messner, 1944.
    Archway, 1985.
Cotton for Jim. By Clara Baldwin. Abingdon, 1954.
West African Vignettes. Dodd, 1963.
Contemporary Black Leaders. Dodd, 1970.
Seventeen Black Artists. Dodd, 1971.
Garvey: The Story of a Pioneer Black Nationalist. Dodd, 1972.
Take a Walk in Their Shoes. By Glennette Tilley Turner. Cobblehill, 1989.

See also Graham (Du Bois), Shirley (Lola); Turner, Glennette Tilley

Feelings, Muriel (Gray)

(1938–)

AUTHOR

Feelings was born in Philadelphia, Pennsylvania, and attended Philadelphia College of Art for one year on a partial scholarship. In 1963, she graduated from California State University at Los Angeles and worked as a teacher in New York. There she met several Africans, and in 1966 the Uganda Mission to the United Nations recruited her to work as an art teacher in a Kampala high school. Her students' work was considered the basis for publishing literature by the Ministry of Education. However, because she believes that factual information on Africa is needed, her first story was *Zamani Goes to Market*.

She married Tom Feelings, who had corresponded with her asking for Kampala folk literature. After returning to America, she taught school in Brooklyn, New York, and introduced African crafts and Swahili. This experience culminated in *Moja Means One: Swahili Counting Book*. In 1971, Feelings and her husband traveled to Guyana to work, and she taught art in two high schools there. Upon her return to the United States, she completed *Jambo Means Hello: Swahili Alphabet Book*. Both books, illustrated by Tom Feelings, have been widely honored, including being designated Caldecott Honor Books. *Jambo . . .* also won a Boston Globe-Horn Book Award for illustration in 1974.

Feelings divorced in 1974. She lives in Philadelphia, Pennsylvania, and is an administrator at Temple University.

BIBLIOGRAPHY

Zamani Goes to Market. Illustrated by Tom Feelings. Seabury, 1970. Houghton, 1979.

Moja Means One: Swahili Counting Book. Illustrated by Tom Feelings. Dial, 1971, 1976.

Jambo Means Hello: Swahili Alphabet Book. Illustrated by Tom Feelings. Dial, 1974, 1985.

See also Feelings, Tom

Feelings, Tom

(1 9 3 3 –)

ILLUSTRATOR

"When I am asked what kind of work I do, my answer is that I am a storyteller in picture form, who tries to reflect and interpret the lives and experiences of the people who gave me life. When I am asked who I am, I say I am an African who was born in America. Both answers connect me specifically with my past and present; therefore, I bring to my art a quality which is rooted in the culture of Africa and expanded by the experience of being Black in America."

Feelings was born and reared in Brooklyn, New York. He received a three-year scholarship to the Cartoonists and Illustrators School after high school. After serving in the United States Air Force (1953–1959), he attended New York's School of Visual Arts. His comic strip, *Tommy Traveler in the World of Negro History,* was a feature of Harlem's newspaper *New York Age.*

In 1964, he worked in Ghana for the Ghana Government Publishing Company. He returned to the United States two years later and began working on children's books on African and African-American subjects. In his work for the Guyana government (1971–1974), he served as a consultant for the Guyanese Children's Book Division and taught Guyanese illustrators.

He illustrated *Moja Means One: Swahili Counting Book* and *Jambo Means Hello: Swahili Alphabet Book,* Caldecott Honor Books written by his former wife, Muriel. His illustrations have won the Coretta Scott King. Award three times—in 1979 for *Something on My Mind,* by Nikki Grimes; in 1994 for *Soul Looks Back in Wonder*; and in 1996 for *The Middle Passage: White Ships, Black Cargo*—and honorable mention in 1982 for *Daydreamers* by Eloise Greenfield. Feelings was awarded a National Endowment for the Arts fellowship in 1982.

He has illustrated more than twenty books and, in addition to the above awards, has also received the School of Visual Arts Outstanding Achievement Award and at least eight certificates of merit from the Society of Illustrators.

His paintings are in the private collections of many notable African Americans, including Maya Angelou, Roberta Flack, the late Alex Haley, and Cicely Tyson. In 1990, he was named artist-in-residence at the University of South Carolina, Columbia.

Feelings received an honorary degree of Doctor of Fine Arts from the School of Visual Arts in New York City in 1996 and the following year received an honorary doctorate of Humane Letters from John Jay College of Criminal Justice in New York City.

He is retired from teaching at the University of South Carolina where he taught for five years and is doing freelance book illustrations full time.

Feelings lives in Columbia, South Carolina.

BIBLIOGRAPHY

Song of the Empty Bottles. By Osmond Molarsky. H.Z. Walck, 1968.

Bola and the Oba's Drummers. By Letta Schatz. McGraw-Hill, 1967.

To Be a Slave. By Julius Lester. Dial, 1968.

The Tuesday Elephant. By Nancy Garfield. Crowell, 1968.

When the Stones Were Soft: East African Fireside Tales. By Eleanor Butler Heady. Funk & Wagnalls, 1968.

Black Folktales. By Julius Lester. R.W. Baron, 1969.

Tales of Temba: Traditional African Stories. Edited by Kathleen Arnott. H.Z. Walck, 1969.

Zamani Goes to Market. By Muriel Feelings. Seabury, 1970. Houghton, 1979.

Moja Means One: Swahili Counting Book. By Muriel Feelings. Dial, 1971, 1976.

Black Pilgrimage. Lothrop, 1972.

Jambo Means Hello: Swahili Alphabet Book. By Muriel Feelings. Dial, 1974. Reprint, 1985.

Something on My Mind. By Nikki Grimes. Dial, 1978.

Daydreamers. By Eloise Greenfield. Dial, 1981.

Now Sheba Sings the Song. By Maya Angelou. Dial, 1987.

Tommy Traveler in the World of Black History. Black Butterfly, 1991.

Soul Looks Back in Wonder. Edited by Phyllis Fogelman. Dial, 1993.

The Middle Passage: White Ships, Black Cargo. Dial, 1995.

See also Feelings, Muriel (Gray); Greenfield, Eloise (Glynn Little); Grimes, Nikki; Lester, Julius

Ferguson, Amos

(1920–)

ILLUSTRATOR

Ferguson, who prefers to be called Mr. Amos Ferguson, was born in Exuma, the Bahamas. He was one of fourteen children, and his preacher father, who was also a carpenter, inspired his Bible reading. Ferguson left home as a teenager and moved to Nassau, where he polished furniture, learned to paint houses, and then decided to work as a house painter.

The subject matter of his paintings reflects his Bahamian background and origin. His paintings are rich with the colors depicting the flora and fauna of the Bahamas, and many display his deep religious bent and interest in Bible readings.

His exhibition at the Wadsworth Atheneum in Hartford, Connecticut, in 1985 traveled around the United States for two years. The Connecticut Public Television documentary on this island artist received an Emmy nomination. Ferguson's religious convictions are evident in his artwork, some of which is displayed at the Pompey Museum's permanent exhibition in the Bahamas.

He won a Coretta Scott King Honor Book Award in 1989 for his illustration of *Under the Sunday Tree*. During a brief 1978 visit, New Yorker Sukie Miller bought one of his paintings, the first in a series which led to the 1985 Wadsworth Atheneum exhibition "Paint By Mr. Amos Ferguson." He is now well represented in significant collections worldwide.

He is married and lives in Nassau, Bahamas.

BIBLIOGRAPHY

Under the Sunday Tree. By Eloise Greenfield. Harper, 1988.

See also Greenfield, Eloise (Glynn Little)

Ferguson, Dwayne J.

(1965–)

AUTHOR, ILLUSTRATOR

Ferguson was born in Jersey City, New Jersey, and has been dreaming of reaching beyond the stars ever since. In 1984, when he was nineteen and in his sophomore year at Rutgers College, *Hamster Vice*, his popular fourteen-issue comic book series, was published. The first issue, *Hamster Vice: Rumble Roach*, sold 42,000 copies in one month and placed Ferguson's feet into the door of professional comics.

Ferguson then created the futuristic detective Captain Africa. In November 1990, Ferguson's publishing company, African Price Productions, released the 120-page illustrated novel *Captain Africa: The Battle for Egyptica*. The book sold well and caught the eye of Africa World Press publisher Kassahun Checole, who picked up the publishing chores on Ferguson's next five novels.

A recipient of the Outstanding Young Men of America Award, Ferguson continues to develop a large portfolio of achievements.

He is married and lives in Glen Ridge, New Jersey.

BIBLIOGRAPHY

Captain Africa: The Battle for Egyptica. Africa World, 1992.
The Amazing Adventures of Abiola. By Jeffrey J. and Debra A. Dean. Africa World, 1994.
Captain Africa and the Fury of Anubis. Africa World, 1994.
Kid Caramel, Private Investigator: Case of the Missing Ankh. Just Us Books, 1997.

Flournoy, Valerie (Rose)

(1 9 5 2–)

AUTHOR

"I was always a voracious reader ever since my earlier elementary years. I real-ized that although I had favorite books or characters during my grammar school years, I couldn't recall reading or seeing any fictional books with Black charac-ters. I think it was then that I knew I wanted to be a part of anything that would bring books to young Black children that would either lift self-esteem, open imaginations, reveal previously unknown facts, or just plain entertain in a new way or light. With these goals in mind, I am continually motivated by the joy of taking one little thought or idea and stretching it into what I hope will be a memorable story that all people can enjoy."

Born in Camden, New Jersey, the author is the third of five children. Her twin sister, Vanessa, is the author of *All-American Girl,* a Silhou-ette First Love published in 1983 under the name Vanessa Payton.

Flournoy received her bachelor's degree and teacher's certifica-tion in social studies (grades seven to twelve) from Hobart and Will-iam Smith College in Geneva, New York. She became senior editor for Silhouette Romance Books/Pocket Books and editorial consultant for another romance line. Her book *The Patchwork Quilt* received a Chris-topher Wood Award and the 1986 Ezra Jack Keats New Writer Award. The illustrations by Jerry Pinkney won the 1986 Coretta Scott King Award.

Flournoy is a former member of the board of directors for the Perkins Center for the Arts of South Jersey. She is also a former mem-ber of Black Women in Publishing and was associated with Vis a Vis Publishing in Palmyra, New Jersey, where she lives. Flournoy travels and writes full time.

BIBLIOGRAPHY

The Best Time of Day. Illustrated by George Ford. Random House, 1978, 1992.

The Twins Strike Back. Dial, 1978. Just Us Books (Illustrated by Melodye Rosales), 1994.

The Patchwork Quilt. Illustrated by Jerry Pinkney. Dial, 1985.

Celie and the Harvest Fiddler. With Vanessa Flournoy. Illustrated by James Ransome. Tambourine, 1995.

Tanya's Reunion. Illustrated by Jerry Pinkney. Dial, 1995.

See also Ford, George (Cephas); Pinkney, Jerry; Ransome, James (Earl); Rosales, Melodye (Benson)

Ford, Bernette G(oldsen)

(1 9 5 0 –)

AUTHOR

Born in New York City, Ford recalls that she was a "dreamy child" who buried herself in books and was constantly reading. She grew up on Long Island, New York, the child of an interracial couple. Both parents were deeply involved in the civil-rights movement. Her mother, an African American, and her father, a European American, instilled in her, her brother, and her sister a strong sense of identity and Black pride.

Ford's cousin, playwright Douglas Turner Ward, was the founder of the Negro Ensemble Company, and she remembers how proud she was in junior high school when he elected to display her review of one of its earliest plays on the theater's bulletin board for months.

Ford's interest in books led to a career in publishing after graduation from Connecticut College. She began work as an editorial assistant in the children's-book division at Random House and held various editorial positions from 1972 to 1979, when she moved to Golden Press, where she was a senior editor. In 1983, she became editorial director for Grosset and Dunlap, where she stayed for six years, and was vice president and publisher when she left in 1989. She now works at Scholastic, where she is a vice president and editorial director, and has started her own imprint, Cartwheel Books for the Very Young.

She and her husband, illustrator George Ford, have a daughter, Olivia, and live in Brooklyn, New York.

BIBLIOGRAPHY

Bright Eyes, Brown Skin. With Cheryl Willis Hudson. Illustrated by George Ford. Just Us Books, 1990.

The Hunter Who Was King and Other African Folk Tales. Illustrated by George Ford. Hyperion, 1994.

See also Ford, George (Cephas); Hudson, Cheryl Willis

Ford, George (Cephas)

(1936–)

ILLUSTRATOR

"For an illustrator whose subject is the portrayal of Black life and Black children, it's important to use the story as a beginning, an opportunity to arouse in himself, and express to his readers, those broader human qualities that have helped us to survive this long—those qualities that are positive, full of energy and enthusiasm. All of these things I hope come out automatically, and inspire, and uplift, the young people who read the books.

The object of the drawing is not just to elicit admiration for one's technique, or admiration of any kind. Experimentation with techniques is valuable in the execution of a work and in tapping one's intuition, one's own creativity. But that is not the primary aim. The content and the emotion in the work are far more important than stylistic innovation or anything of that sort. I strive to touch my readers at an emotional level, and thereby change their lives."

Ford was born in Brooklyn, New York, and spent part of his early childhood in Barbados. His vivid memories include those of his Bajan maternal grandmother, who drew amazing portraits of friends and family on slate with chalk. He credits her with inspiring him to become an artist, and his sister Marguerita, a children's librarian, with encouraging him to illustrate children's books.

He studied in New York City at the Art Students League, Pratt Institute, Cooper Union, and the School of Visual Arts and graduated from the City College of New York with a bachelor of science degree in education. His drawings and paintings have appeared in *Harper's* magazine and the Brooklyn Museum, including the 1971 exhibition, Black Artists in Graphic Communications.

Ford was art director at Eden Advertising in New York City and design director of *Black Theater* magazine. In 1974, he was awarded the first Coretta Scott King Award for illustration, for *Ray Charles* by Sharon Bell Mathis.

Ford is married to author Bernette G. Ford. They have one daughter, Olivia, and live in Brooklyn, New York.

BIBLIOGRAPHY

Little Boy Black. By Alfred W. Wilkes. Scribner, 1971.

The Singing Turtle and Other Tales from Haiti. By Phillipe Thoby-Marcelin. Farrar, 1971.

Walk On. By Mel Williamson and George Ford. Third Press, 1972.

Ray Charles. By Sharon Bell Mathis. Crowell, 1973.

Ego Tripping and Other Poems for Young People. By Nikki Giovanni. Revised Edition. Lawrence Hill, 1974.

Paul Robeson. By Eloise Greenfield. Crowell, 1975.

Far Eastern Beginnings. By Olivia Vlahos. Viking, 1976.

The Best Time of Day. By Valerie Flournoy. Random House, 1978, 1992.

Baby's First Picture Book. Random House, 1979.

Darlene. By Eloise Greenfield. Methuen, 1980.

Alesia. By Eloise Greenfield and Alesia Revis. Philomel, 1981.

Afro-Bets First Book About Africa. By Veronica F. Ellis. Just Us Books, 1990.

Bright Eyes, Brown Skin. By Cheryl Willis Hudson and Bernette G. Ford. Just Us Books, 1990.

Jamal's Busy Day. By Wade Hudson. Just Us Books, 1991.

Good Morning, Baby. By Cheryl Willis Hudson. Scholastic, 1992.

Good Night, Baby. By Cheryl Willis Hudson. Scholastic, 1992.

Willie's Wonderful Pet. By Mel Cebulash. Scholastic, 1993.

The Hunter Who Was King and Other African Tales. By Bernette G. Ford. Hyperion, 1994.

Animal Sounds for Baby. By Cheryl Willis Hudson. Scholastic, 1995.

Baby Jesus, Like My Brother. By Margery Wheeler Brown. Just Us Books, 1995.

Let's Count, Baby. By Cheryl Willis Hudson. Scholastic, 1995.

The Story of Ruby Bridges. By Robert Coles. Scholastic, 1995.

Wild, Wild Hair. By Nikki Grimes. Scholastic, 1996.

See also Brown, Margery Wheeler; Ellis, Veronica F.; Flournoy, Valerie; Ford, Bernette G.; Giovanni, Nikki (Yolanda Cornelia); Greenfield, Eloise (Glynn Little); Grimes, Nikki; Hudson, Cheryl Willis; Hudson, Wade; Mathis, Sharon Bell

Forman, James

(1928–)

AUTHOR

Forman was born in Chicago, Illinois, and attended Roosevelt University there, receiving a bachelor's degree in public administration in 1957. He earned a master's degree in professional studies/African and Afro-American affairs from Cornell University, Ithaca, New York, in 1980 and a doctorate in political history from the Union Institute, Cincinnati, Ohio, in 1982.

Forman served as executive secretary of the Student Non-Violent Coordinating Committee from 1961 to 1966 and was its international-affairs director from 1966 to 1969.

He is the recipient of many awards and honors, including the 1990 Fannie Lou Hamer Freedom Award from the National Council of Black Mayors and a 1991 certificate of appreciation from the University of Michigan, Ann Arbor.

The author lives in Washington, D.C.

BIBLIOGRAPHY

Self-Determination: An Examination of the Question and Its Application to the African-American People. Open Hand, 1981.
The Making of Black Revolutionaries. Open Hand, 1985.
Sammy Younge, Jr: The First Black College Student to Die in the Black Liberation Movement. Open Hand, 1986.
High Tide of Black Resistance and Other Political and Literary Writings. Open Hand, 1994.

Franklin, Harold L(eroy)
Chikuyo Alimayo

(1 9 3 4 –)

AUTHOR, ILLUSTRATOR, FILMMAKER

Franklin was born in Mobile, Alabama, an only child. His childhood creative expression began with art, for which he won numerous awards. Upon graduating from high school, he was awarded a full scholarship to the Philadelphia College of Art, where he was graduated with honors. He also served in the United States Army, assigned to Special Services. His award-winning design of Fort Eustis's newspaper masthead was used for many years after he left the Army. He has chosen the African name of Chikuyo Alimayo but publishes under the name of Harold L. Franklin.

Franklin is a graphic design specialist for the city of Philadelphia. In addition to his full-time position, he has done freelance artwork for many local and national publications, including the *Philadelphia Inquirer* and the *New York Times* newspapers and *Business Week* magazine.

He illustrated the award-winning children's book *Boss Cat,* written by Kristin Hunter Lattany, and has also written, illustrated, and published three books of his own. *Once Around the Track* was developed into a motion picture, which he filmed, directed, and edited and for which he composed the music score. It has been broadcast on several Public Broadcasting System (PBS) stations.

Franklin lives in Philadelphia, Pennsylvania.

BIBLIOGRAPHY

Which Way to Go. EKO, 1969.
Boss Cat. By Kristin Hunter. Scribner, 1971.
A Garden on Cement. EKO, 1973.
Once Around the Track. EKO, 1974.
A Trip Back to Elmwood. EKO, 1991.

See also Hunter (Lattany), Kristin

Freeman, Chester D(aniel)

(1 9 5 1 –)

AUTHOR

"My approach to children's literature is through the sensory world of the non-reader with the words and symbols of the reader. I have always seen books as a means of transportation to take me out of one world so that I can experience another. It is my hope that the books I write will inform, amuse, and stimulate the reader."

Freeman was born in Belhaven, North Carolina. As a chaplain at Amherst College, he began making stuffed animals, and students urged him to participate in a faculty craft show. He chose teddy bears to be the perfect entry because they seemed to be everywhere in the student dormitories. He later began to use teddy bears while ministering to the sick at Hartford Hospital. As more and more people wished to purchase the bears, he began to refocus his vocation on making bears.

He received a special honor from the state of New York in 1994 when the legislature adopted a resolution put forth by Senator John R. Kuhl recognizing him as "a nationally known teddy bear artist" and honoring him for his recently published children's book, *Runaway Bear.* A collection of his bears was purchased by the curatorial staff of the world's largest children's museum in Indianapolis, Indiana. Freeman made his television debut in 1997 on the Carol DuVall show on Home and Garden Television.

He lives in Geneva, New York.

BIBLIOGRAPHY

Runaway Bear. Illustrated by Rachel Kuper. Pelican, 1993.

Fufuka, Karama
Sharon Antonia Morgan

(1 9 5 1 –)

AUTHOR

Fufuka was born in Chicago, Illinois, and attended Loop City College, one of the Chicago city colleges. She has a variety of interests and work experiences as secretary, receptionist, and associate director of the Provident Community Development Corporation. She has contributed articles to *Ebony Jr., Essence,* and *Lifestyles,* and has been an editor of the *Woodburn Community Observer* since 1975.

BIBLIOGRAPHY

My Daddy Is a Cool Dude and Other Poems. Illustrated by Mahiri Fufuka. Dial, 1975.

Fullen-Collins,
Marilyn Kaye

(1 9 5 4 –)

AUTHOR

"My opinion of current trends in children's books is [that] the rise of multiculturalism . . . is fine but because of it, books geared toward children on various ethnicities are sorely lacking. That causes a tremendous void!"

Fullen-Collins was born in Los Angeles, California. She is a social worker for the Church Council of Greater Seattle Homelessness Project in Seattle, Washington, providing direct service to homeless mothers and their children.

She has been published in many magazines, including *Before Columbus* and *Moreno.* Her book, *Pathblazers,* chronicles the lives and achievements of eight African American women and men and their participation and accomplishments in the civil-rights movement, the field of education, and the arts.

She is a regular contributor to the *Quarterly Black Review of Books,* and her work has appeared in *Sisterfire, Black Womanist Fiction and Poetry, Divine Mosaic,* and *Women's Images of the Sacred Other.* She is a regular commentator on KUOW, a local public radio Seattle station. She conducts workshops on anger management and conflict resolution and on multicultural issues in Seattle-area schools and universities.

She and her husband have one son and live in Seattle, Washington.

BIBLIOGRAPHY

Pathblazers. Open Hand, 1992.

Gantt, Derrick

(1956–)

AUTHOR

A native of Philadelphia, Pennsylvania, Gantt was educated in the Philadelphia public school system. As the seventh of twelve children, he learned that independence and resourcefulness are the keys to success. After high school, Gantt joined the United States Army, and, through a successful nine-year career in financial printing, he developed a wealth of contacts who encouraged him to launch Songhai Press.

His first book, *The Storyteller,* was the first in a series of four publications that teach African history through mystical tales that offer facts on great kingdoms of the African continent.

Gantt lives in Philadelphia, Pennsylvania, with his wife and children.

BIBLIOGRAPHY

The Storyteller. Illustrated by J. Brian Pinkney and Nanette Wilkens. Songhai, 1981.

Hey Pop-Pop! Songhai, 1993.

The Storyteller II: Candace. Illustrated by Mark Hyman and Darrell Lewis. Songhai, 1993.

Eboni and the Dinosaur. Illustrated by Katy Blander. Songhai, 1994.

My First Week of School. By Derrick Gantt and Joanette Parker. Illustrated by Katy Blander. Songhai, 1996.

See also Pinkney, Brian

Gayle, Addison

(1932–1991)

The author, born in Newport News, Virginia, received his bachelor's degree from the City College of New York and his master's degree from the University of California, Los Angeles.

A teacher of writing and literature, Gayle was a professor of American and African-American literature at the University of Washington and lectured at City College, serving on the chancellor's committee on prisons and the Graduate Center's committee on English programs. He was a consultant to minority writers at Doubleday and Random House publishers and was on the editorial staffs of *Amistad* magazine, Third World Press, and *Black World* magazine. He also sponsored the Richard Wright Award for the minority scholarship program SEEK, given each semester to the student with the highest scholastic average.

Gayle was a member of P.E.N. International and the Authors Guild and a Distinguished Professor of English at Bernard M. Baruch College in New York City.

BIBLIOGRAPHY

Oak and Ivy: A Biography of Paul Laurence Dunbar. Doubleday, 1981.

See also Dunbar, Paul Laurence

Geter, Tyrone

(1945–)

ILLUSTRATOR

Geter was born in Anniston, Alabama, the third of three children. He received a master of fine arts degree and taught at several colleges and universities. In 1988, Geter joined the faculty of the University of Akron, Ohio, where he is an associate professor in the School of Art.

The first children's book he illustrated, *Irene and the Big, Fine Nickel,* was proclaimed one of 1991's Best Books for Young Readers by *Time* magazine. His second illustrated book, *Dawn's Friends,* was chosen in 1992 by the New England Book Show and the Book Builders of Boston for Best Design and Production.

Geter won First-Place Painting and Best of Show awards at the Akron Art Expo and honorable mention at the Twenty-Fourth Annual Boston Mills Artfest in 1995. His works can be seen at Hikima Creations in Akron, Ohio.

Geter is married and the father of one son, Gerald, and two daughters, Jamila and Hafizah. He lives in Akron, Ohio.

BIBLIOGRAPHY

Irene and the Big, Fine Nickel. By Irene Smalls. Little, Brown, 1991.
Dawn's Friends. By Irene Smalls. D.C. Heath, 1992.
Dawn and the Round To-It. By Irene Smalls. Simon & Schuster, 1994.
My Black Me. Edited by Arnold Adoff. Dutton, 1994.
Can't Scare Me! By Melissa Milich. Delacorte, 1995.
Sound the Jubilee. By Sandra Forrester. Lodestar, 1995.
Willie Jerome. By Alice Faye Duncan. Macmillan, 1995.
A Day for Phyllis Mae. By Laura Pegram. Dial, 1996.
The Little Tree Growin in the Shade. By Camille Yarbrough. Putnam, 1996.
White Socks Only. By Evelyn Coleman. Whitman, 1996.

See also Dunbar, Alice Faye; Smalls, Irene; Yarbrough, Camille

Gibson, Sylvia Ann (Scott)

(1 9 5 3 –)

AUTHOR, ILLUSTRATOR

"My approach to my work is serious. I enjoy seeing children's eyes light up when they are reading and enjoying a good book. I like for children to learn as they enjoy a book."

Gibson was born in Mound Bayou, Mississippi. In 1979, she was awarded a certificate in family day-care management. Her education also includes a degree in nursery-school education received in 1981.

Gibson has received a plaque for special recognition and a certificate from the Drake Park Head Start Program. One of her poems, "Spring," was published in *American Poetry Anthology* in 1990.

Since 1994, she has been a member of the Cite Base Management Team in Fort Worth, Texas, where she lives. She and her husband, James Gibson, have nine children.

BIBLIOGRAPHY

Latawnya, the Naughty Horse, Learns to Say "No" to Drugs. Vantage, 1991.

Gilchrist, Jan Spivey

(1949–)

AUTHOR, ILLUSTRATOR

"As in over twenty years of fine-art works having the same philosophy, I wish to always portray a positive and sensitive image for all children, especially the African American children."

Gilchrist was born in Chicago, Illinois. She obtained her bachelor of science degree in art education at Eastern Illinois University in 1973 and her master of arts degree in painting from the University of Northern Iowa in 1979. In 1990, she received the Coretta Scott King Award for her illustrations in *Nathaniel Talking* by Eloise Greenfield. Her illustrations for another Greenfield book, *Night on Neighborhood Street,* won her a Coretta Scott King Honor Book Award in 1992, as well as the Distinguished Alumni Award from Eastern Illinois University, also in 1992. *Lift Ev'ry Voice and Sing* received a starred review in *Booklist.*

In 1985, Gilchrist received the first award given by the National Academic Artists Association. Her artwork has won five Purchase Awards from the DuSable Museum of African American History in Chicago, Illinois. She is an honorary member of Alpha Kappa Alpha sorority and a member of Phi Delta Kappa.

Gilchrist is the mother of an adult daughter and a young son. Her husband, Dr. Kelvin Gilchrist, is both her literary agent and her strongest supporter. They live in Olympia Fields, Illinois.

BIBLIOGRAPHY

Children of Long Ago. By Lessie Jones Little. Philomel, 1988.
Nathaniel Talking. By Eloise Greenfield. Black Butterfly, 1989.
Big Friend, Little Friend. By Eloise Greenfield. Black Butterfly, 1991.
Everett Anderson's Christmas Coming. By Lucille Clifton. Holt, 1991.

First Pink Light. By Eloise Greenfield. Black Butterfly, 1991.

I Make Music. By Eloise Greenfield. Black Butterfly, 1991.

My Daddy and I. By Eloise Greenfield. Black Butterfly, 1991.

My Doll, Keshia. By Eloise Greenfield. Black Butterfly, 1991.

Night on Neighborhood Street. By Eloise Greenfield. Dial, 1991.

Red Dog, Blue Fly. By Sharon Bell Mathis. Viking, 1991.

Aaron and Gayla's Alphabet Book. By Eloise Greenfield. Black Butterfly, 1992.

Aaron and Gayla's Counting Book. By Eloise Greenfield. Black Butterfly, 1992.

Indigo and Moonlight Gold. Black Butterfly, 1992.

Lisa's Daddy and Daughter Day. By Eloise Greenfield. Black Butterfly, 1991. Sundance, 1993.

William and the Good Old Days. By Eloise Greenfield. HarperCollins, 1993.

Baby. By Monica Greenfield. HarperCollins, 1994.

On My Horse. By Eloise Greenfield. HarperCollins, 1994, 1995.

Sweet Baby Coming. By Eloise Greenfield. HarperCollins, 1994.

Honey, I Love. By Eloise Greenfield. HarperCollins, 1995.

Lift Ev'ry Voice and Sing. By James Weldon Johnson. Scholastic, 1995.

Sharing Danny's Dad. By Angela Shelf Medearis. HarperCollins, 1995.

Mimi's Tutu. By Tynia Thomassie. Scholastic, 1996.

Waiting for Christmas. By Monica Greenfield. Scholastic, 1996.

For the Love of the Game: Michael Jordan and Me. By Eloise Greenfield. HarperCollins, 1997.

Kia Tanisha. By Eloise Greenfield. HarperCollins, 1997.

Kia Tanisha Drives Her Car. By Eloise Greenfield. HarperCollins, 1997.

See also Clifton, (Thelma) Lucille (Sayles); Greenfield, Eloise (Glynn Little); Greenfield, Monica; Johnson, James Weldon; Little, Lessie Jones; Mathis, Sharon Bell; Medearis, Angela Shelf

Giovanni, Nikki (Yolanda Cornelia)

(1 9 4 3 –)

AUTHOR

Giovanni was born in Knoxville, Tennessee, and moved with her family to Cincinnati, Ohio, when she was quite young. She earned her bachelor's degree at Fisk University and later attended the University of Pennsylvania School of Social Work and Columbia University.

Among her awards are a Ford Foundation grant in 1968 and a National Endowment for the Arts grant in 1969. Honorary doctorates from Wilberforce University, Smith College, the University of Maryland, Rockville College, and Widener University, as well as a citation from *Ebony* magazine in 1969 as one of the Ten Most Admired Black Women have made her much in demand on the lecture circuit.

Giovanni has been an assistant professor of Black studies at Queens College of the City University of New York, an associate professor of English at Livingston College, Rutgers University, and an editorial consultant for *Encore* magazine. She is a professor of English at Virginia Tech Institute and State University in Blacksburg, Virginia, where she currently lives.

BIBLIOGRAPHY

Spin a Soft Black Song: Poems for Children. Illustrated by Charles Bible. Hill & Wang, 1971.
Ego Tripping and Other Poems for Young People. Illustrated by George Ford. Revised Edition. Lawrence Hill, 1974.
Vacation Time: Poems for Children. Illustrated by Marisabina Russo. Morrow, 1981.
Grand Mothers: A Multicultural Anthology of Poems, Short Stories and Reminiscences About the Keepers of Our Traditions. Holt, 1994.
Knoxville, Tennessee. Illustrated by Larry Johnson. Scholastic, 1994.

The Genie in the Jar. Illustrated by Chris Raschka. Holt, 1995.
Shimmy Shimmy Shimmy Like My Sister Kate: Looking at the Harlem Renaissance Through Poems. Holt, 1996.
The Sun Is So Quiet. Illustrated by Ashley Bryan. Holt, 1996.

See also Bible, Charles; Bryan, Ashley; Ford, George

Graham, Lorenz (Bell)

(1902–1989)

AUTHOR

Graham was born in New Orleans, Louisiana, and educated at the University of California, Los Angeles. He graduated from Virginia Union University, and attended the New York School of Social Work, and New York University. He taught at Monrovia College, Liberia, from 1925 to 1929.

The religious influence of his minister father is reflected in Graham's early work. His own trip to Liberia to teach in a missionary school heightened his awareness of the African people and inspired him to attempt to dispel some of the stereotypes he had read in books. His first book, *How God Fix Jonah*, was followed by other Bible stories for young readers using the African speech patterns he had heard. It was his sister, author Shirley Graham, the widow of W.E.B. Du Bois, who alerted publishers to her brother's stories.

Later, Graham dealt more directly with race relations in the United States with *South Town, North Town, Whose Town?* and *Return to South Town*. This series relates the continuing saga of a family in a small Southern town and later in an urban setting in the North, where racial tensions were even greater after World War II and the Korean War and the disparities between the races was quite pronounced.

Graham won a Coretta Scott King Honor Book Award in 1971, the Thomas Alva Edison Foundation Citation in 1956, the Charles W. Follett Award in 1958, the Southern California Council of Literature for Children and Young People Award in 1968, and first prize from Book World in 1969.

In 1987, at the age of 85, he was one of two invited authors from the United States to speak at a Symposium on Literature for Children and Young Readers at the University of the Western Cape, South Africa. From that experience, he began a novel, *Cape Town,* which he did not finish.

Although Bell wrote primarily for the young, as did his sister, his reviewers often insisted that his suspenseful, realistic books are also appropriate for adults. Most of Graham's manuscripts are at the University of Minnesota, Minneapolis, and others are in the North Carolina Central University Library in Durham.

He was married to author Ruth Morris-Graham, and they had five children.

BIBLIOGRAPHY

How God Fix Jonah. Illustrated by Letterio Calapai. Reynal & Hitchcock, 1946.
Tales of Momolu. Illustrated by Letterio Calapai. Reynal & Hitchcock, 1947.
South Town. Follett, 1958.
North Town. Crowell, 1965.
I, Momolu. Illustrated by John Biggers. Crowell, 1966.
Whose Town? Crowell, 1969.
Every Man Heart Lay Down. Illustrated by Colleen Browning. Crowell, 1970.
A Road Down in the Sea. Crowell, 1971.
David He No Fear. Illustrated by Ann Grifalconi. Crowell, 1971.
God Wash the World and Start Again. Crowell, 1971.
John Brown's Raid. Scholastic, 1972.
Song of the Boat. Illustrated by Leo and Diane Dillon. Crowell, 1975.
Return to South Town. Crowell, 1976.
John Brown: A Cry for Freedom. Crowell, 1980.

See also Dillon, Leo; Graham, Ruth Morris; Graham (Du Bois), Shirley (Lola)

Graham, Ruth Morris

(1901–1996)

AUTHOR

Born in Charleston, South Carolina, the author was active in Christian work most of her life. Graham was educated at Nyack Missionary College in New York and studied at Shelton College and Hampton Institute in Virginia. She became a teacher and lecturer at the Boydton Institute and Virginia Seminary in Virginia.

Graham traveled widely, visiting more than fifty countries, and in 1969–1970 she made a six-month trip around the world, visiting missions and schools to counsel students, workers, and officials.

In 1975, Graham was awarded the Martin Luther King, Jr., Award by the Pacific Southwest Region, Disciples of Christ Church; in 1987, she received the Los Angeles Mayor's Certificate of Appreciation for Outstanding Service as president of Los Angeles's oldest Black organization of women, the Phys Art Lit Mor Club. She was also profiled in 1978 in *The World Who's Who of Women.*

She was married to Lorenz Graham, noted author, world traveler, and missionary to West Africa, who died in 1989. They had five children (one predeceased her), fifteen grandchildren and sixteen great-grandchildren. *Notable Americans,* a volume of books by the American Biographical Institute, profiled Graham in 1997. She was interviewed and appeared in the film "W.E.B. DuBois: A Biography in Four Voices," produced for television in 1995 by the Public Broadcasting System.

She was the sister-in-law of author Shirley Graham (Mrs. W.E.B. Du Bois). Graham died in Claremont, California, in 1996.

BIBLIOGRAPHY

The Happy Sound. Illustrated By Hans Zander. Follet, 1970.

Penny Savings Bank: The Story of Maggie L. Walker. Houghton, 1976.
Big Sister. Illstrated By Julie Downing. Houghton, 1981.

See also Graham, Lorenz (Bell); Graham (Du Bois), Shirley (Lola)

Graham (Du Bois), Shirley (Lola)

(1906–1977)

AUTHOR

Professionally known as Shirley Graham, Mrs. W.E.B. Du Bois was born in Indianapolis, Indiana. She studied music in Paris, obtained a French certificate from the Sorbonne, and earned her bachelor's and master's degrees from Oberlin College. She also studied at Yale University Drama School and received an honorary doctorate of letters from the University of Massachusetts in 1973.

Graham's many talents are reflected in the variety of positions she held in her career, including head of the Fine Arts Department of Tennessee State College, director of the Chicago Federal Theater, director of the YWCA, field secretary for the National Association for the Advancement of Colored People (NAACP), director of Ghana Television, founding editor of *Freedomways* magazine, and English editor in 1968 of the Afro-Asian Writers Bureau in Beijing, China.

She received many awards, including Rosenwald and Guggenheim fellowships from Yale University Drama School for historical research and in 1950 the Julian Messner Award for *There Was Once a Slave*. She also wrote five additional adult books.

She married twice and had two sons (one died in his twenties) from her first marriage. Her brother was author Lorenz Graham. Noted Black educator and author W.E.B. Du Bois became her second husband in 1951. She died in Beijing, China, on March 27, 1977. A biography, *DuBois: A Pictorial Biography,* was published posthumously in 1978 by Johnson Publishing Company.

BIBLIOGRAPHY

Dr. George Washingon Carver, Scientist. Illustrated by Elton C. Fax. Messner, 1944.

Paul Robeson, Citizen of the World. Messner, 1971.

There Once Was A Slave: The Heroic Story of Frederick Douglass. Messner, 1947.

The Story of Phyllis Wheatley. Illustrated by Robert Burns. Messner, 1949.

Jean Baptiste Pointe de Sable, Founder of Chicago. Messner, 1953.

The Story of Pocahontas. Grosset & Dunlap, 1953. Messner, 1955.

Booker T. Washington: Educator of Hand, Head and Heart. Messner, 1955.

His Day Is Marching On: A Memoir of W.E.B. Du Bois. Lippincott, 1971.

Gamal Abdel Nasser, Son of the Nile. Third Press, 1972.

Julius K. Nyerere: Teacher of Africa. Messner, 1975.

Du Bois: A Pictorial Biography. By Shirley Graham Du Bois. Johnson, 1978.

See also Fax, Elton C.; Graham, Lorenz (Bell); Graham, Ruth Morris

Green, Jonathan

(1 9 5 5–)

ILLUSTRATOR

"I believe there is inadequate literature for Black children in churches, schools, and day-care centers. It is during these formative years that children are in the process of developing their identity. Without ethnically and culturally relevant children's books with which the children can identify, I believe there will be educational as well as unfortunate developmental lags."

Green was born in Gardens Corner, South Carolina. He graduated in 1982 with a bachelor of fine arts degree from the School of the Art Institute of Chicago, Illinois. From 1982 through 1996, he had four traveling exhibitions throughout the United States, thirty solo exhibitions including eight museums, and thirty-two group exhibitions including sixteen museums. His work and contributions have been noted in more than 125 publications.

Among his numerous awards, he has received recognition for Outstanding Contributions to the Arts in 1991 and the Martin Luther King, Jr., Humanitarian Award for the Arts in 1993.

He served from 1993 to 1995 on the board of directors of Share our Strength, an organization that distributes grants from hunger relief, and was vice-president of the Collier County United Arts Council in Naples, Florida, from 1992 to 1994. He received an honorary doctorate in Fine Art in 1996 from the University of South Carolina at Columbia.

Green is a full-time artist who works from his studio. He lives in Naples, Florida.

BIBLIOGRAPHY

Father and Son. By Denizé Lauture. Philomel, 1992.

Noah. By Patricia A. Gauch. Philomel, 1994.
Crosby. By Dennis Haseley. Harcourt, 1996.

See also Lauture, Denizé

Greenfield, Eloise (Glynn Little)

(1 9 2 9 –)

AUTHOR

"The problems that existed in children's literature when my first book was pub-lished more than twenty years ago still face us today. Therefore, my major goals for my work have changed very little since that time. I want to depict African American people in the variety and complexity in which we appear in real life. I want to counteract the stereotypes with which we are bombarded daily by books, films, and television and provide a mirror in which African American children can find themselves and their families. I write with the hope that my work will inspire in readers a love for themselves, a love for language and lit-erature, and a commitment to humane values."

Greenfield was born Eloise Glynn Little in Parmele, North Carolina, to Weston Wilbur Little, Sr., and Lessie Jones Little, who collaborated in later years with her in writing two children's books.

Greenfield grew up in Washington, D.C., where she had moved with her family at the age of four months. From 1949 to 1971, she held a number of secretarial and administrative-assistant positions in the District of Columbia and federal governments. She began writing when she was in her twenties and had her first publication, a poem in the *Hartford Times,* in 1962. Her first children's book was published in 1972.

Now the author of more than thirty books, Greenfield continues to live in Washington. Under the auspices of the D.C. Commission on the Arts and Humanities, she has taught creative writing to children. She has received more than forty awards and citations for her books, includ-ing the first Carter G. Woodson Award, in 1974, from the National Council for Social Studies for *Rosa Parks,* the 1978 Coretta Scott King Award for *Africa Dream,* and the 1990 Recognition of Merit Award from the George G. Stone Center for Children's Books for *Honey, I Love.*

In 1993, she received the Ninth Annual Celebration of Black Writing Lifetime Achievement Award from Moonstone, Incorporated.

She received an award for Excellence in Poetry for Children in 1997 from the National Council of Teachers of English given for her body of works and the 1997 Humanist of the Year award given by the Washington, D.C., Humanities Council. She is a member of the African American Writers Guild and the Authors Guild.

Greenfield, who was formerly married to Robert J. Greenfield, has a son, Steven, a daughter, Monica, who also writes children's books, and four grandchildren. Greenfield lives in Washington, D.C.

BIBLIOGRAPHY

Bubbles. Illustrated by Eric Marlow. Drum & Spear, 1972.

Rosa Parks. Illustrated by Eric Marlow. Crowell, 1973.

She Come Bringing Me That Little Baby Girl. Illustrated by John Steptoe. Lippincott, 1974.

Sister. Illustrated by Moneta Barnett. Crowell, 1974.

First Pink Light. Illustrated by Moneta Barnett. Crowell, 1975. Black Butterfly (Illustrated by Jan Spivey Gilchrist), 1991.

Me and Neesie. Illustrated by Moneta Barnett. Crowell, 1975.

Paul Robeson. Illustrated by George Ford. Crowell, 1975.

Africa Dream. Illustrated by Carole Byard. HarperCollins, 1977.

Good News. Illustrated by Pat Cummings. Coward, 1977.

Mary McLeod Bethune. Illustrated by Jerry Pinkney. Crowell, 1977.

Honey, I Love. Illustrated by Leo and Diane Dillon. Crowell, 1978. HarperCollins (Illustrated by Jan Spivey Gilchrist), 1995.

I Can Do It by Myself. With Lessie Jones Little. Illustrated by Carole Byard. Crowell, 1978.

Talk About a Family. Illustrated by James Calvin. Lippincott, 1978.

Childtimes: A Three-Generation Memoir. With Lessie Jones Little. Illustrated by Jerry Pinkney. Harper, 1979.

Darlene. Illustrated by George Ford. Methuen, 1980.

Grandmama's Joy. Illustrated by Carole Byard. Philomel, 1980.

Alesia. With Alesia Revis. Illustrated by George Ford. Philomel, 1981.

Daydreamers. Illustrated by Tom Feelings. Dial, 1981.

Grandpa's Face. Illustrated by Floyd Cooper. Philomel, 1988.

Under the Sunday Tree. Illustrated by Amos Ferguson. Harper, 1988.

Nathaniel Talking. Illustrated by Jan Spivey Gilchrist. Black Butterfly, 1989.

Big Friend, Little Friend. Illustrated by Jan Spivey Gilchrist. Black Butterfly, 1991.

I Make Music. Illustrated by Jan Spivey Gilchrist. Black Butterfly, 1991.

Lisa's Daddy and Daughter Day. Illustrated by Jan Spivey Gilchrist. Black Butterfly, 1991. Sundance, 1993.

My Daddy and I. Illustrated by Jan Spivey Gilchrist. Black Butterfly, 1991.

My Doll, Keshia. Illustrated by Jan Spivey Gilchrist. Black Butterfly, 1991.

Night on Neighborhood Street. Illustrated by Jan Spivey Gilchrist. Dial, 1991.

Aaron and Gayla's Alphabet Book. Illustrated by Jan Spivey Gilchrist. Black Butterfly, 1992.

Aaron and Gayla's Counting Book. Illustrated by Jan Spivey Gilchrist. Black Butterfly, 1992.

Koya DeLaney and the Good Girl Blues. Scholastic, 1992.

William and the Good Old Days. Illustrated by Jan Spivey Gilchrist. HarperCollins, 1993.

On My Horse. Illustrated by Jan Spivey Gilchrist. HarperCollins, 1994, 1995.

Sweet Baby Coming. Illustrated by Jan Spivey Gilchrist. HarperCollins, 1994.

For the Love of the Game: Michael Jordan and Me. Illustrated by Jan Spivey Gilchrist, HarperCollins, 1997.

Kia Tanisha. Illustrated by Jan Spivey Gilchrist. HarperCollins, 1997.

Kia Tanisha Drives Her Car. Illustrated by Jan Spivey Gilchrist. HarperCollins, 1997.

See also Barnett, Moneta; Byard, Carole; Cooper, Floyd (Donald); Cummings, Pat; Dillon, Leo; Feelings, Tom; Ferguson, Amos; Ford, George (Cephas); Gilchrist, Jan Spivey; Little, Lessie Jones; Pinkney, Jerry; Steptoe, John (Lewis); Woodson, Carter G(odwin)

Greenfield, Monica

(1958–)

AUTHOR

Greenfield was born in Washington, D.C. As a child, she wrote poetry and loved to read and draw. She also loves music and has sung all of her life and hopes one day to combine the two careers. Her first book *Baby*, illustrated by Jan Spivey Gilchrist, was chosen by the American Booksellers Association as a Pick of the List book for 1994.

Greenfield worked for many years as a secretary at Howard University, the Children's Defense Fund, and other organizations. She is the mother of a young daughter, Kamaria, and is herself the daughter of the prominent children's author Eloise Greenfield.

She lives in Washington, D.C.

BIBLIOGRAPHY

Baby. Illustrated by Jan Spivey Gilchrist. HarperCollins, 1994.
Waiting for Christmas. Illustrated by Jan Spivey Gilchrist. Scholastic, 1996.

See also Gilchrist, Jan Spivey; Greenfield, Eloise (Glynn Little)

Griffin, Judith Berry

AUTHOR

Educated at the University of Chicago, Griffin received a bachelor of science and a master of arts degree in psychology. She also earned a master of arts degree in special education from Columbia University. After leaving a career as an elementary school teacher and principal, Griffin became director of A Better Chance, an organization that searches out and identifies achieving minority youth who may be qualified to enter private or preparatory schools in the United States. The board of A Better Chance is composed of corporation heads and individuals who help in the funding and provision of the scholarships for these students, many of whom are African American. It is possible that Griffin's own attendance at the Lab School at the University of Chicago helped prepare her for this job.

She lives in White Plains, New York.

BIBLIOGRAPHY

Nat Turner. Illustrated by Leo Carty. Coward, 1970.
The Magic Mirrors. Illustrated by Ernest Crichlow. Coward, 1971.
Phoebe and the General. Illustrated by Margot Tomes. Coward, 1971.
Phoebe the Spy. Scholastic, 1979.

See also Carty, Leo; Crichlow, Ernest

Griffith, Gershom

(1960-)

ILLUSTRATOR

The artist was born in Barbados, West Indies, the fourth of five children. He started drawing at the age of seven. When he was eleven years old, he and his family moved to New York City. Griffith attended the New York High School of Art and Design and also studied at the Art Students League.

The Brooklyn Public Libraries have exhibited his artwork for Black History Month, and his books have been reviewed by *School Library Journal, Publishers Weekly, Booklist,* and *Kirkus Reviews.*

Griffith is single and lives in Far Rockaway, New York.

BIBLIOGRAPHY

Pearl Bailey: With a Song in Her Heart. By Keith Brandt. Troll, 1992.

Rosa Parks: Fight for Freedom. By Keith Brandt. Troll, 1993.

Thurgood Marshall: Fight for Justice. By Rae Baines. Troll, 1993.

Journey to Freedom: A Story of the Underground Railroad. By Courtni C. Wright. Holiday House, 1994.

Jumping the Broom. By Courtni C. Wright. Holiday House, 1994.

A Picture Book of Sojourner Truth. By David A. Adler. Holiday House, 1994.

Toussaint L'Ouverture: Lover of Liberty. By Laurence Santrey. Troll, 1994.

I Can Swim. By David McCoy. Modern Curriculum, 1995.

Off to School. By Gwendolyn Battle-Lavert. Holiday House, 1995.

Wagon Train: A Family Goes West in 1865. By Courtni C. Wright. Holiday House, 1995.

Takiya and Thunderheart's Life Garden. By J. Victor McGuire. Spice of Life, 1997.

See also Battle-Lavert, Gwendolyn; Wright, Courtni C(rump)

Grimes, Nikki

(1 9 5 0–)

AUTHOR

"Within the realm of literature for Black children, I find there are not enough anthologies of contemporary African American children's authors and illustrators. Too few of the books I read growing up gave me back a mirror image of myself or of my childhood experiences. I write for today's children in jeopardy with a desire to validate their experiences, their feelings. Realizing that many of these children are reluctant readers, I strive to write books which are linguistically simple, though they may be emotionally complex. I hope my work gives readers some of the joy, inspiration, and healing I found in books as a child."

Grimes was born in Harlem, New York. She has worked at different times as a secretary, a library assistant, a literary consultant, a children's-book editor, a photographer, and a radio producer/host. Grimes majored in English and studied African languages at Livingston College and Rutgers University. She received a Ford Foundation grant in 1974 that enabled her to spend a year in Tanzania collecting folk tales and poetry. Journalism, photography, and poetry writing have kept her busy since 1975. Her poetry often appears in anthologies of modern American poetry.

Her book *Growin'* was named a Child Study Associations Best Book in 1977. *Something on My Mind* was selected in 1978 as an American Library Association Notable Book, a Library of Congress Children's Book, a Coretta Scott King Honor Book for its illustrations by Tom Feelings, a *Saturday Review* Best Book of the Season, and the *Philadelphia Inquirer* Best Book of the Year. *Malcolm X: A Force for Change* was a 1993 Image Award finalist, and *Meet Danitra Brown* was a Coretta Scott King Honor Book for illustration in 1995, an American Library Association Notable Book in the same year and received several starred reviews. *C Is for City* was included in the 1995 New York

Public Library list of Children's Books—100 Titles for Reading and Sharing. *Come Sunday* was named an American Library Association Notable Book in the category of poetry for all ages in 1996. Grimes writes full time and lives in Seattle, Washington.

BIBLIOGRAPHY

Growin'. Illustrated by Charles Lilly. Dial, 1977.
Something on My Mind. Illustated by Tom Feelings. Dial, 1978.
Malcolm X: A Force for Change. Fawcett, 1992.
From a Child's Heart. Illustrated by Brenda Joysmith. Just Us Books, 1993.
Meet Danitra Brown. Illustrated by Floyd Cooper. Lothrop, 1994.
Come Sunday. Illustrated by Michael Bryant. Eerdmanns, 1996.
Wild, Wild Hair. Illustrated by George Ford. Scholastic, 1996.
It's Raining Laughter. Illustrated by Myles C. Pinkney. Dial, 1997.

See also Bryant, Michael; Cooper, Floyd (Donald); Cummings, Pat; Feelings, Tom; Ford, George (Cephus); Lilly, Charles

Guirma, Frederic

Guirma was born in Ouagadougou, Upper Volta, in West Africa. He claims Naba Koumdoum 'ue,' the eighth emperor of the Mois people in the fourteenth century, as one of his ancestors. Guirma attended an elementary school taught by the Sisters of Our Lady of Africa and later the Seminary of Padre. He received his bachelor's degree in France and a master's degree from Loyola University in Los Angeles, California.

He has been secretary of the French Embassy in Ghana and served as vice consul in Kumesi, Ghana. When Upper Volta (which is now known as Burkina Faso) became an independent nation in 1960, he was its first ambassador to the United Nations and Washington, D.C. He has also been senior political affairs officer at United Nations headquarters in New York City.

In his spare time, Guirma writes and paints. His book *Princess of the Full Moon*, which he wrote and illustrated, is based on folklore of Upper Volta.

BIBLIOGRAPHY

Princess of the Full Moon. Macmillan, 1970.
Tales of Mogho: African Stories from Upper Volta. Macmillan, 1971.

Gunning, Monica (Olwen)

(1930–)

AUTHOR

"I write for children and young people because I love children's literature. I approach my work realizing that children deserve the best to develop their language and writing skills and a love of literature."

Born in Jamaica, West Indies, Gunning loved to read and recite poetry as a child. When she was twelve years old, she won a scholarship to attend Mannings High School in Jamaica. After high school, she came to the United States and graduated from City College of New York with a bachelor of science degree in education in 1957.

Gunning taught preschool through sixth grade in Los Angeles, California, and she was named to the organization of Outstanding Elementary Teachers of America. Fluent in Spanish, she traveled extensively in Mexico and studied at the Institute of Cuernavaca and the University of Guadalajara and holds a bilingual teaching credential.

She is affiliated with a number of writing groups, including the Society of Children's Book Writers and Illustrators; Women Writers West of Los Angeles; the Southern California Council on Literature for Children and Young People; and is active in the Toastmaster's Club where she was elected president of the Beverly Hills chapter.

Her book, *Not a Copper Penny in Me House,* was named a National Council of Teachers of English Notable Book for 1994 and received excellent reviews as a multicultural book.

She and her husband Elon have two sons and live in Toluca Lake, California.

BIBLIOGRAPHY

Not a Copper Penny in Me House. Illustrated by Frané Lessac. Boyds Mills, 1993.

Guy, Rosa (Cuthbert)

(1 9 2 5 –)

AUTHOR

Rosa Guy was born in Trinidad, West Indies. She was brought to the United States in 1932, grew up in Harlem, New York, and later attended New York University. She also studied at the American Negro Theater.

Guy is a founder and former president of the Harlem Writers Guild. She writes adult books and novels as well as children's books.

The Friends, first of a trilogy of novels for young people, was cited among the Best Books for Young Adults by the American Library Association and selected as the *New York Times* Outstanding Book of the Year in 1973. Other books in the trilogy are *Ruby* and *Edith Jackson.*

Guy's book for younger children, *Mother Crocodile = Maman–Caiman* was an American Library Association Notable Book and won the 1982 Coretta Scott King Award for its illustrations by John Steptoe. A musical play, *Once on This Island,* was based on a short novel by Guy titled *My Love, My Love.* The play was performed on Broadway during the 1991 season. She has one son, Warner, and is the widow of Warner Guy. She lives in New York City.

BIBLIOGRAPHY

The Friends. Holt, 1973.
Ruby. Viking, 1976.
Edith Jackson. Viking, 1978.
The Disappearance. Delacorte, 1979.
Mother Crocodilee = Maman–Caiman. By Birago Diop. Translated and adapted by Rosa Guy. Illustrated by John Steptoe.
Mirror of Her Own. Delacorte, 1981.
New Guys Around the Block. Viking, 1983.
Paris, Pee Wee and Big Dog. Illustrated by Caroline Binch. Delacorte, 1984.

And I Heard a Bird Sing. Delacorte, 1987.
The Ups and Downs of Carl Davis III. Delacorte, 1989.
Billy the Great. Illustrated by Caroline Binch. Dell, 1992.
The Music of Summer. Delacorte, 1992.

See also Diop, Birago (Ismael); Steptoe, John (Lewis)

Hall, Beverly Hawkins

(1 9 4 6 –)

ILLUSTRATOR

Born in Denver, Colorado, Hall began drawing paper dolls in elementary school. What began as a playtime activity developed into a career and lifelong love.

Hall's talent for drawing and design led in 1964 to a scholarship to the Colorado Institute of Arts, where she completed her formal training. After graduating with a degree in advertising, design and illustration, she was first employed with Denver's Neusteters Department Store as a designer/illustrator. Over the next ten years, she worked in both Denver and Los Angeles, designing product packaging and advertising pieces for major advertising agencies, cosmetics, fashion, and publishing companies.

In 1977, Hall settled in Los Angeles, where she accepted a position with the Los Angeles Community College District as a graphic designer, discontinuing for two years to work as an illustrator/designer for the *Los Angeles Times*.

With the publication of *Black Women for Beginners* by Saundra Sharp in 1993, Hall's illustrations won widespread recognition.

Hall and her husband live in Los Angeles, California, with their two children.

BIBLIOGRAPHY

Black Women for Beginners. By Saundra Pearl Sharp. Writers & Readers, 1993.

Hall, LaVerne C(orine) Williams

AUTHOR, ILLUSTRATOR

Born in Austin, Texas, Hall is the founder and producer of Holiday Festival of Black Dolls, the largest and oldest touring Black doll festival in the world. Among other activities, she is an associate in a marketing and management consulting firm and president of the Carter G. Woodson Group, an organization she founded to preserve and promote Black history. In addition, Hall is a licensed Baptist minister and conducts a prison ministry. She has been written about not only locally but also nationally in such publications as *Vogue*, *Essence*, and *Glamour* magazines and *USA Today*.

In 1985, the National Council of Negro Women and Frito-Lay chose her from more than 130 nominees as one of the fifteen semifinalists in the national Salute to Black Women Who Make It Happen. Her name and biography are included in the 1985 edition of the *World's Who's Who of Women and Personalities of America*. In 1981, Hall created and designed the My Little Mahji Paper Doll. Since that time, the doll has been marketed worldwide.

Hall is the author of several books and the publisher of one of the first magazines to feature African American doll artists, designers, and collectors, *DOLL-E-GRAM*.

The mother of Mahji Hall, she lives in Bellevue, Washington.

BIBLIOGRAPHY

Mahji, Ami, Jahmi. VELB, 1985.
Hair's What It's All About. VELB, 1993.
The Quiet Brilliance of Onyx. VELB, 1995.

See also Hall, Mahji (B'Vance); Woodson, Carter G(odwin)

Hall, Mahji (B'Vance)

(1976–)

AUTHOR, ILLUSTRATOR

Hall was born in Seattle, Washington, and signed a contract with Open Hand Publishing when she was ten years old. She illustrated her first book with her pre-school and early childhood artwork, which was published in 1988 in Spanish and English. The Regional Library of Texas put her book on audiocassettes and provides complimentary tapes to the visually impaired.

She has traveled all over the country, autographing her book, and has spoken at several schools in the Seattle–King County area. Active in her church, she attends the Saturday Ethnic School, sang in the Junior Choir, and now sings in the Chapel Choir. She is also a member of the Educational Excellence Program and of the Youth Credit Union Board.

Hall graduated from Sammamish High School, received a college tuition scholarship, and attended Bellevue Community College.

The daughter of the Reverend LaVerne Corine Hall and the late Ellsworth Connye Hall, she lives in Seattle, Washington.

BIBLIOGRAPHY

T Is Terrific: Mahji's ABC Book. Open Hand, 1988.

See also Hall, LaVerne C. (Williams)

Hamilton, Virginia (Esther)

(1936–)

AUTHOR

Hamilton was born in southern Ohio, Yellow Springs, where her maternal ancestors settled after the Civil War. John Rowe Townsend, in *Written for Children,* describes Virginia Hamilton as "the most subtle and interesting of today's Black writers for children." Hamilton's books have always centered on Black heritage and more personally on her own family history. Her themes go beyond family experiences, weaving mysticism, fantasy, and realism.

Hamilton has received many major literary awards and much recognition for her children's books. *M.C. Higgins, the Great* won the 1975 Newbery Medal, the National Book Award, and the 1974 Boston Globe-Horn Book Award. *The Planet of Junior Brown* and *Sweet Whispers, Brother Rush* were also Newbery Honor Books, as was *In the Beginning: Creation Stories from Around the World.* Hamilton won the Coretta Scott King Award in 1983, 1986, and 1996, the latter for *Her Stories: African American Folktales, Fairy Tales and True Tales,* and Boston Globe-Horn Books Awards in 1974, 1983, and 1988. The Virginia Hamilton Lectureship on Minority Experiences in Children's Literature at Kent State University in Ohio was established in her honor. Her novel *The House of Dies Drear* was produced for television by the Public Broadcasting System (PBS).

In 1995, Hamilton won the Laura Ingalls Wilder Body of Work Medal and was also the first children's writer to be named a MacArthur Fellow.

She now resides in Yellow Springs, Ohio, with her husband, poet Arnold Adoff.

BIBLIOGRAPHY

Zeely. Macmillan, 1967.

The House of Dies Drear. Collier, 1968.

The Time-Ago Tales of Jadhu. Macmillan, 1968.

The Planet of Junior Brown. Macmillan, 1971.

Time-Ago Lost: More Tales of Jahdu. Illustrated by Ray Prather. Macmillan, 1973.

M.C. Higgins, the Great. Macmillan, 1974.

Paul Robeson: The Life and Times of a Free Black Man. Harper, 1974.

The Writing of W.E.B. Du Bois. Edited by Virginia Hamilton. Crowell, 1975.

Jahdu. Illustrated by Jerry Pinkney. Greenwillow, 1980.

Sweet Whispers, Brother Rush. Philomel, 1982.

The Magical Adventures of Pretty Pearl. Harper, 1983.

A Little Love. Philomel, 1984.

Junius Over Far. Harper, 1985.

The People Could Fly: American Black Folktales. Illustrated by Leo and Diane Dillon. Knopf, 1985.

The Mystery of Drear House. Greenwillow, 1987.

Anthony Burns: The Defeat and Triumph of a Fugitive Slave. Knopf, 1988.

In the Beginning: Creation Stories from Around the World. Illustrated by Barry Moser. Harcourt, 1988.

The Bells of Christmas. Illustrated by Lambert Davis. Harcourt, 1989.

Cousins. Philomel, 1990.

The Dark Way: Stories from the Spirit World. Illustrated by Lambert Davis. Harcourt, 1990.

The All Jadhu Storybook. Illustrated by Barry Moser. Dial, 1991.

Drylongso. Illustrated by Jerry Pinkney. Harcourt, 1992.

Many Thousand Gone: African Americans from Slavery to Freedom. Illustrated by Leo and Diane Dillon. Knopf, 1992.

Plain City. Scholastic, 1993.

Her Stories: African American Folktales, Fairy Tales and True Tales. Scholastic, 1995.

Jaguarundi. Illustrated by Floyd Cooper. Scholastic, 1995.

When Birds Could Talk and Bats Could Sing: The Adventures of Broh Sparrow, Sis Wren and their Friends. Illustrated by Barry Moser. Blue Sky, 1996.

See also Cooper, Floyd (Donald); Dillon, Leo; Pinkney, Jerry; Prather, Ray

Hanna, Cheryl (Irene)

(1951-)

ILLUSTRATOR

"Illustrations should be visual joys uplifting children who don't always have other sources of formal beauty around them. The African image is often not seriously introduced in positive ways for all children. For the African American child, the illustrations should be as love letters."

Hanna was born in Ann Arbor, Michigan, the daughter of a local dentist, Leonard Morton Hanna. She remembers drawing seriously from about age five, encouraged to continue by her parents, grandmother, and younger brother. After attending Cass Technical High School in Detroit, Michigan, from which she graduated in 1969, the artist attended Pratt Institute in New York City from 1969 to 1973.

An Enchanted Hair Tale by Alexis De Veaux, for which Hanna did the illustrations, was cited as an American Library Association Notable Book in 1987, awarded a Social Studies Citation, named a Coretta Scott King Honor Book in 1988, and selected as a review book on the Public Broadcasting System's *Reading Rainbow. Hard to Be Six* was chosen as a Children's Book of the Year by the Child Study Children's Book Committee at Bank Street College.

Some of her artwork from books was seen in the acclaimed exhibitions organized by the National Museum of Women in the Arts, *Through Sister's Eyes* (1991–1994), and *Brave Little Girls*, which opened in 1995.

Hanna received the 1996 Sunshine State Young Readers Award for her illustrations in *Donavan's Word Jar* by Monalisa DeGross. She lives in Brooklyn, New York.

BIBLIOGRAPHY

An Enchanted Hair Tale. By Alexis De Veaux. Harper, 1987.

Hard to Be Six. By Arnold Adoff. Lothrop, 1991.

Next Stop, Freedom. By Dorothy and Thomas Hoobler. Silver Burdett, 1991.

Phillis Wheatley: Poet. By Garnet Nelson Jackson. Modern Curriculum, 1993.

Selma Burke: Artist. By Garnet Nelson Jackson. Modern Curriculum, 1994.

Donavan's Word Jar. By Monalisa DeGross. HarperCollins, 1994.

The Story of Stagecoach Mary Fields. By Robert H. Miller. Stories from the Forgotten West Series. Silver Burdett, 1995.

See also De Gross, Monalisa; De Veaux, Alexis; Jackson, Garnet Nelson; Miller, Robert H(enry)

Hansen, Joyce (Viola)

(1942-)

AUTHOR

"Some writers have recurring or favorite themes—mine are the importance of family, belief in self, maintaining a sense of hope and a determination to overcome obstacles, and being responsible for oneself and other living things."

Hansen was born in New York City, attended Pace University, and received her master's degree from New York University in 1978. She worked as an administrative assistant at Pace University until 1995 and as a teacher of remedial reading and English for the New York City Board of Education.

Her novel *The Gift Giver* received the Spirit of Detroit Award and was also designated a Notable Children's Trade Book in the field of social studies in 1980. In 1986, *Yellow Bird and Me* received the Parents Choice Award. Hansen received a Coretta Scott King Honor Book Award for *Which Way Freedom?* in 1987 and for *The Captive* in 1995.

Her memberships include the Society of Children's Book Writers and Illustrators and the Harlem Writers Guild.

Hansen won the 1998 Coretta Scott King Honor Book Award for *I Thought My Soul Would Rise and Fly: The Diary of Patsy, a Freed Girl.*

She is married to Matthew Nelson and lives in West Columbia, South Carolina.

BIBLIOGRAPHY

The Gift Giver. Clarion, 1980.
Home Boy. Clarion, 1982.
Which Way Freedom? Walker, 1986.
Yellow Bird and Me. Clarion, 1986.

Out from This Place. Walker, 1988.

Between Two Fires. Watts, 1993.

The Captive. Scholastic, 1994.

I Thought My Soul Would Rise and Fly: The Diary of Patsy, a Freed Girl. Scholastic, 1997.

Hanson, Regina

(1944–)

AUTHOR

Hanson was born and reared in Jamaica, West Indies. During her childhood years, television had not yet reached the island. The family cherished books for entertainment as well as for education. After high school, she worked as a trainee journalist at the *Daily Gleaner* in Kingston, Jamaica. The family migrated to the United States in 1963.

In 1967, Hanson graduated from Hunter College in New York City, Phi Beta Kappa, with a bachelor of arts degree in English. She then returned to Jamaica to teach high school English. In 1970, she moved to Boulder, Colorado, where she served on the staff of the University of Colorado until 1992. Hanson's first children's story appeared in *Highlights* and was voted Best of the Issue by the magazine, which named her Author of the Month for February 1995.

The Tangerine Tree, Hanson's first picture book, was reviewed in *School Library Journal, Kirkus Reviews, Booklist, Publishers Weekly,* and *Children's Book Review Service,* all in the year of publication. Hanson's realistic, cultural fiction has been described as "both topical and universal." Her second picture book, *The Face at the Window,* received a pointer review in *Kirkus Reviews* in 1997. She is a member of the Society of Children's Book Writers and Illustrators and the National Writers Association.

Hanson lives in Boulder, Colorado.

BIBLIOGRAPHY

The Tangerine Tree. Illustrated by Harvey Stevenson. Clarion, 1995.
The Face at the Window. Illustrated by Linda Saport. Clarion, 1997.

Hart, Ayanna (Kai)

(1971–)

AUTHOR

Hart was born in Lansing, Michigan, the daughter of author Philip S. Hart and producer Tanya Hart, and mastered reading and writing at an early age. In 1990, the family relocated to Los Angeles, California.

Hart has worked in and around the television and film industry since she was a child. Over the years, she has worked with her parents on a variety of projects, including a video press release for the publication of singing group New Kids on the Block's Harvey Comics comic book; a documentary film on the Atlantic slave trade; a documentary film on America's early Black aviators; several infomercials; and other independent film and television projects. In some of these projects, Hart also served as researcher and writer.

Hart has worked at Walt Disney Studios with her parents and other producers. She worked as a production coordinator at E! Entertainment Television in Los Angeles, California from 1995 to 1997. Recently, Hart has accepted a position as a post-production coordinator on a prime time NBC drama.

She has long wanted to be a published author, and her 1995 book for young readers has allowed her to reach this goal.

Hart lives in Los Angeles, California.

BIBLIOGRAPHY

Africans in America. With Earl Spangler. Lerner, 1995.

See also Hart, Philip S.

Hart, Philip S(haw)

(1944-)

AUTHOR

Hart was born in Denver, Colorado, the middle child among three brothers. His mother was a schoolteacher, so reading and writing were priorities in his household.

Hart has been writing and publishing articles since high school. After graduating from East Denver High School, he went on to attend Colorado College for one year before transferring to the University of Colorado, Boulder, where he was a student and an athlete. He graduated cum laude in 1966.

Hart worked on his graduate degrees at Michigan State University, where he earned a master's degree in sociology in 1970 and a doctorate in sociology in 1974. He met his wife, Tanya, while in college, and they began many years of collaboration on television, film, and radio projects. They relocated to Boston, Massachusetts, in 1971, and he joined the faculty of the College of Public and Community Service at the University of Massachusetts, Boston, in 1974. In 1990, the family moved to Los Angeles, California.

While listening to family stories as he was growing up in Denver, Hart became interested in early Black aviators. He helped put together an exhibit titled *Black Wings* for the Smithsonian Institution's National Air and Space Museum in 1982. In 1987, a documentary film he and his wife produced titled *Flyers in Search of a Dream* was broadcast on the Public Broadcasting System (PBS). Among those who saw this film was Reeve Lindbergh, youngest daughter of the famous aviator Charles Lindbergh, who contacted Hart and encouraged him to write these stories in the form of children's books.

Hart's first book under this arrangement, *Flying Free: America's First Black Aviators*, was published in 1992 and received many positive reviews. The book was recognized that same year as a Notable Children's Trade Book in the field of social studies by the National Council for Social Studies and the Children's Book Council Joint Committee. Another book published in 1996 under this arrangement is *Up in the Air: The Story of Bessie Coleman.*

Hart has been developing one of the stories from *Flying Free* into a motion picture screenplay and has also developed a movie treatment based upon the story of Bessie Coleman. Hart is partnered with his wife in a television, film, and radio production company in Los Angeles, and he is a professor of sociology at the University of Massachusetts, Boston.

Hart's daughter, Ayanna Kai, is also a children's-book writer. He lives in Los Angeles, California, and Martha's Vineyard in Cape Cod, Massachusetts.

BIBLIOGRAPHY

Flying Free: America's First Black Aviators. Lerner, 1992.
Up in the Air: The Story of Bessie Coleman. Carolrhoda, 1996.

See also Hart, Ayanna (Kai)

Haskins, James (Jim)

(1 9 4 1 –)

AUTHOR

"My career as a writer began when I was teaching music and special-education classes in Harlem; my first book, Diary of a Harlem Schoolteacher, *was a result of my experiences. So were my first books for young adults. It was the 1960s, and there were very few books on the events of that tumultuous decade written on my students' level. I believe that the same void in literature for Black children continues to this day; and to this day I continue to write such books. Another void I see in literature for Black children is biographies of undeservedly obscure Black people in history; every year, more biographies are published about Mary McLeod Bethune, George Washington Carver, and Booker T. Washington, but where are the biographies of Ella Baker and Bayard Rustin?*

I like to describe my method of writing books as having conversations with myself. I include what interests me, and hope that it also interests young readers. I have not changed the way I write very much over the years, except at the request of editors. My books tend to be shorter now, and I suspect that is a response to the TV and video age and shorter attention spans in all of us. Another trend in young-adult books is to simplify the writing, but I have resisted that trend, believing that young people are willing to stretch their minds to understand books written about people and events that interest them. More than the best TV film or video, books can both enable one to find a private world and open up new worlds."

Born in Demopolis, Alabama, Haskins received a bachelor's degree in psychology from Georgetown University and one in history from Alabama State University. In 1963, he earned a master's degree from the University of New Mexico and a certificate of work of the Stock Exchange after attending the New York Institute of Finance.

Professional memberships include the National Advisory Committee, Statue of Liberty–Ellis Island Commission, the National Book Critics Circle, the Authors Guild, 100 Black Men, and Phi Beta Kappa. *Social Studies* magazine has selected many of his books as Notable Children's Books, and the Child Study Association selected *Barbara Jordan* in 1979. The Coretta Scott King Award was presented to Haskins for the *Story of Stevie Wonder* in 1977, and his books won Coretta Scott King honor citations in 1978, 1980, 1984, and 1991. He received the *Washington Post* Children's Book Council Award for his body of work in nonfiction for young people in 1994 and, also in 1994, the Carter G. Woodson Award for *The March on Washington* at the National Council on the Social Studies Conference in Phoenix, Arizona. Haskin's book *Bayard Rustin: Behind the Scenes of the Civil Rights Movement* was selected as a 1998 Coretta Scott King Honor Book.

He lives in Gainesville, Florida.

BIBLIOGRAPHY

The Creoles of Color. Illustrated by Don Miller. Crowell, 1975.

The Picture Life of Malcolm X. Watts, 1975.

The Story of Stevie Wonder. Lothrop, 1976.

Barbara Jordan. Dial, 1977.

The Life and Death of Martin Luther King, Jr. Lothrop, 1977.

Andrew Young: Young Man with a Mission. Lothrop, 1979.

James Van DerZee: The Picture Takin' Man. Dodd, 1979.

The New Americans: Vietnamese Boat People. Enslow, 1980.

Black Theatre in America. Crowell, 1982.

Lena Horne. Coward, 1983.

Space Challenger: The Story of Guion Bluford. With Kathleen Benson. Carolrhoda, 1984.

Black Music in America: A History Through Its People. Crowell, 1987.

Count Your Way Through China. Illustrated by Dennis Hockerman. Carolrhoda, 1987.

Count Your Way Through Japan. Illustrated by Martin Skoro. Carolrhoda, 1987.

Count Your Way Through Russia. Illustrated by Vera Mednikov. Carolrhoda, 1987.

Count Your Way Through the Arab World. Illustrated by Dana Gustafson. Carolrhoda, 1987.

Bill Cosby: America's Most Famous Father. Walker, 1988.

Winnie Mandela: Life of Struggle. Putnam, 1988.

Count Your Way Through Canada. Illustrated by Steve Michaels. Carolrhoda, 1989.

Count Your Way Through Korea. Illustrated by Dennis Hockerman. Carolrhoda, 1989.

Count Your Way Through Mexico. Illustrated by Helen Beyers. Carolrhoda, 1989.

Black Dance in America: A History Through Its People. HarperCollins, 1990.

Count Your Way Through Germany. Illustrated by Helen Beyers. Carolrhoda, 1990.

Count Your Way Through Israel. Illustrated by Rick Hanson. Carolrhoda, 1990.

Count Your Way Through Italy. Illustrated by Beth Wright. Carolrhoda, 1990.

Against All Opposition: Black Explorers in America. Walker, 1991.

Outward Dreams: Black Inventors and Their Inventions. Walker, 1991.

Rosa Parks: Mother to a Movement. By Rosa Parks with James Haskins. Dial, 1992.

Freedom Rides: Journey for Justice. Hyperion, 1995.

Count Your Way Through Brazil. With Kathleen Benson. Carolrhoda, 1996.

Count Your Way Through France. With Kathleen Benson. Carolrhoda, 1996.

Count Your Way Through Ireland. With Kathleen Benson. Carolrhoda, 1996.

The Harlem Renaissance. Millbrook, 1996.

Louis Farrakhan and the Nation of Islam. Walker, 1996.

Bayard Rustin: Behind the Scenes of the Civil Rights Movement. Hyperion, 1997.

I Am Rosa Parks. With Rosa Parks. Illustrated by Wil Clay. Dial, 1997.

Spike Lee: By Any Means Necessary. Walker, 1997.

See also Clay, Wil; Miller, Don; Woodson, Carter G(odwin)

Higginsen, Vy

AUTHOR

"In all of my professional endeavors, I was struck by the power that the verbal and written word has on the social, cultural, and spiritual psyche of a mass audience. Throughout the national and international tour of the play Mama, I Want to Sing *across the United States, Japan, Europe, and the Caribbean, gospel music reached and touched all audiences with a zest and vibrancy that was both amazing and astounding."*

Higginsen was born in New York City, the daughter of a minister. She attended the Fashion Institute of Technology and began her career working in advertising and sales for *Ebony* magazine. She was an on-air personality in New York City for station WBLS-FM for four years until 1975 and the producer and director of the 1988 play *Let the Music Play Gospel.* That same year, she produced August Wilson's play *Joe Turner's Come and Gone.*

Among her awards are the Candace Award of the Coalition of 100 Black Women, which she received in 1988 for outstanding achievement; the Alumna of the Year Award in 1989 presented by the Association of Junior Colleges in New York; and the Business Woman of the Year Award, also in 1989, presented by the New York City Chamber of Commerce.

Higginsen is married and has one daughter. She lives in New York City.

BIBLIOGRAPHY

Mama, I Want to Sing. With Tonja Bolden. Scholastic, 1992.
This Is My Song. Illustrated by Brenda Joysmith. Crown, 1995.

See also Bolden, Tonya

Hinds, P(atricia) Mignon

AUTHOR

Born in New York City, Hinds is a graduate of Hampton University and received her master's degree from the City University of New York. She began her publishing career in late 1970 at Harper and Row and has also written magazine articles.

In 1980, she created her own corporate communications company, Mignon Creations and Communications, whose clients include an impressive list of Fortune 500 companies. Her company specializes in editorial, public relations, and marketing services. She has received three Communications Excellence to Black Audiences Awards for her work. She is also an educator on primary and college levels, having taught small business management courses at New York University and has been a writing professor at the College of New Rochelle.

Hinds produced an educational television series titled CAHOOTS, and serves on the board of directors of Cinque Gallery in New York City. In 1993, she was selected by Essence Communications to launch Essence Books and also to spearhead a new line of Essence children's books with twelve original titles. She is director of Essence Books.

An avid supporter of several charities, Hinds lives in New York City.

BIBLIOGRAPHY

Animal Affairs. Dell, 1980.
Kittens Need Someone to Love. Western, 1981.
Puppies Need Someone to Love. Western, 1981.
Baby Calf. Longmeadow, 1988. Western, 1988.
Baby Pig. Longmeadow, 1988. Western, 1988.

A Day in the Life of Morgan Freeman. Macmillan, 1994.

What I Want to Be. Illustrated by Cornelius Van Wright. Golden, 1995.

My Best Friend. Illustrated By Cornelius Van Wright. Golden, 1996.

The King's Daughter. Illustrated by Cornelius Van Wright. Golden, 1997.

Hinton, Tim

(1948–)

ILLUSTRATOR

Hinton was born in Chicago, Illinois, and attended schools in Philadelphia, Pennsylvania; Atlanta, Georgia; and Orlando, Florida. After graduating from high school, he enlisted in the United States Marine Corps and served in Vietnam. Hinton was wounded and spent several months in the hospital in Agana, Guam. After being honorably discharged from the Marine Corps, he was employed as an illustrator with the Naval Ship Engineering Center for several years.

Since 1973, he has been recognized nationally for his work, which has been exhibited at the Museum of African Art, the Anacostia Museum at the Smithsonian Institution, the Kennedy Center, and in a one-man show at the Art Fair Gallery. His work is in the permanent collections of the United States Navy Museum, Naval Annex, and IBM, as well as in Howard University and the University of Maryland.

Hinton's works have been used in many publications, including *Architectural Digest, Reader's Digest, Washingtonian,* and the *Washington Post.* His paintings and prints are in many private collections, including former Virginia Governor Douglas Wilder, Barbara Bush, Muriel Humphrey, Donald McHenry, and the boxers Larry Holmes and Muhammad Ali, and his historical art prints are displayed in all of the national monuments in Washington, D.C.

He lives in Upper Marlboro, Maryland.

BIBLIOGRAPHY

Robert Lives with His Grandparents. By Martha Whitmore Hickman. Whitman, 1995.

Holbert, (James) Raymond

(1 9 4 5 –)

ILLUSTRATOR, PHOTOGRAPHER

"I have been interested in the process of art and design since childhood. A three-year diversion into the study of architectural concepts and applications still shows a strong influence in my work. I have exhibited paintings, etchings, collagraphs, serigraphs, and sculpture for the past thirty-five years, but my strongest interest over the past ten years has been works on paper. It is what I consider a specialty. I have a very strong interest in color and its effect on my drawing and in human behavior. I am an educator as well as an artist and I have had many opportunities to work with students and colleagues and I continue to learn as much as possible. Color is one of the primary factors contained in my work and it influences my images, feelings and concepts.

Photography has been a strong lifetime interest and I have been able to include it as a parallel profession, often incorporating the work of the camera directly into my artwork."

Holbert was born in Berkeley, California, the eldest of three children. He attributes the inspiration for his art to his love of science and fantasy. While in college, Holbert concentrated on the areas of painting and printmaking. He received master's of arts and fine arts degrees. Among the many galleries and museums that have exhibited his works are the Collectors Gallery of the Oakland Museum in Oakland, California, in 1995; the Oliver Art Center/California College of Arts and Crafts, also in Oakland; and the Flora Lamson Hewlett Library in Berkeley, California, in 1993–1994.

Holbert is on the faculty at San Francisco City College, where he teaches intermediate drawing and advanced design. An art historian, he also teaches a course in African and African American art history.

Holbert is married, has three children, and lives in Berkeley, California.

BIBLIOGRAPHY

The Barber's Cutting Edge. By Gwendolyn Battle-Lavert. Children's Press, 1994.

See also Battle-Lavert, Gwendolyn

Holley, Vanessa (Diane)

(1 9 5 2 –)

ILLUSTRATOR

Holley was born in Portsmouth, Virginia, the second of four children. She remembers loving to draw as early as the age of three. She studied commercial art and illustration at Pratt Institute in Brooklyn, New York, and, while there, she worked as a freelance layout artist and illustrator for *Encore* magazine. This began her career as a professional illustrator.

Noted for her drawings of children, she is frequently commissioned as a portrait artist. Holley has exhibited her fine art extensively in the New York metropolitan area and has had several one-woman shows. She has work in the collections of Ossie Davis and Ruby Dee, the Pratt Institute, the Afro-American Historical Museum in Jersey City, New Jersey, and in numerous other private collections throughout the country.

Until 1994, Holley worked primarily as a commercial artist. Since then, she has worked full time on her career as a book illustrator and fine artist. As a children's-book illustrator, she is committed to using her art to uplift and inspire children. She believes that the African and African American experience is so rich in information and areas that need to be explored that it will take her a whole lifetime to express it through her art.

She lives in Jersey City, New Jersey.

BIBLIOGRAPHY

The Black Holocaust for Beginners. By S.E. Anderson. Writers & Readers, 1995.
Jazz for Beginners. By Ron David. Writers & Readers, 1995.
Kai: A Mission For Her Village (Girlhood Journeys Series). By Dawn C. Thomas. Simon & Schuster 1996.

See also Davis, Ossie; Dee, Ruby (Ruby Ann Wallace); Thomas, Dawn C.

Hoston, James (Harry)

(1963–)

ILLUSTRATOR

Hoston was born in Freeport, Long Island, New York, the younger of two children. During his childhood, he was always drawing. He attributes his persistence to his mother, also artistic, and to his Uncle Edward, who supplied him with endless materials. He had only one art class during his junior and senior years in high school, but by the end of his senior year he had decided to pursue art.

After receiving an associate degree in advertising art and design, he attended Pratt Institute in Brooklyn, New York, where he studied illustration and graduated with a bachelor of fine arts degree.

For the following five years, he worked part-time at various jobs and did illustrations in textbooks, Black and White children's books for small publishers, some product illustrations for toy companies, and various magazine editorials.

In 1989, he applied for graduate school at the New York Academy of Art and received an Andy Warhol scholarship for two years of study. During this time, he continued to illustrate and attend classes. After graduation, he accepted a full-time production job at Marvel Comics where he worked until 1996. He is currently employed as a painting assistant with artist Jeff Koons.

Hoston is single and lives in Brooklyn, New York.

BIBLIOGRAPHY

The Original Freddie Ackerman. By Hadley Irwin. McElderry, 1992.
The Great Smith House Hustle. By Jane Louise Curry. McElderry, 1993.
Good Luck Gold. By Janet S. Wong. McElderry, 1994.
The Bicycle Thief. By Richard Brightfield. Macmillan, 1996.
The Legend of Mel and Nin. By Bill Grimmette. Sight Productions, 1998.

Howard, Elizabeth Fitzgerald

(1927–)

AUTHOR

"There are so many wonderful, inspiring, funny, sad, heartwarming, heart-tick-ling, meaningful stories about Black families, waiting to be written down. Some of them are in my own family's treasury, and there is still a shortage—a dearth— of children's books about everyday Black families living ordinary lives during the early part of this century. I would like present-day children, Black and White, to know that Blacks have been a part of all of this country's growth since the beginning. And that there were Black grocers and doctors and postmen and teachers and porters and lawyers who celebrated holidays and sat in the bal-cony at the opera and went to church and sent their children to college—and hoped that the American dream included them. And lived as though it did, in spite of everything that might or might not have gone wrong. Of course, Virginia Hamilton and Patricia McKissack and others are telling this story with depth and flair. I hope that I am able in some small measure to contribute to this."

Thus has Elizabeth Fitzgerald Howard, professor emeritus of library science (West Virginia University) since 1993, stated her underlying phi-losophy in her works.

The author was born in Baltimore, Maryland. Howard earned her bachelor of arts degree from Radcliffe College in 1948, her master's degree in library science and her doctorate from the University of Pitts-burgh in 1971 and 1977, respectively. In her senior year at Radcliffe, she was president of her class.

Her memberships include the American Library Association, the Society of Children's Book Writers and Illustrators, and Links, Incor-porated. In the American Library Association, Howard has served on the Caldecott Committee, the Hans Christian Andersen Committee, the Teachers of Children's Literature Discussion Group, and the American

Library Association Children's Book Council Liaison Committee. She has served for many years on the board of trustees of Magee Women's Hospital in Pittsburgh, Pennsylvania, and has also been a member of the boards of QED Communications, Beginning with Books, the Ellis School, Three Rivers' Youth, and the Radcliffe Alumnae Association.

She is married to Dr. Lawrence C. Howard and lives in Pittsburgh, Pennsylvania. They have three daughters and two grandchildren.

BIBLIOGRAPHY

The Train to Lulu's. Illustrated by Robert Casilla. Bradbury, 1988.

Chita's Christmas Tree. Illustrated by Floyd Cooper. Bradbury, 1989.

Aunt Flossie's Hats (and Crab Cakes Later). Illustrated by James Ransome. Clarion, 1991.

Mac and Marie and the Train Toss Surprise. Illustrated by Gail Gordon Carter. Four Winds, 1993.

Papa Tells Chita a Story. Illustrated by Floyd Cooper. Four Winds, 1995.

What's in Aunt Mary's Room? Illustrated by Cedric Lucas. Clarion, 1996.

Lulu's Birthday. Illustrated by Pat Cummings. Greenwillow, 1999.

Virgie Goes to School. Illustrated by E.B. Lewis. Simon & Schuster, 1999.

When Will Sarah Come? Illustrated by Nina Crews. Greenwillow, 1999.

See also Carter, Gail Gordon; Cooper, Cummings, Floyd (Donald); Pat(ricia Marie); Lucas, Cedric; Ransome, James (Earl)

Howard, Moses Leon
Musa Nagenda

(1928–)

AUTHOR

The author, who uses the pseudonym of Musa Nagenda, was born in Copiah County, Mississippi. He received his bachelor's degree at Alcorn A and M College and his master's degree from Case Western Reserve University. He did further graduate study at the University of Alaska, New York University, and Columbia University.

Howard has worked as a steelworker, a biology and chemistry instructor, and a Science Department head at the National Teachers' College in Uganda, and served at the African Ministry of Education in Kampala, Uganda. He also taught public school in Seattle, Washington.

Howard was named Outstanding Educator of the Year in Washington state in 1981.

BIBLIOGRAPHY

Dogs of Fear. Illustrated by Floyd Sowell. Holt, 1972. (Published under the name Musa Nagenda.)

The Human Mandolin. Illustrated by Barbara Morrow. Holt, 1974.

The Ostrich Chase. Illustrated by Barbara Seuling. Holt, 1974.

Hudson, Cheryl Willis

(1 9 4 8 –)

AUTHOR

"African American children have a right to see themselves portrayed positively and accurately in the literature of this society. Just Us Books specializes in books and learning material for children that focus on the African American experience."

Hudson believes that she and her husband, Wade Hudson, have achieved this goal in the books that they publish in the company they founded, Just Us Books.

The author was born in Portsmouth, Virginia, and for more than twenty years worked in publishing as a graphic designer and art director. She has worked with the Macmillan Company in New York City and with the Educational Division of Houghton Mifflin in Boston, Massachusetts, both major publishing houses.

A graduate of Oberlin College, where she received a bachelor of arts degree, she also took publishing courses at Radcliffe College and a post-baccalaureate in 1972 at Northeastern University with study in graphic-arts management. From 1973 to 1975, she pursued further studies at the Parsons School of Design in New York City.

Some of Hudson's poetry for children and her illustrations have appeared in *Ebony Jr.* and *Wee Wisdom* magazines. She is a member of the Multicultural Publishing Educational Council and the National Association of Black Book Publishers.

She and her husband, Wade, live in East Orange, New Jersey.

BIBLIOGRAPHY

Afro-Bets 123 Book. Illustrated by Culverson Blair. Just Us Books, 1987.
Afro-Bets ABC Book. Illustrated by Culverson Blair. Just Us Books, 1987.

Bright Eyes, Brown Skin. With Bernette G. Ford. Illustrated by George Ford. Just Us Books, 1990.

Good Morning, Baby. Illustrated by George Ford. Scholastic, 1992.

Good Night, Baby. Illustrated by George Ford. Scholastic, 1992.

Animal Sounds for Baby. Illustrated by George Ford. Scholastic, 1995.

Hold Christmas in Your Heart. Compiled by Cheryl Willis Hudson. Scholastic, 1995.

How Sweet the Sound: African-American Songs for Children. Illustrated by Floyd Cooper. Selected by Wade Hudson and Cheryl Willis Hudson. Scholastic, 1995.

Let's Count, Baby. Illustrated by George Ford. Scholastic, 1995.

In Praise of our Mothers and Fathers. Compiled by Cheryl Willis Hudson and Wade Hudson. Just Us Books, 1996.

The Kids' Book of Wisdom. Compiled by Cheryl Willis Hudson and Wade Hudson. Just Us Books, 1996.

See also Blair, Culverson; Ford, Bernette G.; Ford, George (Cephas); Hudson, Wade

Hudson, Wade

(1 9 4 6 –)

AUTHOR

"One can never take any image for granted. Images, whether in print, film, tele-vision, or on the stage, are constantly shaping the way we feel and what we think and believe. This is particularly crucial to the African American community that has been deliberately given negative images of its history and culture. I find it rewarding to help reshape and change those negative images to reflect truth. I think the struggle to present the correct images, the truth, is the most crucial one facing us all."

Hudson, president and CEO of Just Us Books, the publishing company he and his wife founded, was born in Mansfield, Louisiana, and attended the Southern University in Baton Rouge, Louisiana. He was active as a field worker during the civil-rights movement of the 1960s. He has also been a sports writer, a sports editor, and a playwright.

He and his wife, Cheryl, also a children's book author, live in East Orange, New Jersey.

BIBLIOGRAPHY

Beebe's Lonely Saturday. New Dimension, 1967.

Freedom Star. Macmillan, 1968.

Afro-Bets Book of Black Heroes from A to Z. With Valerie Wilson Wesley. Just Us Books, 1988.

Afro-Bets Alphabet Rap Song. Just Us Books, 1990.

Jamal's Busy Day. Illustrated by George Ford. Just Us Books, 1991.

Afro-Bets Kids: I'm Gonna Be! Illustrated by Culverson Blair. Just Us Books, 1992.

I Love My Family. Illustrated by Cal Massey. Scholastic, 1993.

Pass It On: African-American Poetry for Children. Compiled by Wade Hudson. Illustrated by Floyd Cooper. Scholastic, 1993.

Great Black Heroes. Illustrated by Ron Garnett. Scholastic, 1994.

How Sweet the Sound: African-American Songs for Children. Selected by Wade Hudson and Cheryl Willis Hudson. Illustrated by Floyd Cooper. Scholastic, 1995.

In Praise of our Mothers and Fathers. Compiled by Wade Hudson and Cheryl Willis Hudson. Just Us Books, 1996.

The Kids' Book of Wisdom. Compiled by Cheryl Willis Hudson and Wade Hudson. Just Us Books, 1996.

See also Blair, Culverson; Cooper, Floyd (Donald); Ford, George (Cephas); Hudson, Cheryl Willis; Massey, Cal(vin Levi)

Hughes, (James) Langston

(1902–1967)

AUTHOR

Dubbed the Negro Poet Laureate, Langston Hughes, a product of the Harlem Renaissance of the 1920s and 1930s, was a prolific writer. He was born in Joplin, Missouri, and lived with his grandmother in Kansas after his parents' separation. When his mother remarried, young Hughes lived with her and his stepfather in Cleveland, Ohio.

In 1929, he graduated from Lincoln University. In 1935, he won a Guggenheim fellowship, and in 1941 a Rosenwald fellowship, the first of a host of honors he received for his writing. Hughes wrote poetry, short stories, plays, newspaper articles and columns, a novel, essays, lyrics for a successful musical, and children's books. His poetry is a mix of blank verse, dialect, and lyric verse. His prize works demonstrate his political and social activism and his disapproval of civil injustices against his people. His work is distinguished by its brilliant humor and witty satire.

In 1946, he was elected a member of the National Institute of Arts and Letters. He was a visiting professor of creative writing at Atlanta University in 1947–1948 and poet in residence at the Laboratory School of the University of Chicago in 1949–1950. His honorary doctorates were awarded by Lincoln University and Case Western Reserve University.

BIBLIOGRAPHY

The Dream Keeper and Other Poems. Illustrated by Helen Sewell. Introduction by Augusta Baker. Knopf, 1932, 1994 (illustrated by Brian Pinkney).
Famous Negro Music Makers. Dodd, 1954.
Famous American Negroes. Dodd, 1954.
The First Book of Africa. Watts, 1964.

Black Misery. Erikson, 1969.

Not Without Laughter. Knopf, 1930. Collier, 1969.

Don't You Turn Back. Selected by Lee Bennett Hopkins. Knopf, 1969.

Jazz (formerly, *The First Book of Jazz*). Updated Edition. Watts, 1982.

A Pictorial History of Black Americans. With Milton Meltzer and C. Eric Lincoln. Fifth Revised Edition. Crown, 1984.

The Block. Illustrated by Romare Bearden. Selected by Lowery S. Sims and Daisy Murray Voigt. Viking, 1995.

See also Baker, Augusta (Braxston); Bearden, Romare H(oward); Pinkney, Brian

Humphrey, Margo

(1942-)

AUTHOR, ILLUSTRATOR

"Although my work covers a broad spectrum of subjects, many subjects are used as icons, as testament to the triumph of existence. My artwork and stories deal with empowerment and the nobility of culture."

Born in Oakland, California, Humphrey is primarily an artist. She was awarded an undergraduate fellowship to the Whitney Museum of American Art summer program in 1971. Since graduating from Stanford University in 1972 with honors and a master of fine arts degree in printmaking, she has been the recipient of numerous fellowships and awards, among them the James D. Pheland Award, two National Endowment of the Arts fellowships, and a Ford Foundation fellowship.

Humphrey began her career in teaching at the University of California in 1973. She has since taught at the San Francisco Art Institute and has served as visiting professor at the School of Art Institute of Chicago. She joined the faculty of the Department of Art at the University of Maryland in 1989 and served as graduate director of the department from 1991 to 1993.

In addition to Humphrey's impressive credits for her teaching, her accomplishments as an artist and educator have also been recognized. She was honored as the first African American woman to teach studio courses at the University of Texas at San Antonio, and her children's book, *The River That Gave Gifts: An Afro-American Story,* was read in the San Antonio public schools and shared with the San Antonio community. In recognition of these accomplishments, she was proclaimed Artist of the Muses by Mayor Henry Cesneros. The book was nominated by then First Lady Barbara Bush for National Literacy Week and read by Mrs. Bush on the national television program *Working Women.*

Humphrey's works are included in national and international permanent collections, including the Museum of Modern Art in New York City, the Smithsonian Institution in Washington, D.C., and the private collection of Drs. William and Camile Cosby.

Humphrey teaches at the University of Maryland, College Park. She has two children and lives in Hyattsville, Maryland.

BIBLIOGRAPHY

The River That Gave Gifts: An Afro-American Story. Children's Press, 1987.

Hunter (Lattany), Kristin

(1 9 3 1 –)

AUTHOR

"There is no fantasy for Black children, and there are no superhero stories. We need more contemporary Black American heroes—real or fictional—with whom children can identify, and less about kings and queens in remote African cultures of the past. More folklore and humor would be welcome, too, I think. How about some Black Cinderellas, dancers and Kung Fu masters, some aviators and community activists? You don't have to be superhuman to be heroic, but I'd like to read about someone who beats up on the Klan and wins. We need more "brain" stories like M.C. Higgins, the Great, *also. . . . The lists of available Black children's literature have dropped something like 75 percent since the 1960s and 1970s."*

Hunter was born in Philadelphia, Pennsylvania, the only child of two New Jersey schoolteachers who expected her to become a public school teacher, too. Instead, upon graduation from the University of Pennsylvania, she went into advertising and became a copywriter for the Lavenson Bureau of Advertising in Philadelphia, and later for the Wermen and Schorr Agency.

A John Hay Whitney fellowship allowed her to take a year off and write her first adult book, *God Bless the Child,* which was published in 1964. In 1964 and 1965, she was an information officer for the city of Philadelphia, writing press releases for the city's health and welfare departments. After the publication in 1966 of her second adult novel, *The Landlord,* which was made into a United Artists film, she was supported by her writing for seven years.

She married John I. Lattany in 1968; that same year, her novel for teens, *The Soul Brothers and Sister Lou,* was published.

Sister Lou was inspired by the impromptu *a cappella* street-corner singing she heard while living in Philadelphia, by the author's love of music, and also by her own experiences as a lonely adolescent who seldom felt that she fit in. One of the first books for Black teens, it was a big hit with the generation of young African American women who are now in their thirties, some of whom still tell the author how much the book meant to them. It won a number of awards, including the Council on Interracial Books for Children's prize as the Best Book of the Year for older children.

Hunter wrote two more adult novels, *The Survivors* and *The Lakestown Rebellion,* and several more children's books. Two of the latter won Coretta Scott King Honor Book Awards, *Lou in the Limelight* in 1982 and *Guests in the Promised Land* in 1974. The lively interaction she enjoys with children and the opportunity to influence them are among the great rewards of writing for a young audience, rewards that those who write only for adults do not enjoy.

In 1972, Hunter joined the English Department faculty of her alma mater, the University of Pennsylvania, as a lecturer in creative writing. Over twenty-three years of teaching, she was promoted to adjunct associate professor and then to senior lecturer, a position from which she retired in 1995.

Hunter lives in Magnolia, New Jersey.

BIBLIOGRAPHY

The Soul Brothers and Sister Lou. Scribner, 1968.
Boss Cat. Illustrated by Harold L. Franklin. Scribner, 1971.
The Pool Table War. Houghton, 1972.
Uncle Daniel and the Raccoon. Houghton, 1972.
Guests in the Promised Land. Scribner, 1973.
Lou in the Limelight. Scribner, 1981.

See also Franklin, Harold L. (Chikuyo Alimayo)

Hyppolite, Joanne

(1969–)

AUTHOR

"I read tons of age-graded children's literature when I was young, and it taught me English, it taught me humor, and it taught me respect for the genre. I was also influenced by Haitian traditions, culture and language (kreyol). My mother's storytelling ("contes") and her memories of her life in Haiti are a great inspiration. I live and I write through them. I have been influenced by children's writer Kristin Hunter and other children's book authors."

Hyppolite was born in Haiti, and her family settled in the United States when she was four years old. She grew up in Boston, Massachusetts, and graduated in 1991 from the University of Pennsylvania with a bachelor of arts degree in creative writing. In 1994, she received a master's degree in Afro-American studies from the University of California, Los Angeles. She is a doctoral student in Caribbean literature at the University of Miami.

Her fiction addresses the Haitian-American experience. *Seth and Samona,* her first novel, was published in 1995 and won the second annual Marguerite de Angeli Prize from Delacorte Press.

Hyppolite lives in Miramar, Florida.

BIBLIOGRAPHY

Seth and Samona. Illustrated by Colin Bootman. Delacorte, 1995.
Ola Shakes It Up. Delacorte, 1998.

Jackson, Garnet Nelson

(1944–)

AUTHOR

The middle child of a family of three daughters, Jackson was born and reared in New Orleans, Louisiana, where she enjoyed a middle-class upbringing. Her early education consisted of private and Catholic schools.

Jackson began writing during her teen years, and, after having written several short stories, poems, and a book, she delayed her writing career and dedicated her early adulthood to teaching. During her college years, Jackson worked as a postal clerk. She received a bachelor of arts degree in education from Dillard University in 1968 and began her teaching career in Flint, Michigan.

In 1980, she began writing poetry again. After joining the Rejoti Writers Club of New Jersey, she had several poems published and received an honorable mention for her poem "A Composite of Experiences," published in *The Griot Speaks* in 1986.

In 1989, after an unsuccessful search for books about African American achievers written for young children, she decided to write for her first-grade students. She wrote five biographies of great achievers that were enjoyed and appreciated by her students. In 1990, after seeking in vain for a publisher, she published them herself in the series African Like Me Books. They were later published by Modern Curriculum Press, Simon and Schuster's education group. They also published more than a dozen books she has written in a series entitled Beginning Biographies: African Americans. Jackson has also written a weekly column about issues concerning young children in the *Flint Journal* newspaper.

The many honors and awards she has received for her literary contributions include the National Association for the Advancement of Colored People's 1991 Harambee Medal; the Educator of the Year

Award in 1991; a proclamation from the office of the mayor of Flint, Michigan, declaring February 26, 1992, as Garnet Jackson Day; and the Zeta Phi Beta Finer Womanhood Hall of Fame Award in 1993. She has completed a novel for adults and writes full-time.

Jackson lives in Grand Blanc, Michigan, and has an adult son.

BIBLIOGRAPHY

I Am an African American Child. Illustrated by Inez Goodman. African Like Me Books, 1990.

The Little African King. Illustrated by Inez Goodman and Ken Ross. African Like Me Books, 1990.

Benjamin Banneker: Scientist. Illustrated by Rodney Pate. Modern Curriculum, 1993.

Elijah McCoy: Inventor. Illustrated by Gary Thomas. Modern Curriculum, 1993.

Frederick Douglass: Freedom Fighter. Illustrated by Keaf Holliday. Modern Curriculum, 1993.

Garrett Morgan: Inventor. Illustrated by Thomas Hudson. Modern Curriculum, 1993.

Phillis Wheatley: Poet. Illustrated by Cheryl Hana. Modern Curriculum, 1993.

Rosa Parks: Hero of Our Times. Illustrated by Tony Wade. Modern Curriculum, 1993.

Charles Drew: Doctor. Illustrated by Gary Thomas. Modern Curriculum, 1994.

Mae Jemison: Astronaut. Illustrated by Fred Willingham. Modern Curriculum, 1994.

Maggie Walker: Business Leader. Illustrated by Keaf Holliday. Modern Curriculum, 1994.

Selma Burke: Artist. Illustrated by Cheryl Hanna. Modern Curriculum, 1994.

Shirley Chisholm: Congresswoman. Illustrated by Thomas Hudson. Modern Curriculum, 1994.

Thurgood Marshall: Supreme Court Justice. Illustrated by Higgins Bond. Modern Curriculum, 1994.

Toni Morrison: Author. Illustrated by Higgins Bond. Modern Curriculum, 1995.

See also Bond, Higgins (Barbara)

Jackson, Jesse

(1908–1983)

AUTHOR

The author was born in Columbus, Ohio, and attended Ohio State University, where he was active in boxing and track. He entered the Olympic trials and planned to become a professional boxer, but he later changed his mind. His summers were spent at various jobs: boxing in a carnival, working on a steamer on the Great Lakes, and "jerking sodas" in Atlantic City, New Jersey. He worked in boys' camps and with private youth agencies, served as a juvenile probation officer, and worked for the Bureau of Economic Research.

His first writing venture was in collaboration with artist Calvin Bailey on a series of articles on boxers. The articles were sold to New York newspapers. He said his first book for children, *Call Me Charley*, was written as "a small tribute to the good people who somehow or other succeed in making bad things better."

In 1974, he became a lecturer at Appalachian State University in North Carolina. Among his awards were a MacDowell Colony fellowship and the National Council for Social Studies Carter G. Woodson Award in 1975.

BIBLIOGRAPHY

Call Me Charley. Illustrated by Doris Spiegel. Harper, 1945.
Anchor Man. Illustrated by Doris Spiegel. Harper, 1947.
Room for Randy. Illustrated by Frank Nicholas. Friendship, 1957.
Charley Starts from Scratch. Harper, 1958.
Tessie. Illustrated by Harold James. Harper, 1968.
The Sickest Don't Always Die the Quickest. Doubleday, 1971.
The Fourteenth Cadillac. Doubleday, 1972.

Make a Joyful Noise unto the Lord: The Life of Mahalia Jackson. Crowell, 1974.
Queen of Gospel Singers. Crowell, 1974.

See also Woodson, Carter G(odwin)

Jenkins, Leonard L(arry)

(1960–)

ILLUSTRATOR

"I was just obsessed with drawing my whole life. I knew what I wanted to be in the third grade."

The artist was born in Chicago, Illinois, the sixth of eight children. By the time he reached the third grade, his work had won him praise and awards from his peers and teachers alike. One teacher shared his work with the chairperson of the Art Department at the University of Wisconsin, who was equally impressed. Jenkins became a child prodigy on the campus, but, because his mother believed he should remain in the traditional setting of an elementary school, she declined the university's offer. This began a local art career that spanned the next ten years. Jenkins earned monetary rewards for his art throughout his senior year in high school from local clients and one-person shows.

After graduation in 1978, committed to his work, Jenkins enrolled in the School of the Art Institute in Chicago for a year, then accepted a three-year scholarship to Chicago's American Academy of Art. Jenkins says, "At a certain point, your art must go beyond how good you can paint. It has to go to the soul. Clarity is my inspiration for a deeper self in my art." Jenkins lived in Kansas City, Missouri, from 1981 to 1986 and while there, a New York-based publisher, Kirchoff Shaw and Wohlberg, commissioned Jenkins to illustrate children's textbooks. Advancing with the project also exposed his talents to Lockhart and Pettus, Uniworld, the Mingo Group, and other leading Black advertising agencies. In 1992, he experienced a major breakthrough in children's illustration when Clarion Books, G.P. Putnam, Simon and Schuster, and HarperCollins publishers, among others, sought his skills and talents for ongoing projects.

Jenkins was commissioned in 1984 and 1985 to paint the Miller Gallery of Greats. His work also has been exhibited in the DuSable Museum of African-American History in Chicago, the Martin Luther King Center in Washington, D.C., and numerous galleries throughout the New York tri-state area.

Jenkins's work has won many awards and glowing book reviews. He has been honored with the Communications Excellence to Black Audiences Award and the Award for Excellence in Advertising in 1984, 1988, and 1989. Book reviews for his illustrations in several award-winning children's books appeared in 1994 in *Booklist, Books for Young People, Publishers Weekly,* and *School Library Journal,* among others.

Jenkins has one child and lives in New York City.

BIBLIOGRAPHY

HeartBreak. By Walter Dean Myers. Steck-Vaughn, 1993.

Mayfield Crossing. By Vaunda Micheaux Nelson. Putnam, 1993.

The Man Who Knew Too Much: A Moral Tale from the Baila of Zambia. By Julius Lester. Clarion, 1994.

Taste of Salt. By Frances Temple. HarperCollins, 1994.

Crazy Lady. By Jane Leslie Conly. HarperCollins, 1995.

Sambalena Show-Off and the Iron Pot. By Phillis Gershator. Simon & Schuster, 1995.

Blue Tights. By Rita Williams Garcia. Puffin, 1996.

The Genuine Half Moon Kid. By Michael Williams. Puffin, 1996.

If I Only Had a Horn. By Roxane Orgil. Houghton, 1997.

See also Lester, Julius (Bernard); Myers, Walter Dean; Nelson, Vaunda Micheaux

Johnson, Angela

(1 9 6 1–)

AUTHOR

"My writing has allowed a change to come over me. I no longer see the world as good or bad, with rules emblazoned in stone. I no longer have such a definite opinion on everything in the world. There is so much more gray in the spectrum of life. Thankfully this will make my writing grow."

Johnson was born in Tuskegee, Alabama, and attributes her storytelling skills to her father and grandfather, both of whom frequently told stories to the children in the family. She began writing poetry in Windham High School in Ohio and continued while attending Kent State University. Her first book, *Tell Me a Story, Mama,* is described in a *School Library Journal* review as a "touching picture book in both language and art."

Johnson believes that there should be more Black-oriented literature for children and senses the need for Black children to see their own images in books. She placed her own Aunt Rosetta as a character in *Tell Me a Story, Mama.*

Her book *When I Am Old with You* won a 1991 Coretta Scott King Honor Book Award and the American Library Association Social Responsibilities Round Table Award, and, that same year, she also won the Ezra Jack Keats New Writer Award. She received the Northern Ohio Live Writers Award in 1991 and the Alabama Author Award in 1993, and, in 1994, *Toning the Sweep* won the Coretta Scott King Award, and the PEN-Norma Klein Award in 1995.

She has been a Volunteers in Service to America (VISTA) volunteer at the King-Kennedy Community Center, a volunteer at the Kent Head Start Program, and also worked as a nanny for four years in Kent, Ohio.

Johnson is single and lives and writes full time in Kent, Ohio.

BIBLIOGRAPHY

Tell Me a Story, Mama. Illustrated by David Soman. Orchard, 1989.

Do Like Kyla. Illustrated by James Ransome. Orchard, 1990.

When I Am Old with You. Illustrated by David Soman. Orchard, 1990.

One of Three. Illustrated by David Soman. Orchard, 1991.

The Leaving Morning. Illustrated by David Soman. Orchard, 1992.

The Girl Who Wore Snakes. Illustrated by James Ransome. Orchard, 1993.

Julius. Illustrated by Dav Pilkey. Orchard, 1993.

Toning the Sweep. Orchard, 1993.

Joshua by the Sea. Illustrated by Rhonda Mitchell. Orchard, 1994.

Joshua's Night Whispers. Illustrated by Rhonda Mitchell. Orchard, 1994.

Mama Bird, Baby Bird. Illustrated by Rhonda Mitchell. Orchard, 1994.

Rain Feet. Illustrated by Rhonda Mitchell. Orchard, 1994.

Humming Whispers. Orchard, 1995.

Shoes Like Miss Alice's. Illustrated by Ken Page. Orchard, 1995.

The Aunt in Our House. Illustrated by David Soman. Orchard, 1996.

Daddy Calls Me Man. Illustrated by Rhonda Mitchell. Orchard, 1997.

The Rolling Store. Illustrated by Peter Cat. Orchard, 1997.

See also Ransome, James (Earl)

Johnson, Dolores

(1949–)

AUTHOR, ILLUSTRATOR

Johnson was born in New Britain, Connecticut, the third of three children. She attended public schools until she went to college in Boston, Massachusetts, and studied art at Boston University School of the Arts, graduating with a bachelor of fine arts degree.

Within a year of graduating from college, she moved to Los Angeles, California. Johnson had been a sculpture major in college and found few jobs available in her field; her first jobs were clerical. Eventually, she found work as a production artist and production manager at various advertising agencies.

Johnson started making pottery and stained glass windows at home then she did some painting and writing until a friend suggested that she pursue the writing and illustration of children's books. After taking courses, she found an agent and submitted manuscripts and dummies to publishers until she was finally awarded a contract in 1989 to illustrate her first book, *Jenny*, written by Beth P. Wilson.

She has continued to write and/or illustrate many other books, including *What Will Mommy Do When I'm at School?*, *What Kind of Baby-Sitter Is This?*, and *Your Dad Was Just Like You* (books about contemporary children and their worlds); *Now Let Me Fly: The Story of a Slave Family*, and *Seminole Diary: Remembrances of a Slave* (period fiction); and *The Children's Book of Kwanzaa* and *Bessie Coleman: She Dared to Fly* (nonfiction).

Johnson teaches children's-book illustration in the Otis College of Art and Design Continuing Education Program in Los Angeles.

She lives in Inglewood, California.

BIBLIOGRAPHY

Jenny. By Beth P. Wilson. Macmillan, 1990.

What Will Mommy Do When I'm at School? Macmillan, 1990.

What Kind of Baby-Sitter Is This? Macmillan, 1991.

The Best Bug to Be. Macmillan, 1992.

Who Fed the Chickens? By Ella Jenkins. Scott Foresman, 1992.

Calvin's Christmas Wish. By Calvin Miles. Viking, 1993.

Your Dad Was Just Like You. Macmillan, 1993.

Now Let Me Fly: The Story of a Slave Family. Macmillan, 1993.

Papa's Stories. Macmillan, 1994.

Seminole Diary: Remembrances of a Slave. Macmillan, 1995.

Bessie Coleman: She Dared to Fly. Marshall Cavendish, 1996.

Big Meeting. By Dee Palmer Woodtor. Atheneum, 1996.

The Children's Book of Kwanzaa: A Guide to Celebrating the Holiday. Atheneum, 1996.

Grandma's Hands. Benchmark, 1998.

See also Miles, Calvin; Wilson, Beth P(ierre)

Johnson, Georgia A(nna) (Lewis)

(1930–)

AUTHOR

Johnson was born in Chicago, Illinois, and grew up in Van Buren County, Michigan. She attended South Haven High School, graduated from Western Michigan University, and received her M.D. degree from the University of Michigan in 1956.

She received the Distinguished Alumnus Award in 1972 from Western Michigan University. Between 1955 and 1969, Johnson served a rotating internship at Evanston Hospital, Evanston, Illinois, and was a resident of internal medicine and Hematology Fellow at Detroit Receiving Hospital and staff physician at Ypsilanti State Hospital. Between 1969 and 1985, Johnson was assistant professor in the Department of Internal Medicine at Michigan State University, as well as director of adolescent services and staff physician at Olin Health Center. She is now retired from medicine and is conducting research, writing, and publishing.

Active in community affairs, Johnson is a member of the editorial board of the Post-Graduate Medicine Audit Committee and on the board of directors of the Comprehensive Family Health Project. A member of Alpha Kappa Alpha sorority, she also belongs to several professional societies, including the American Medical Association, the Michigan State Medical Society, the Alpha Epsilon Iota medical fraternity, and the Black Faculty and Administrators Association.

Johnson lives in Lansing, Michigan, and is a docent at Kresge Art Museum at Michigan State University.

BIBLIOGRAPHY

Towpath to Freedom. Georgia A. Johnson, 1989.
Webster's Gold. Georgia A. Johnson, 1990.
The Baby Who Knew Too Much. Georgia A. Johnson, 1993.

Johnson, Herschel (Lee)

(1948–)

AUTHOR

"Children's books seem to provide opportunities for stories with elements of fantasy. This particular book made me aware that there were few books for African American children in the literature for children. When I was asked to work with Romare Bearden, it was the best opportunity."

Johnson was born in Birmingham, Alabama. A graduate of Dartmouth College in 1970, he later attended Columbia University School of Journalism. He was associate editor of *Ebony* magazine and a freelance writer from 1974 to 1976 for *Black Enterprise* magazine, where he had worked as assistant and associate editor from 1972 to 1974. In 1971–1972 he was assistant editor and researcher at *Newsweek*.

Among the publications in which his poetry has appeared are the *Young Black Poets Anthology* and *Blackout,* a literary magazine. He does public relations work for AT&T in New York City where he lives.

BIBLIOGRAPHY

A Visit to the Country. Illustrated by Romare Bearden. Harper, 1989.

See also Bearden, Romare H(oward)

Johnson, James Weldon

(1871–1938)

AUTHOR

Johnson was born in Jacksonville, Florida, where he attended city schools. After graduation from Atlanta University, he became an elementary school principal, developing the school program until it became a high school. He then received a law degree and practiced law in Florida.

He and his brother J. Rosamond Johnson moved to New York City and worked together on writing songs and musicals. During this time, Johnson attended Columbia University for graduate study in drama and literature. Johnson was the first Black to pass the Florida bar examination since Reconstruction. In 1898 he formed a law practice with his friend, J.D. Wetmore which dissolved in 1901.

Johnson is probably best known for the "national Negro anthem," "Lift Every Voice and Sing." He wrote the words, and his brother, the music. While serving as U.S. consul at Corinto in Venezuela and Nicaragua, he wrote *The Autobiography of an Ex-Coloured Man.* He contributed articles to magazines, translated the libretto of the Spanish opera *Coyescas,* and served for many years as secretary and field secretary of the National Association for the Advancement of Colored People (NAACP). He was one of the primary shapers of the artistic movement of the 1920s and 1930s called the Harlem Renaissance and was awarded the Spingarn Medal in 1925.

Johnson died in a tragic automobile collision with a train in Wiscasset, Maine, in 1938.

BIBLIOGRAPHY

God's Trombones. Illustrated by Aaron Douglas. Viking, 1927.
Along This Way. Viking, 1968.

Lift Every Voice and Sing. With J. Rosamond Johnson. Illustrated by Mozelle Thompson. Hawthorne, 1970.

Lift Ev'ry Voice and Sing. By James Weldon Johnson. Illustrated by Jan Spivey Gilchrist. Scholastic, 1995.

The Creation. Illustrated by James Ransome. Holiday House, 1994.

See also Gilchrist, Jan Spivey; Ransome, James (Earl)

Jones, (Joan) Jewell

(1942-)

AUTHOR

Jones was born and reared in Cleveland, Ohio. The oldest of six children, she graduated from East Tech Senior High School and attended Bowling Green State University for one year, where she met her future husband, Willis Jones, Jr.

Several years after moving to Akron, Ohio, Jones finished her college education at the University of Akron. She felt that her first responsibility was to her family and took only one or two courses a semester, finally graduating with honors.

She was an elementary school teacher for nine years, then turned to writing. Inspired by the publication of a book of poetry, she completed another book of poetry and has been working on stories for children.

Jones began writing poems about her children and things they did as they were growing up. Never dreaming that the poems would one day be published, she saved them, along with short stories she had also written. Her book *My Skin's Just Right!* parallels the growth and maturing of her daughters. The book is a story about a family told through poetry.

In addition to writing, the former teacher does poetry readings of her work and the works of other Black poets. She also does presentations of African American literature, using poetry, storytelling, and dramatic readings to teach African American history and literature to schoolchildren.

Jones and her husband are the parents of two daughters, and they have one grandson. They live in a suburb of Akron, Ohio.

BIBLIOGRAPHY

My Skin's Just Right! Telcraft, 1994.

Jones, K(enneth) Maurice

(1958–)

AUTHOR

An editor, journalist, poet, and performance artist, Jones was born in Highland Park, Michigan. He grew up addicted to the rhythm, blues, and jazz soul of Motown. He began his career as an editor for the *Cass Technician* at Cass Technical High School in Detroit, Michigan, and has been writing ever since. His first book, the award-winning *Say It Loud! The Story of Rap Music,* was published in 1994. It was voted a Best Book for Young Adults, nonfiction, by the American Library Association.

A graduate of the University of Michigan and the Columbia School of Journalism, Jones has traveled, reported, and lectured extensively throughout southern Africa and the Caribbean. He has taught at the College of New Rochelle, Hunter College, and the Africa Literature Center in Kitwe, Zambia. His articles have appeared in the *Rochester Times Union, Black Enterprise* and *Essence* magazines, the *Michigan Chronicle, Monthly Detroit,* the *Detroit News,* the *Quarterly Black Book Review, Ebony Man,* and *Scholastic* magazine, where he holds the position of media editor.

Jones has appeared at the Nuyorican Poets Cafe in New York City with percussionist Eli Fountain and tap dancer Savion Glover in "an experimental fusion of jazz, tap, and verse." He is cochair of the Africa Outreach Committee for the New York chapter of the National Association of Black Journalists; other affiliations include UNICEF's (United Nations Children's Fund) Day of the African Child, TransAfrica, Fellowship Chapel United Church of Christ in Detroit, and St. Paul Community Baptist Church in Brooklyn, New York.

Jones lives in Detroit, Michigan.

BIBLIOGRAPHY

Say It Loud! The Story of Rap Music. Millbrook, 1994.

Spike Lee and the African American Filmmakers: A Choice of Colors. Millbrook, 1996.

Jordan, June (Meyer)

(1 9 3 6 –)

AUTHOR

Jordan was born in New York City. She attended Barnard College and the University of Chicago and then taught English at Connecticut College, City College, City University of New York, Sarah Lawrence College, and the State University of New York (SUNY) at Stony Brook.

Her publications include essays, poetry, newspaper articles, and books for young people. Her work has appeared in the *New York Times, Partisan Review,* the *Village Voice,* and the *Nation.* She has worked in films, with Mobilization for Youth, and as codirector of the Voice of the Children and its writers' workshop. Among her awards are a Rockefeller Foundation fellowship in creative writing, the Rome Prize fellowship in environmental design, 1970–1971, and a C.A.P.S. grant in poetry. *His Own Where,* published in 1971, was a National Book Award finalist and an American Library Association Best Book for Young Adults. *The Voice of the Children* was a 1971 Coretta Scott King Honor Book.

In 1982, Jordan was awarded a National Endowment of the Arts fellowship in poetry. In 1985, she received a New York Foundation of the Arts fellowship and an award from the Massachusetts Council on the Arts in contemporary arts. In 1986, she received an achievement award for national reporting from the National Association of Black Journalists.

Jordan was an associate professor of English at SUNY at Stony Brook from 1982 to 1987 and a director of its Creative Writing Program. Since 1989, she has been at the University of California, Berkeley, as professor of African American studies and of English.

She is a member of several organizations, including the Center for Constitutional Rights, the New York Foundation of the Arts (where she serves on the board of governors), and the Nicaraguan Culture Alliance (where she is also on the board of directors).

Jordon lives in Berkeley, California. She has one son.

BIBLIOGRAPHY

Who Look at Me. Crowell, 1969.
Soulscript: Afro-American Poetry. Edited by June Jordan. Doubleday, 1970.
The Voice of the Children. Collected with Terri Bush. Holt, 1970.
His Own Where. Crowell, 1971.
Some Changes. Dutton, 1971.
Dry Victories. Holt, 1972.
Fannie Lou Hamer. Crowell, 1972.
New Life: New Room. Crowell, 1975.
Kimako's Story. Houghton, 1981.

Joseph, Lynn

AUTHOR

The author was born and reared on the island of Trinidad in the West Indies. She moved to the United States with her family and received a bachelors' degree from the University of Colorado. In 1994 she won the Book America's Award presented by the Consortium of Latin American Studies for *The Mermaid's Twin Sister*.

She lives in Richmond Hill, New York, with her family.

BIBLIOGRAPHY

Coconut Kind of Day. Illustrated by Sandra Speidel. Lothrop, 1990.
A Wave in Her Pocket: Stories from Trinidad. Illustrated by Brian Pinkney. Clarion, 1991.
An Island Christmas. Illustrated by Catherine Stock. Clarion, 1992.
Jasmine's Parlour Day. Illustrated by Ann Grifalconi. Lothrop, 1994.
The Mermaid's Twin Sister: More Stories from Trinidad. Illustrated by Donna Perrone. Houghton, 1994.

See also Pinkney, Brian

Keens-Douglas, Ricardo

AUTHOR

"At night, my family would sit on the veranda telling stories and jokes. We had picnics on the beach and ate mangoes until our bellies were full. There was always laughter and a strong sense of living."

Keens-Douglas was born in Grenada, the Isle of Spice. As the youngest of seven children, he has fond memories of growing up. He is a storyteller, playwright, radio and television show host and actor. Now he is exploring new ground—as an author of children's books. His first title, *The Nutmeg Princess,* teaches an important message to children: "Follow your dreams, and if you believe in yourself all things are possible."

He attended the Dawson Theatre School and has appeared in films and on radio and television across the country, including the Stratford Shakespearean Company. He performed his famous creation story, *Mama God, Papa God,* for Princess Diana aboard the British royal yacht *Britannia* during her 1991 visit to North America.

As a storyteller, Keens-Douglas has thrilled audiences in the United States and the Caribbean and at international storytelling festivals. His storytelling cabaret production of *Once Upon an Island* was a Sterling Award nominee for Best Touring Production in Edmonton, Alberta, Canada, in 1991.

Many of Keens-Douglas's stories are now in print and are anthologized in *Take Five* and *Fiery Spirits.* Three fables for young readers, *The Nutmeg Princess, LaDiablesse and the Baby,* and *Freedom Child of the Sea,* have been translated into French and Spanish.

He lives in Toronto, Ontario, Canada.

BIBLIOGRAPHY

The Nutmeg Princess. Annick, 1992.
Freedom Child of the Sea. Annick, 1995.
LaDiablesse and the Baby. Annick, 1995.
Grandpa's Visit. Annick, 1996.

Kirkpatrick, Oliver Austin
John Canoe

(1911–1988)

AUTHOR

The author, who was also known by his pseudonym, John Canoe, was born and educated in Jamaica. After coming to the United States, he attended New York University, the New School for Social Research, and Columbia University, where he obtained his master's degree in library science.

Kirkpatrick was a columnist and sports editor for the *Jamaica Standard* and a newscaster on radio Jamaica ZQI before working as a librarian in the New York Public Library and a supervising librarian in the Brooklyn Public Library, from which he retired.

He received the Joyce Kilmer Award from New York University for creative writing.

He lived in Brooklyn, New York.

BIBLIOGRAPHY

Naja the Snake and Magnus the Mongoose. Doubleday, 1970.

Lauture, Denizé

(1946–)

AUTHOR

Lauture was born in Haiti, the first of thirteen children, and migrated from Haiti to the United States in 1968. He was then twenty-two years old, a welder, and without a high school diploma.

He worked as a welder in Harlem, New York, and attended evening classes at the City College of New York. He earned a bachelor of arts degree in sociology and a master of science degree in bilingual education. His poetry has been published in many countries, including the West Indies, Spain, and Canada. In the United States, his poetry has appeared in various literary magazines, including *Callaloo, Black American Literature Forum,* and *African Commentary.* The main source for his children's books is his childhood in rural Haiti.

Father and Son was one of five books nominated to receive the National Association for the Advancement of Colored People's (NAACP) 1993 Image Award. Lauture teaches at Saint Thomas Aquinas College in Sparkill, New York, where he was the recipient of the 1994 Board of Trustees' Award for Excellence. *Running the Road to ABC* won the 1997 Coretta Scott King Honor Award for illustration.

He has two sons, Charles and Conrad, and lives in the Bronx, New York.

BIBLIOGRAPHY

Father and Son. Illustrated by Jonathan Green. Philomel, 1993.
Running the Road to ABC. Illustrated by Reynold Ruffins. Simon & Schuster, 1996.

See also Green, Jonathan; Ruffins, Reynold

Lawrence, Jacob

(1 9 1 7–)

ILLUSTRATOR, AUTHOR

One of the most outstanding contemporary artists, Lawrence has been called "the nation's foremost Negro painter." His work has been compared favorably with that of Picasso, Daumier, Orozco, and especially Hogarth. His style, described as a series of large flat forms, with no depth, and no details, is known for the use of pure colors: blues, reds, yellows. Each picture has a title so that the series in sequence resembles a story's script.

He was born in Atlantic City, New Jersey. His mother later moved the family to Philadelphia, Pennsylvania, and then to New York City when Lawrence was twelve years old.

Lawrence studied at the American Artists School in New York on a full scholarship. His spare time was spent at the 135th Street branch of the New York Public Library and at the Schomburg Collection to gather material for a pictorial biography of Frederick Douglass. In 1940, he received a Rosenwald fellowship to research Southern migrants in the North after World War I. His Rosenwald Foundation grant in 1941–1942 enabled him to produce his *Life of John Brown* with a series of twenty-two paintings. A Guggenheim fellowship in 1945 helped him produce, in 1947, fourteen paintings of World War II. The United States Coast Guard Archives houses his World War II pictures.

In December 1983, Lawrence was elected to the American Academy of Arts and Letters, an honor acknowledging the contribution of his art and teaching over the many years. He is Professor Emeritus at the University of Washington. Lawrence lives with his wife, artist Gwendolyn Knight, in Seattle, Washington.

BIBLIOGRAPHY

Harriet and the Promised Land. Simon & Schuster, 1968.

The Great Migration: An American Story. HarperCollins, 1993.

John Brown: One Man Against Slavery. By Gwen Everett. Rizzoli, 1993.

Toussaint L'Ouverture: The Fight for Haiti's Freedom. By Walter Dean Myers. Simon & Schuster, 1996.

Aesop's Fables. University of Washington Press, 1997.

See also Myers, Walter Dean

Lee, Judith Lynn (Blackwell)

(1957–)

AUTHOR

Lee was born and reared in Akron, Ohio, the eighth of nine children. Her first children's book, *Look at Me,* is a book of motivational poetry. Although she has always loved reading poems, she did not think of writing poetry herself until she tried it as a way of gaining a better understanding and a more interesting way of reading the Bible. It was then that she found her talent for writing. Her poems are used in many schools, churches, and organizations.

Lee works through the drug-rehabilitation programs in her community doing what she can to make a positive difference. She also shares her time in the fight for equal opportunities by working for and supporting the Akron branch of the National Association for the Advancement of Colored People (NAACP). The Parent Teachers Association is another organization in which Lee spends much of her time, working with the schools that her children attend, as president of the association.

Lee is pursuing a bachelor's degree in communications at Akron University.

She lives in Akron, Ohio, with her husband and two daughters.

BIBLIOGRAPHY

Look at Me. Telcraft, 1995.

Lester, Julius (Bernard)

(1939–)

AUTHOR

The author was born in St. Louis, Missouri, but his family moved to Kansas City, Missouri, and then to Nashville, Tennessee, during his early adolescence. Lester earned his bachelor's degree in English in 1960 at Fisk University. He attributes his interest in Southern rural traditions and Black folklore to his father, a Methodist minister and a captivating storyteller.

Lester has had a varied work experience. Since 1971, he has been a professor at the University of Massachusetts, Amherst, where he teaches in the Judaic Studies, English, and History Departments. He hosted a radio talk show on WBAI-FM in New York City from 1968 to 1975 and a live television talk show on WNET from 1971 to 1973.

His political activities include experience in the late 1960s as a field secretary and head of the Photo Department for the Student Non-Violent Coordinating Committee (SNCC). In 1967, he took photographs of North Vietnam to show the effects of U.S. bombing there, and also attended the Organization of Latin American Solidarity Conference in Cuba with SNCC activist Stokely Carmichael.

As a father, he felt the need to write the sort of books unavailable during his own childhood. Lester has also written books for adults and articles that have appeared in newspapers and journals such as the *Village Voice*, *The New Republic*, *Ebony*, the *New York Times Book Review Forward*, and *Parents' Choice*. He has also written poetry. His interest in music is evident in his work with folksinger Pete Seeger on the instructional book *The 12-String Guitar as Played by Leadbelly*.

To Be a Slave was a Newbery Honor Book in 1969, and *Long Journey Home: Stories from Black History* (1972) and *Black Folktales* (1969) were on the *New York Times* list of Outstanding Books of the

Year. *Long Journey Home* was nominated for a National Book Award in 1973, and *John Henry,* illustrated by Jerry Pinkney, received both the Caldecott Honor Book Award and the Boston Globe-Horn Book Award in 1995. In addition, Lester won Coretta Scott King Honor Book Awards for *This Strange New Feeling* in 1983 and *The Tales of Uncle Remus: The Adventures of Brer Rabbit* in 1988.

Lester has five children and lives in Belchertown, Massachusetts.

BIBLIOGRAPHY

To Be a Slave. Illustrated by Tom Feelings. Dial, 1968.

Black Folktales. Illustrated by Tom Feelings. R.W. Baron, 1969.

The Knee-High Man and Other Tales. Illustrated by Ralph Pinto. Dial, 1972.

Long Journey Home: Stories from Black History. Dial, 1972.

Two Love Stories. Dial, 1972.

Who I Am. Photopoems by Julius Lester and David Gahr. Dial, 1974.

This Strange New Feeling. Dial, 1982.

The Tales of Uncle Remus: The Adventures of Brer Rabbit. Illustrated by Jerry Pinkney. Dial, 1987.

More Tales of Uncle Remus: Further Adventures of Brer Rabbit, His Friends, Enemies and Others. Illustrated by Jerry Pinkney. Dial, 1988.

How Many Spots Does a Leopard Have? Illustrated by David Shannon. Scholastic, 1989.

Further Tales of Uncle Remus: The Misadventures of Brer Rabbit, Brer Fox, Brer Wolf, the Doodang and Other Creatures. Illustrated by Jerry Pinkney. Dial, 1990.

John Henry. Illustrated by Jerry Pinkney. Dial, 1994.

The Last Tales of Uncle Remus. Illustrated by Jerry Pinkney. Dial, 1994.

The Man Who Knew Too Much: A Moral Tale from the Baila of Zambia. Illustrated by Leonard Jenkins. Clarion, 1994.

Othello: A Novel. Scholastic, 1995.

Sam and the Tigers. Illustrated by Jerry Pinkney. Dial, 1996.

From Slave Ship to Freedom Road. Illustrated by Rod Brown. Dial, 1997.

See also Feelings, Tom; Jenkins, Leonard; Pinkney, Jerry

Lewis, Dennis E(arl)

(1 9 4 9 –)

ILLUSTRATOR

Lewis was born in St. Louis, Missouri. At the early age of seven, he knew immediately upon doing his first drawing in class, that he would pursue a career in art. He soon found art to be a positive vehicle for self-expression.

His parents were always encouraging and always found the time to give him proper guidance and understanding. Lewis credits his mentor, artist Robert A. Wright, as his inspiration. He was able to obtain a grant and a loan just before graduation from high school for the California Institute of the Arts (Choutnard Art Institute) and earned a bachelor of fine arts degree in commercial illustration.

Lewis's first job as a professional artist was working in the retail business as a layout artist for one of the major department stores in the Los Angeles, California, area. After much experience, he became a freelance illustrator, taking on all types of jobs and opening his first art studio with another illustrator.

He lives in Bellevue, Washington, with his wife and three children.

BIBLIOGRAPHY

The African Question Collection. By Linda Schwartz. Learning Works, 1994.

Lilly, Charles

ILLUSTRATOR

The illustrator of *Philip Hall Likes Me, I Reckon Maybe,* Lilly studied in New York City at the School of Visual Arts, where he also taught a painting class. His work has appeared in magazines and as bookjacket illustrations, and his art has been recognized by awards of merit from the Society of Illustrators, the Art Directors Club, and Publication Designers.

Lilly lives in New York City.

BIBLIOGRAPHY

Mukasa. By John Nagenda. Macmillan, 1973.

The Peppermint Pig. By Nina Bawden. Lippincott, 1975.

Soup and Me. By Robert N. Peck. Knopf, 1975.

Growin'. By Nikki Grimes. Dial, 1977.

Philip Hall Likes Me, I Reckon Maybe. By Bette Greene. Dial, 1977.

Runaway to Freedom: A Story of the Underground Railroad. By Barbara Smucker. HarperCollins, 1979.

Escape from Slavery: Five Journeys to Freedom. By Doreen Rappaport. HarperCollins, 1991.

See also Boyd, Candy (Marguerite) Dawson; Childress, Alice; Grimes, Nikki

Lindamichellebaron

(1950–)

AUTHOR

One of two children, Lindamichellebaron was born in New York City, the daughter of a pastor.

She has authored and published two books of poetry, one in 1971 while still a junior at New York University, and the other in 1977. Shortly after, she received the Martin Luther King Service Award for Achievement in Arts and Letters for the year 1978.

She became an educational sales representative for the McGraw-Hill publishing company in 1978, and her reputation as a "take care of business" salesperson allowed her to be welcomed at two other major publishing houses, Harcourt Brace Jovanovich and Silver Burdett. In 1988, she began working for herself as a publisher, performing artist, motivational speaker, consultant, and "edu-tainer."

She received the New York State Small Business Development Center's Entrepreneur of the Year Award in 1993 and the Business Recognition Award for Outstanding Business Achievement and Its Impact on Community Life, presented in 1991 by the Black Business and Professional Women. She received the 1992 National Association for the Advancement of Colored People's (NAACP) President's Award and was named Educator of the Year in 1995 by the New York Association of Black Educators.

Lindamichellebaron appears nationally as a keynote speaker at colleges and universities and social and political organizations and has been featured on both radio and television. She is on the board of directors for the multicultural Publishing Exchange and Black Women in Publishing, and she is a member of many professional and social organizations, including the Theta Iota Omega chapter of Alpha Kappa Alpha sorority. She is working toward her doctorate in cross categorical studies at Columbia University Teacher's College.

Lindamichellebaron lives in Hempstead, New York.

BIBLIOGRAPHY

Black Is Beautiful. Lindamichellebaron, 1971.

Going Through Changes. Illustrated by Leola Young. Lindamichellebaron, 1977.

Rhythm and Dues. Illustrated by Jorge Domenech. Harlin Jacque, 1981, 1990, 1995.

The Sun Is On. Illustrated by Jorge Domenech. Harlin Jacque, 1981, 1990, 1995.

Little, Lessie Jones

(1906–1986)

AUTHOR

Little was born in Parmele, North Carolina. A 1924 graduate of Higgs Roanoke Seminary, she also attended North Carolina State Normal School (now Elizabeth City State University). After graduation, she began teaching in her home state, and two years later she married her childhood sweetheart, Weston W. Little, Sr. They moved to Washington, D.C., in 1929 and later became parents of five children.

Little's daughter, children's author Eloise Greenfield, has noted that her mother had a special love for people and for the arts and enjoyed bringing these together through her writing. Although Little entered this field late in her life (she was almost seventy), she was diligent in studying the craft and took seriously what she saw as her responsibility to pass on to children messages of truth and hope.

She developed a Harriet Tubman crossword puzzle, which appeared in *Ebony Jr.'s* June/July 1973 issue, and this experience became the stimulus for writing. Her own book of poetry, *Love: A Lamp Unto My Feet,* was published in 1982.

Among her awards during her brief writing career are the Boston Globe-Horn Book Honor Book Award in 1980 for *Childtimes: A Three-Generational Memoir* which she coauthored with her daughter, and the 1988 Parents Choice Award for *Children of Long Ago.*

She died leaving several unpublished manuscripts—picture books and poetry for children and a novel for adults.

BIBLIOGRAPHY

I Can Do It by Myself. With Eloise Greenfield. Illustrated by Carole Byard. Crowell, 1978.

Childtimes: A Three-Generation Memoir. With Eloise Greenfield. Illustrated by
 Jerry Pinkney. Harper, 1979.
Children of Long Ago. Illustrated by Jan Spivey Gilchrist. Philomel, 1988.

See also Byard, Carole; Gilchrist, Jan Spivey; Greenfield, Eloise
(Glynn Little); Pinkney, Jerry

Lloyd, Errol

(1943-)

AUTHOR, ILLUSTRATOR

Lloyd was born in Jamaica and attended Munro College, Jamaica, London University, and the Council of Education in London, England. He became interested in art when he was about sixteen years old. He had already decided on a legal career, and he did start to study law in 1964, but his love of art outweighed this pursuit and he never completed his studies.

His illustrations for *My Brother Sean,* written by Petronella Breinburg, were commended for the Kate Greenaway Medal in England in 1974.

BIBLIOGRAPHY

My Brother Sean. By Petronella Breinburg. Bodley Head, 1973.
Shawn Goes to School. By Petronella Breinburg. HarperCollins, 1973.
Doctor Shawn. By Petronella Breinburg. HarperCollins, 1975.
Shawn's Red Bike. By Petronella Breinburg. Crowell, 1976.
Nini at Carnival. Crowell, 1978.
Nandy's Bedtime. Bodley Head, 1982.
Sasha and the Bicycle Thieves. Barron's, 1989.

See also Breinburg, Petronella

Lucas, Cedric

(1962–)

ILLUSTRATOR

Lucas was born in New York City, and as far back as he can remember, even as a young child, art was always an area of interest. He attributes his motivation to become an artist to the early support of his family and teachers.

After graduating from the New York High School of Art and Design, he attended the School of Visual Arts in New York City on a foundation scholarship in 1979, earning a bachelor's degree. He earned a master's degree from Lehman College in 1993 and also studied media arts, winning many awards, among them the Society of Illustrators National Student Competition Gyo Fujikawa Award, and the Art Directors Club New Talent Competition Award.

In 1984, Lucas began a career as a freelance illustrator and an art teacher for the New York City Board of Education. He was honored by the United Federation of Teachers with an innovative-teaching grant in 1992. His interest in art as it relates to educational literature led him to illustrating children's books.

Lucas is fast becoming a well-known illustrator, and he gives lectures to educators on the process of illustrating children's books and making connections between content reading, content writing, and art. He is the chairperson of a middle-school art department.

Reviews of his children's book *Frederick Douglass: The Last Day of Slavery* appeared in *Publishers Weekly* and in *Booklist* in 1995.

Lucas lives in Yonkers, New York, with his wife and children.

BIBLIOGRAPHY

Frederick Douglass: The Last Day of Slavery. By William Miller. Lee & Low, 1995.

What's in Aunt Mary's Room? By Elizabeth Fitzgerald Howard. Clarion, 1996.
Big Wind Coming! By Karen English. Whitman, 1996.

See also Howard, Elizabeth Fitzgerald

Lynch, Lorenzo

(1 9 3 2 –)

ILLUSTRATOR, AUTHOR

The artist took a correspondence course from Art Instruction, Incorporated, Minneapolis, Minnesota, from 1946 to 1950. He then attended the Art Students League and the School of Visual Arts in New York City. He worked as an artist with Fisher Advertising in Brooklyn, New York, at Olivetti in New York City, at Martin's Department Store in Brooklyn, and at New York's Annivette Studios.

He lives in Brooklyn, New York.

BIBLIOGRAPHY

The Hot Dog Man. Bobbs-Merrill, 1970.
Baba and Mr. Big. By C. Everard Palmer. Bobbs-Merrill, 1972.
A Bottle of Pop. By James Holding. Putnam, 1972.
The Fastest Quitter in Town. By Phyllis Green. HarperCollins, 1972.
The Black Is Beautiful Beauty Book. By Melba Miller. Prentice-Hall, 1974.
Big Sister Tells Me That I'm Black. By Arnold Adoff. Holt, 1976.

See also Palmer, C(yril) Everard

Madhubuti, Safisha

Jewel Latimore
Johari M. Amini

(1935–)

AUTHOR

Formerly Jewel Latimore, Safisha Madhubuti changed her name legally to Johari M. Amini. The daughter of a clergyman, she is married to Haki Madhubuti (Don L. Lee), the poet and publisher, and was a cofounder of Third World Press. She and her husband are parents of two sons and a daughter.

Madhubuti attended Chicago City College, from which she received an associate of arts degree, and later the University of Chicago, where she obtained her bachelor of arts degree in 1970. She has worked as an editor for the Third World Press and contributed numerous articles to the periodicals *Black World* and *Negro Digest*. She has also been assistant editor for the *Black Books Bulletin*. Her work appears in more than a dozen anthologies.

From 1965 to 1966, she worked at the Chicago City College. For the period 1970–1972, she was an instructor in psychology and a lecturer in Black literature at the college. She has been the director of the successful New Concept Development Center in Chicago, an affirmative African American educational institution.

Her memberships include the Institute of Positive Education, the African Heritage Studies Association, and the Organization of Black American Culture. Madhubuti and her husband, Haki Madhubuti, poet and literary critic, live in Chicago, Illinois.

BIBLIOGRAPHY

The Story of Kwanzaa. Illustrated by N. DePillars. Third World, 1989.

Magubane, Peter

(1932–)

ILLUSTRATOR, AUTHOR

Photographer Magubane was born in Johannesburg, South Africa. He started his career as a photographer in 1956 on the magazine *Drum* and was a staff member in 1956 of the *Rand Daily Mail,* a Johannesburg newspaper. For more than twenty years, he was the only major Black South African news photographer. His experiences, recorded in *Magubane's South Africa,* portray his arrests, banning orders, solitary confinement, and other experiences under the apartheid system.

His *Black Child* won the 1983 Coretta Scott King Award for illustration.

He still has a home in Dupkloof, a section of the Black township of Soweto, outside Johannesburg, South Africa.

BIBLIOGRAPHY

Black Child. Knopf, 1982.

Martin, Linda

(1961–)

AUTHOR, ILLUSTRATOR

Martin was born in Colorado Springs, Colorado, the second of seven children. As a young child she preferred reading Edward Lear, Carl Sandburg, Robert Louis Stevenson, and Lewis Carroll. While in college, Martin began illustrating various small publications and doing portraits for extra income. Her first illustration job was a comic strip published in a local Black "minizine" called *The Marketplace*. This led to having illustrations published in a textbook covering English as a second language for Oxford University.

She continued to illustrate more textbooks and manuals and, in 1993, established an African doll and art business named MAKI. She is a member of the Colorado Springs Art Guild and the Art Students League.

Martin lives in Colorado Springs, Colorado.

BIBLIOGRAPHY

Fast Forward, USA. Oxford University Press, 1989.
When Dinosaurs Go Visiting. Chronicle, 1993.
Watch Them Grow. Dorling Kindersley, 1994.
Ready, Set, Go! Libraries Unlimited, 1995.

Massey, Cal(vin Levi)

(1926–)

ILLUSTRATOR

"I paint because I have to; it's my way of communicating with the world around me."

Massey was born in Philadelphia Pennsylvania. He attended and graduated from the Hussian School in Philadelphia, majoring in life drawing and illustration. He later joined the faculty for a three-year tenure.

His illustrations have appeared in the *Saturday Evening Post* and have been used by several publishing companies, including Scott Foresman, Random House, Scholastic, and Just Us Books. Among his designs and sculptures, he has created the crest and class rings for the United States Naval Air Force Military Academy, the MacArthur Memorial Medal, and a bas-relief sculpture commemorating the restoration of Ellis Island for the Statue of Liberty Foundation. He designed fifty medallions for the Madison Collection from 1990 to 1991.

Massey has had several one-man shows: at John Wanamaker's Fine Arts Gallery in 1979, the Makler Gallery in Philadelphia, Pennsylvania, in 1979, and Swarthmore College between 1983 and 1984, among others. He was commissioned to do a portrait of Gloria Chisum in 1993 for the Philadelphia Library, and his work can be found in many private collections.

Massey lives in Moorestown, New Jersey.

BIBLIOGRAPHY

Tom B and the Joyful Noise. By Jerome Cushman. Westminster, 1970.
What Harry Found When He Lost Archie. By Jean Horton Berg. Westminster, 1970.
My First Kwanzaa Book. By Deborah M. Newton Chocolate. Scholastic, 1992.
I Love My Family. By Wade Hudson. Scholastic, 1993.

See also Chocolate, Debbi (Deborah Mique Newton); Hudson, Wade

Mathenge, Judy (Wanjiku)

(1971–)

ILLUSTRATOR

Born in Nairobi, Kenya, Mathenge went to Nairobi Primary School and Kenya High School for Girls. Inspired by her secondary school art teacher, and encouraged by her father to pursue a career in art, she entered Kenyatta University and graduated in 1994 with a bachelor's degree in fine art. Mathenge has been associated with the publishing house Jacaranda Designs since it first began operation in 1991, working part-time as an illustrator until her graduation, when she became a full-time member of the art staff.

In 1995, she was selected as the illustrator for the book *What Causes Bad Memories* by the trauma team of UNICEF (United Nations Children's Fund), which was working with displaced and orphaned children in Rwanda. A trained and qualified teacher and artist, Mathenge was selected to run the Healing Arts Program, which organizes groups of Kenyan secondary-school art students to paint the walls in the children's wards of Nairobi hospitals.

At the Pan African Book Fair in Nairobi, she conducted a painting workshop in 1994 and was a facilitator in computer graphic design in 1995.

She lives in Nairobi, Kenya.

BIBLIOGRAPHY

Mcheshi Goes to the Market. By the Jacaranda House Team. Jacaranda Designs, 1993.

Beneath the Rainbow: Princess Rainbow. By Kariuki Gakuo. Jacaranda Designs, 1994.

Mcheshi Goes on a Journey. By the Jacaranda House Team. Jacaranda Designs, 1994.

Zamani: Flight of the Firehawk. By Tom Nevin. Jacaranda Designs, 1995.

What Causes Bad Memories. By UNICEF. UNICEF, 1995.

Mcheshi Goes to School. By The Jacaranda House Team. Jacaranda Designs, 1995.

Mcheshi Goes to a Farm. By The Jacaranda House Team. Jacaranda Designs, 1996.

Mathis, Sharon (Yvonne) Bell

(1937–)

AUTHOR

Mathis was born in Atlantic City, New Jersey, the first of four children. As a child and young adult, she enjoyed reading her books on an iron fire escape suspended above the backyard. The books of Black writers were greatly appreciated in Mathis's home, and she had the additional advantage of watching her mother draw pictures and create poems.

Mathis graduated from Morgan State University, Baltimore, Maryland, in 1958, and in 1975 she received a master of science degree in library science from Catholic University in Washington, D.C. After five years as a fifth-grade teacher for the archdiocese of Washington, ten years as a special-education teacher, and twenty years as a school library media specialist, Mathis retired from the District of Columbia public schools in 1995.

A former columnist for *Ebony Jr.* magazine, Mathis has contributed fiction to *Negro Digest, Essence,* and *Scholastic* magazines. She has reviewed books for the *Washington Post* and *Black Books Bulletin. Sidewalk Story* was a Child Study Association of America's Children's Book of the Year in 1970. Several of her works have been American Library Association Notable Books. *The Hundred Penny Box* was a Newbery Honor Book in 1976, and *Ray Charles* won the Coretta Scott King Award in 1974 for both text and illustration. *Red Dog, Blue Fly* won the American Bookseller Association Pick of the List in 1991 and Bank Street College's Children's Books for the year 1991.

The divorced mother of three daughters, she lives in Fort Washington, Maryland.

BIBLIOGRAPHY

Brooklyn Story. Illustrated by Charles Bible. Hill & Wang, 1970.

Sidewalk Story. Illustrated by Leo Carty. Viking, 1971.
Teacup Full of Roses. Viking, 1972.
Ray Charles. Illustrated by George Ford. Crowell, 1973.
Listen for the Fig Tree. Viking, 1974.
The Hundred Penny Box. Illustrated by Leo and Diane Dillon. Viking, 1975.
Cartwheels. Illustrated by Norma Holt. Scholastic, 1977.
Red Dog, Blue Fly. Illustrated by Jan Spivey Gilchrist. Viking, 1991.
Running Girl: The Diary of Ebonee Rose. Browndeer, 1997.

See also Bible, Charles; Carty, Leo; Dillon, Leo; Ford, George (Cephas); Gilchrist, Jan Spivey

Matthews, Debbie M.

AUTHOR

Matthews was born in Akron, Ohio, and began to write poetry while in college. Her writing is greatly inspired by her family.

Matthews is a schoolteacher, a model, and a writer. Her poetry has been published in the anthologies *Spirit of the Age* and *Reflections of Light*. A review of her children's book, *Why Polly Wants a Cracker!*, appeared in the *Akron Beacon Journal* newspaper. She has also made several book-signing appearances. Matthews teaches in the Columbus public schools and is completing a master's degree in administration at Ohio State University.

She and her husband, author Robert Decatur, live in Columbus, Ohio.

BIBLIOGRAPHY

Why Polly Wants a Cracker! Illustrated by Martin K. Riley, Jr. Dibora, 1995.

See also Riley, Martin K., Jr.

Mbugua, Kioi wa

(1962–)

AUTHOR

Mbugua was born in Ngong near Nairobi, Kenya, the third in a family of seven children. He grew up in an ethnically mixed environment among the Kikuyu and the culture-loving Maasai peoples. This played an essential role in his development, inculcating a deep appreciation of cultural diversity and a love of the rich, traditional African heritage.

Mbugua graduated from Nairobi University in 1988 with a bachelor's degree in African languages. He worked for two years as a journalist with the Kenya News Agency and continues to contribute articles, short stories, and book reviews. He is an active member of the Kenya Oral Literature Association, an organization that promotes professional collection and publication of Kenyan folklore.

In 1991, he received a postgraduate diploma in film production from the Kenya Institute of Mass Communication. In 1995, he worked as a script consultant on two educational video productions: *Roots of Rhythm* and *Enkishon: The Maasai Child of Kenya*.

Since 1991, he has been a resident writer and editor with Jacaranda Designs and has actively participated in training workshops for African writers and illustrators from other countries. Mbugua has translated several of their books into Swahili and is a senior member of the editorial board.

He lives in Nairobi, Kenya.

BIBLIOGRAPHY

Inkishu: Myths and Legends of the Maasai. Jacaranda Designs, 1994.
Inkishu: Nkai's Great Gift. Illustrated by Kang'ara wa Njambi. Jacaranda Designs, 1994.

Inkishu: The Forest of the Lost Child. Illustrated by Samwel Ngoje. Jacaranda Designs, 1994.

Fumo Liyongo: A Hero of the Swahili. Jacaranda Designs, 1996.

See also Ngoje, Samwel; Njambi, Kang'ara wa

McCannon, Dindga

(1947–)

ILLUSTRATOR, AUTHOR

McCannon was born in Harlem, New York, and studied at the Art Students League and the City University of New York. At seventeen, she exhibited her work in a one-woman show, followed by other exhibitions at the PAX Gallery, as a participant in Genesis II, the Black Expo, and the Harlem Outdoor Art Show. She is cofounder of the Black women's art collective Where We At.

McCannon has also worked as a dress designer, a teacher of printmaking, and a jewelry designer.

BIBLIOGRAPHY

Omar at Christmas. By Edgar White. Lothrop, 1973.
Sati the Rastifarian. By Edgar White. Lothrop, 1973.
Children of Night. By Edgar White. Lothrop, 1974.
Peaches. Lothrop, 1974.
Wilhemina Jones: Future Star. Delacorte, 1980.

See also White, Edgar

McConduit, Denise Walter

(1950–)

AUTHOR

"*I was the fourth in a family of thirteen children. By the time I was nine, there were nine children, including three sets of twins, under me. My mother always praised me for being her biggest helper, and I just assumed the role of entertaining my younger sisters and brothers. As a child, I loved to read stories and put on plays. My mother enjoyed writing and drawing and would often write stories for us to read. My daddy was a very humorous man who was known for telling the funniest stories. I guess I got my writing ability from my mother and my storytelling humor from my father.*

I love to write because I've always felt that I had something to say. As a child, my stories were about my sisters and brothers. There were no stories about African American children in the library. I read the encyclopedia when I had nothing else to read. When I had children, I created stories about them and about the New Orleans culture, such as the Mardi Gras. I am very grateful that I have been able to make a contribution to the world of literature. I guess that the old saying is true, that if you do something long enough, and work hard enough, one day it's going to pay off."

Born in New Orleans, Louisiana, McConduit loved drawing and reading, and at about the age of twelve she started writing poetry. In high school, she was staff artist for the school paper and was on a local television show every week as a teen dancer. She attended Xavier University for one year, married, and started working at Shell Oil Company, where she has been for more than twenty-five years.

McConduit has had articles published in *Black New Orleans* and *Essence* magazines. She is a member of the New Orleans Poetry Forum.

Conduit lives in New Orleans, Louisiana.

BIBLIOGRAPHY

D.J. and the Zulu Parade. Illustrated by Emile F. Henriquez. Pelican, 1995.

McKissack, Fredrick (Lemuel)

(1939–)

AUTHOR

"If you don't know the stories and lore of your people, then it is difficult to participate in the culture."

McKissack, a civil engineer, was born in Nashville, Tennessee. He has owned his own construction company for many years. Now, he believes, his writing "builds bridges with books." He comes from a long line of builders. His great-grandfather, Moses McKissack, was the first licensed Black architect in the state of Tennessee and the founder of a company that bore his name as partner. His grandfather was one of the first African American builders known particularly for his design of doors. His father, Lewis Winter McKissack, was also an architect.

McKissack attended Tennessee State University (formerly Tennessee Agricultural and Industrial State University) and obtained his bachelor of science degree in civil engineering in 1964. He is a member of the African Methodist Episcopal Church, where he is a steward on the church board and a member of the male chorus. He also belongs to the National Writers Guild and the Society of Children's Book Writers and Illustrators and is co-owner of All-Writing Services with his wife, Patricia.

He has shared honors with his wife for many books, including *Abram, Abram, Where Are We Going?*, which won the C.S. Lewis Silver Medal Award from the Christian Educators Association in 1985; *A Long Hard Journey: The Story of the Pullman Porter,* which won the Jane Addams Children's Book Award and the Coretta Scott King Award in 1990; *Sojourner Truth: Ain't I a Woman?,* which won a Boston Globe-Horn Book Award in 1993 and was a Coretta Scott King Honor Book that same year; and *Christmas in the Big House, Christmas in the Quarters,* which won the Coretta Scott King Award in 1995. *Rebels Against*

Slavery:American Slave Revolts was named a 1997 Coretta Scott King Author Honor Book.

McKissack has been called "one of the best" researchers in the business, and with good reason. The photo research for the book *A Long Hard Journey: The Story of the Pullman Porter* has been widely acclaimed because of the previously unpublished photographs he secured from a private collection. In 1993, he was honored as Tennessee Author of the Year by the *Nashville Banner* newspaper for his research.

In addition to writing, McKissack and his wife are often speakers at educational meetings, workshops, and seminars. Both received honorary doctorate degrees in 1994 from the University of Missouri.

He lives in St. Louis, Missouri, with his wife, Patricia McKissack. They have three adult children.

BIBLIOGRAPHY

Abram, Abram, Where Are We Going? With Patricia C. McKissack. David Cook, 1984.

It's the Truth, Christopher. With Patricia C. McKissack. Augsburg, 1984.

Lights Out, Christopher. With Patricia C. McKissack. Illustrated by Bartholomew. Augsburg, 1984.

Michael Jackson: Superstar. With Patricia C. McKissack. Children's Press, 1984.

Paul Laurence Dunbar: A Poet to Remember. With Patricia C. McKissack. Children's Press, 1984.

The Civil Rights Movement in America from 1865 to the Present. With Patricia C. McKissack. Children's Press, 1987, 1991 (Second Edition).

Frederick Douglass: The Black Lion. With Patricia C. McKissack. Children's Press, 1987.

Constance Stumbles. With Patricia C. McKissack. Children's Press, 1988.

Messy Bessey. With Patricia C. McKissack. Illustrated by Richard Hackney. A Big Book. Children's Press, 1988.

God Made Something Wonderful. With Patricia C. McKissack. Illustrated by Ching. Augusburg, 1989.

A Long Hard Journey: The Story of the Pullman Porter. With Patricia C. McKissack. Walker, 1990.

Taking a Stand Against Racism and Racial Discrimination. With Patricia C. McKissack. Watts, 1990.

W.E.B. Du Bois. With Patricia C. McKissack. Watts, 1990.

Carter G. Woodson. With Patricia C. McKissack. Enslow, 1991.

Frederick Douglass: Leader Against Slavery. With Patricia C. McKissack. Enslow, 1991.

George Washington Carver: The Peanut Scientist. With Patricia C. McKissack. Enslow, 1991.

Ida B. Wells-Barnett: A Voice Against Violence. With Patricia C. McKissack. Enslow, 1991.

Louis Armstrong: Jazz Musician. With Patricia C. McKissack. Enslow, 1991.

Marian Anderson: A Great Singer. With Patricia C. McKissack. Enslow, 1991.

Martin Luther King, Jr.: Man of Peace. With Patricia C. McKissack. Enslow, 1991.

Mary Church Terrell: Leader for Equality. With Patricia C. McKissack. Enslow, 1991.

Ralph J. Bunche: Peacemaker. With Patricia C. McKissack. Enslow, 1991.

Booker T. Washington: Leader and Educator. With Patricia C. McKissack. Enslow, 1992.

Jesse Owens: Olympic Star. With Patricia C. McKissack. Enslow, 1992.

Langston Hughes: Great American Poet. With Patricia C. McKissack. Enslow, 1992.

Madam C.J. Walker: Self-Made Millionaire. With Patricia C. McKissack. Enslow, 1992

Paul Robeson: A Voice to Remember. With Patricia C. McKissack. Enslow, 1992.

Satchel Paige: The Best Arm in Baseball. With Patricia C. McKissack. Enslow, 1992.

Sojourner Truth: Ain't I a Woman? With Patricia C. McKissack. Scholastic, 1992.

Zora Neale Hurston: Writer and Storyteller. With Patricia C. McKissack. Enslow, 1992.

Tennessee Trailblazers. With Patricia C. McKissack. March Media, 1993.

African-American Inventors. With Patricia C. McKissack. Millbrook, 1994.

Christmas in the Big House, Christmas in the Quarters. With Patricia C. McKissack. Scholastic, 1994.

The Royal Kingdoms of Ghana, Mali and Songhay: Life in Medieval Africa. With Patricia C. McKissack. Holt, 1994.

Red-Tail Angels: The Story of the Tuskegee Airmen of World War II. With Patricia C. McKissack. Walker, 1995.

Rebels Against Slavery: American Slave Revolts. With Patricia C. McKissack. Scholastic, 1996.

Ma Dear's Apron. Illustrated by Floyd Cooper. Knopf, 1997.

Can You Imagine? Photographs by Miles Pinkney. Owen, 1997.

Run Away Home. Scholastic, 1998.

See also McKissack, Patricia C(arwell)

McKissack, Patricia C(arwell)

(1944-)

AUTHOR

"Good books—fiction and nonfiction—written for, by, and about African Americans are needed if we are to help young readers develop a healthy self-image and an open attitude about other cultures different from their own. That is my goal. To reach it, however, I begin by writing an appealing story. When youngsters have an enjoyable reading experience, they are most likely to choose a similar book . . . and another. By providing interesting and lively written materials for children, the above goal can be achieved."

The author was born in Nashville, Tennessee. McKissack attended Tennessee Agricultural and Industrial State University, now Tennessee State University, where she obtained her bachelor of arts degree in 1964. She earned a master of arts in 1975 from Webster University in St. Louis, Missouri, and married writer Fredrick McKissack in 1964. From 1968 to 1975, she worked as a junior high school teacher in Kirkwood, Missouri, and in 1975 she was a part-time instructor in English at Forest Park College in St. Louis.

McKissack is co-owner of All-Writing Services with her husband and has been an instructor of children's literature at the University of Missouri. She was a writer for a preschool series, *L Is for Wishing*, broadcast by KWMU radio from 1975 to 1977. She has written radio and television scripts and been a contributor to the magazines *Friend*, *Happy Times*, and *Evangelizing Today's Child*.

McKissack won the Helen Keating Ott Award from the National Church and Synagogue Librarians Association in 1980 for her editorial work at Concordia Publishing House and a Coretta Scott King Award in 1993 for her book *The Dark-Thirty: Southern Tales of the Supernatural*. In addition, in 1989 Jerry Pinkney won a Caldecott Honor Book

Award and the Coretta Scott King Award for his illustration of McKissack's book *Mirandy and Brother Wind.*

McKissack has also shared honors with her husband on many books, including *Abram, Abram, Where Are We Going?*, which won the C.S. Lewis Silver Medal Award from the Christian Educators Association in 1985; *A Long Hard Journey: The Story of the Pullman Porter,* which won the Jane Addams Children's Book Award and the Coretta Scott King Award in 1990; *Sojourner Truth: Ain't I a Woman?*, which won a Boston Globe-Horn Book Award in 1993 and was a Coretta Scott King Honor Book that same year; and *Christmas in the Big House, Christmas in the Quarters,* which won the Coretta Scott King Award in 1995.

McKissack's memberships include Alpha Kappa Alpha sorority, the Tennessee State Alumni Association, the Authors Guild, and the Society for Children's Book Writers and Illustrators.

In 1991, McKissack wrote her first movie script with award-winning author Marvis Jukes. The movie, produced by Disney Educational Productions, titled *Who Owns the Sun,* won several major film awards and a starred review from Kirkus. In 1994 she and her husband received honorary doctorate degrees from the University of Missouri.

McKissack lives in St. Louis, Missouri, with her husband, Fredrick McKissack. They have three adult sons. Their oldest son Fredrick, Jr., co-author with her of *Black Diamond: The Story of the Negro Baseball League,* is an editor for *The Progressive Magazine* in Madison, Wisconsin. Their son Robert wrote a text for the educational division of Houghton Mifflin Publishers, and John Patrick is an engineer in Memphis, Tennessee.

BIBLIOGRAPHY

Who Is Who? Illustrated by Elizabeth M. Allen. Children's Press, 1983.

Abram, Abram, Where Are We Going? With Fredrick McKissack. David Cook, 1984.

It's the Truth, Christopher. With Fredrick McKissack. Augsburg, 1984.

Lights Out, Christopher. With Fredrick McKissack. Illustrated by Bartholomew. Augsburg, 1984.

Michael Jackson: Superstar. With Fredrick McKissack. Children's Press, 1984.

Paul Laurence Dunbar: A Poet to Remember. With Fredrick McKissack. Children's Press, 1984.

Flossie and the Fox. Illustrated by Rachel Isadora. Dial, 1986.

When Do You Talk to God? Prayers for Small Children. Illustrated by Gary Gumble. Augsburg, 1986.

The Civil Rights Movement in America from 1865 to the Present. With Fredrick McKissack. Children's Press, 1987, 1991 (Second Edition).

Frederick Douglass: The Black Lion. With Fredrick McKissack. Children's Press, 1987.

Constance Stumbles. Illustrated by Tom Dunnington. With Fredrick McKissack. Children's Press, 1988.

Messy Bessey. With Fredrick McKissack. Illustrated by Richard Hackney. A Big Book. Children's Press, 1988.

Mirandy and Brother Wind. Illustrated by Jerry Pinkney. Knopf, 1988.

Monkey–Monkey's Trick: Based on an African Folk Tale. Illustrated by Paul Meisel. Random House, 1988.

God Made Something Wonderful. With Fredrick McKissack. Illustrated by Ching. Augsburg, 1989.

Jesse Jackson: A Biography. Scholastic, 1989.

Nettie Jo's Friend. Illustrated by Scott Cook. Knopf, 1989.

James Weldon Johnson: Lift Every Voice and Sing. Children's Press, 1990.

A Long Hard Journey: The Story of the Pullman Porter. With Fredrick McKissack. Walker, 1990.

Taking a Stand Against Racism and Racial Discrimination. With Fredrick McKissack. Watts, 1990.

W.E.B. Du Bois. With Fredrick McKissack. Watts, 1990.

Who Is Coming? Illustrated by Clovis Martin. Children's Press, 1990.

Carter G. Woodson. Illustrated by Ned Ostendorf. With Fredrick McKissack. Enslow, 1991.

Frederick Douglass: Leader Against Slavery. Illustrated by Ned Ostendorf. With Fredrick McKissack. Enslow, 1991.

George Washington Carver: The Peanut Scientist. Illustrated by Ned Ostenforf. With Fredrick McKissack. Enslow, 1991.

Ida B. Wells-Barnett: A Voice Against Violence. Illustrated by Ned Ostendorf. With Fredrick McKissack. Enslow, 1991.

Louis Armstrong: Jazz Musician. Illustrated by Ned Ostendorf. With Fredrick McKissack. Enslow, 1991.

Marian Anderson: A Great Singer. Illustrated by Ned Ostendorf. With Fredrick McKissack. Enslow, 1991.

Martin Luther King, Jr.: Man of Peace. Illustrated by Ned Ostendorf. With Fredrick McKissack. Enslow, 1991.

Mary Church Terrell: Leader for Equality. Illustrated by Ned Ostendorf. With Fredrick McKissack. Enslow, 1991.

Ralph J. Bunche: Peacemaker. Illustrated by Ned Ostendorf. With Fredrick McKissack. Enslow, 1991.

Booker T. Washington: Leader and Educator. With Fredrick McKissack. Enslow, 1992.

The Dark-Thirty: Southern Tales of the Supernatural. Illustrated by Brian Pinkney. Knopf, 1992.

Jesse Owens: Olympic Star. With Fredrick McKissack. Enslow, 1992.

Langston Hughes: Great American Poet. With Fredrick McKissack. Enslow, 1992.

Madam C.J. Walker: Self-Made Millionaire. With Fredrick McKissack. Enslow, 1992.

A Million Fish . . . More or Less. Illustrated by Dena Schutzer. Knopf, 1992.

Paul Robeson: A Voice To Remember. With Fredrick McKissack. Enslow, 1992.

Satchel Paige: The Best Arm in Baseball. With Fredrick McKissack. Enslow, 1992.

Sojourner Truth: Ain't I a Woman? With Fredrick McKissack. Scholastic, 1992.

Zora Neale Hurston: Writer and Storyteller. With Fredrick McKissack. Enslow, 1992.

Tennessee Trailblazers. With Fredrick McKissack. March Media, 1993.

African-American Inventors. With Fredrick McKissack. Millbrook, 1994.

Black Diamond: The Story of the Negro Baseball League. With Fredrick McKissack, Jr. Scholastic, 1994.

Christmas in the Big House, Christmas in the Quarters. Illustrated by John Thompson. With Fredrick McKissack. Scholastic, 1994.

The Royal Kingdoms of Ghana, Mali and Songhay: Life in Medieval Africa. With Fredrick McKissack. Holt, 1994.

Red-Tail Angels: The Story of the Tuskegee Airmen of World War II. With Fredrick McKissack. Walker, 1995.

Rebels Against Slavery: American Slave Revolts. With Fredrick McKissack. Scholastic, 1996.

Ma Dear's Aprons. Illustrated by Floyd Cooper. Knopf, 1997.

See also Cooper, Floyd (Donald); McKissack, Fredrick (Lemuel); Pinkney, Brian; Pinkney, Jerry

McPherson, James (Alan)

(1943-)

AUTHOR

McPherson was born in Savannah, Georgia. He attended Morris Brown College, studying English and history, and earned a bachelor of arts degree in 1965. He earned a law degree from the Harvard University Law School, received a master of fine arts degree in 1971 from the University of Iowa, and was a visiting scholar at the Yale University Law School, in 1978.

He taught at the University of Iowa from 1968 to 1969; lectured at the University of California, Santa Cruz, for the following two years; and was an assistant professor at Morgan State University from 1975 to 1976 and an associate professor at the University of Virginia from 1976 to 1981. Since then, he has been a professor of English at the University of Iowa. He has lectured internationally at Meiji University in Japan, Tsuda College at Chiba University, lectures in Osaka Kyoto, Japan and at the American Centers in Tokyo and Fukuoka.

His essays, stories, and reviews have appeared in the *Harvard Advocate, Atlantic, Ploughshares, Nimrod*, the *University of Toledo Law Review*, the *New York Times, Playboy, Harvard* magazine, *Esquire, Reader's Digest*, and *Newsday*, among others. Additional essays and stories have been published in a variety of anthologies, including *The Best American Short Stories, O'Henry Prize Stories, The Best American Essays*, and *Southern* magazine.

McPherson has received many awards and honors, among them the Pulitzer Prize for Fiction in 1978 and an honorary doctor of letters degree from Morris Brown College, the MacArthur Prize Fellows Award in 1981, and the Award for Excellence in Teaching from the University of Iowa in 1990. He is listed in *Who's Who in America; Who's Who in The Midwest; Who's Who in Education;* and *Who's Who in The World*.

He was elected to the American Academy of Arts and Sciences in 1995 and is also professionally associated with the American Civil Liberties Union, the Writers Guild, and the National Association for the Advancement of Colored People (NAACP).

In 1995 he was elected to the American Academy of Arts and Sciences.

McPherson has one daughter. He lives in Iowa City, Iowa.

BIBLIOGRAPHY

Hue and Cry. Little, Brown, 1968.

Railroad: Trains and Train People in American Culture. Edited by James Alan McPherson and Miller Williams. Random House, 1976.

Elbow Room. Little, Brown, 1977.

Medearis, Angela Shelf

(1956–)

AUTHOR

"I love introducing children all over the world to all the different aspects of African-American history, folklore and culture. I love picture books because they are a challenge to convey complex ideas in a simple form for children. I really enjoy factually and vividly presenting history in a thirty-two or forty-eight-page book. It's wonderful to be able to hold a child's attention and teach them something important.

Picture books are a child's first step into a lifetime of reading. That's why I feel that my job is important. I want to write about history in such an interesting and exciting way that the memory of reading my book and the information it contained about a particular historical event will linger with them for a lifetime. I love children and I like to write books especially for them. I really love writing books. I enjoy that wonderful feeling you get when you have a great idea and can't wait to get started to work on it. I enjoy thinking about all of the children that have read my work. I have books in Africa and England and other places. It's fun to think that someone, somewhere, is reading one of my books or checking them out of the library.

Most people think I'm funny. I like to make people laugh. I really, really like to make kids laugh. It's one of the happiest sounds in the world."

Medearis was born in Hampton, Virginia, and attended Southwest Texas University for one year. *Picking Peas for a Penny*, written in rhyme, and the sequel, *Dancing with the Indians*, are based on family stories told to her by her mother. *Dancing with the Indians* was a Reading Rainbow selection and winner of the Violet Crown Literary Award and the Notable Social Studies Book Award. *The Zebra-Riding Cowboy* was an ABA Pick of the List.

Medearis has published more than twenty books, including *The*

Singing Man, which was a Coretta Scott King Honor Book Award winner for illustration in 1995, and has received numerous awards for her work. She is the founder of Book Boosters, a multicultural, multiethnic reading motivational/tutorial program designed for elementary students in the Austin, Texas, Independent School District, and was curator of two African American history exhibits for the George Washington Carver Museum in Austin.

She is a member of the Society of Children's Book Writers and Illustrators, the Texas Library Association, and the Texas Institute of Letters.

She and her husband, Michael, daughter Deanna, and granddaughter Anysa live in Austin, Texas.

BIBLIOGRAPHY

Picking Peas for a Penny. State House, 1990.

Dancing with the Indians. Holiday House, 1991.

The Zebra-Riding Cowboy. Illustrated by Maria Cristina Brusca. Holt, 1992.

Come This Far to Freedom: A History of African Americans. Illustrated by Terea D. Shaffer. Atheneum, 1993.

Annie's Gifts. Illustrated by Anna Rich. Just Us Books, 1994.

Dare to Dream: The Story of Coretta Scott King. Illustrated by Anna Rich. Lodestar, 1994.

Little Louis and the Jazz Band: The Story of Louis Armstrong. Lodestar, 1994.

Our People. Illustrated by Michael Bryant. Atheneum, 1994.

The Seven Days of Kwanzaa. Scholastic, 1994.

The Singing Man. Illustrated by Terea Shaffer. Holiday House, 1994.

The Adventures of Sugar and Junior. Illustrated by Nancy Poydar. Holiday House, 1995.

Bye, Bye Babies. Candlewick, 1995.

Eat Babies Eat. Illustrated by Patrice Aggs. Candlewick, 1995.

The Freedom Riddle. Illustrated by John Ward. Lodestar, 1995.

The 100th Day. Scholastic, 1995.

Poppa's New Pants. Illustrated by John Ward. Holiday House, 1995.

Sharing Danny's Dad. Illustrated by Jan Spivey Gilchrist. HarperCollins, 1995.

Skin Deep and Other Teenage Reflections. Illustrated by Michael Bryant. Macmillan, 1995.

Too Much Talk. Illustrated by Stefano Vitale. Candlewick, 1995.

Treemonisha. Illustrated by Michael Bryant. Holt, 1995.

We Play on a Rainy Day. Scholastic, 1995.

The Ghost of Sifty-Sifty Sam. Scholastic, 1996.

Here Comes the Snow. Illustrated by Maxie Chambliss. Scholastic, 1996.

Nannie. Atheneum, 1996.

Shari and the Musical Monster. Atheneum, 1996.
We Eat Dinner in the Bathtub. Scholastic, 1996.
Dance. With Michael R. Medearis. Holt, 1997.
Music. With Michael R. Medearis. Holt, 1997.
Rum-A-Tum Tum. Illustrated by James Ransome. Holiday House, 1997.
Princess of the Press: The Story of Ida B. Wells-Barnett. Lodestar, 1997.
Poppa's Itchy Christmas. Illustrated by John Ward. Holiday House, 1998.

See also Bryant, Michael; Gilchrist, Jan Spivey; Ransome, James (Earl); Ward, John (Clarence)

Mendez, Phil

(1947–)

AUTHOR, ILLUSTRATOR

Mendez was born in Bridgeport, Connecticut. In the animation business, he is known as an artist. He has created cartoons for the Walt Disney Studios, Marvel Productions, Disney's subsidiary, WED, Hanna-Barbera Productions, Chuck Jones, and Pantomime Pictures, among others.

Phil Mendez Productions is his own studio, where he and his wife, Karen, write and conceive ideas for children's books. Mendez has been an art director for commercial television accounts such as Cocoa Puffs and Cheerios; directed accounts for the 1982 World Olympics; created two animated shows for NBC Saturday morning cartoons, *Kissyfur* and *Foofur;* and designed toys, greeting cards, and some fine-arts lithographs. His hobby is painting in watercolors and oils.

He and his wife live in Sierra Madre, California, with their daughter.

BIBLIOGRAPHY

The Puggle Tales. By Glenn Duncan. Price Stern, 1984.
Kissyfur and His Dad. By Dina Anastasio. Scholastic, 1986.
Kissyfur and the Big Contest. By Suzanne Lord. Scholastic, 1986.
Kissyfur and the Birthday Hugs. By Larry Weinberg. Scholastic, 1986.
Kissyfur of Paddlecab County. By Suzanne Lord. Scholastic, 1986.
The Kissyfur Treasury. By Dina Anastasia. Scholastic, 1986.
Kissyfur and Fun at the Circus. By Nancy E. Kurlik. Scholastic, 1988.
The Black Snowman. Illustrated by Carole Byard. Scholastic, 1989.

See also Byard, Carole

Meriwether, Louise

(1923–)

AUTHOR

Meriwether was born in Havestraw, New York, received her bachelor's degree from New York University and, in 1965, received her master's degree from the University of California, Los Angeles. She has worked as a story analyst at Universal Studios in California, a legal secretary, and a freelance writer, publishing articles and short stories in magazines. Her memberships included the Watts Writers Workshop, the Authors Guild, and the Harlem Writers Guild. She is a freelance writer in New York City where she lives.

BIBLIOGRAPHY

Daddy Was a Number Runner. Pyramid, 1971.
The Freedom Ship of Robert Small. Prentice-Hall, 1971.
Don't Ride the Bus on Monday: The Rosa Parks Story. Prentice-Hall, 1973.

Miles, Calvin

(1942–)

AUTHOR

"One of the things we need to have in order to start to fill the void in the realm of literature for Black children is more material written by Black people for Black people, stories that tell about the Black life and experience not only in America but throughout the world."

Miles, born in Gaston, North Carolina, is a teacher in the field of adult and family literacy, working with adults and parents who are coming back to school in order to learn to read and write. He helps adults and parents validate their stories and teaches them how to share them with their children.

His book, *Calvin's Christmas Wish,* was written when he was thirty-nine years old and was learning to read and write as a student at Literacy Volunteers of New York City. He studied there with a group of adults like himself. Memories of his childhood came back to him when the group members decided to write about Christmas.

The editors at Viking Children's Books saw *When Dreams Came True,* which was originally published in paperback by Literacy Volunteers of America and illustrated with photographs, and it became a children's book with the title of *Calvin's Christmas Wish.*

Miles lives in Brooklyn, New York.

BIBLIOGRAPHY

Calvin's Christmas Wish. Illustrated by Dolores Johnson. Viking, 1993.

See also Johnson, Dolores

Millender, Dharathula H(ood)

(1920–)

AUTHOR

Millender was born in Terre Haute, Indiana. She graduated from Indiana State University and completed additional study at Indiana and Purdue Universities and at the Catholic University of America.

She was a teacher and a librarian in South Carolina and Maryland, a reference assistant at the Library of Congress in Washington, D.C., a librarian at a military reservation, and a junior high school librarian in Baltimore, Maryland, and Gary, Indiana. During 1962–1964 and 1966–1967, she chaired Negro History Week Observance in Gary. She wrote a daily newspaper column, "Yesterday in Gary," edited the *Gary Crusader,* and contributed to *Education and Changing Education.*

She has been a member of the American Federation of Teachers, the Negro Cultural Achievement Committee, the Indiana School Library Association, the Indiana State Teachers Association, Alpha Kappa Alpha, and the National Association for the Advancement of Colored People (NAACP).

BIBLIOGRAPHY

Louis Armstrong: Young Music Maker. Bobbs-Merrill, 1972.
Crispus Attucks: Black Leader of Colonial Patriots. Illustrated by Gray Morrow. Simon & Schuster, 1986.
Martin Luther King, Jr.: Young Man with a Dream. Illustrated by Al Fiorentino. Simon & Schuster, 1986.

Miller, Don

(1923–)

The artist was born in Jamaica and grew up in Montclair, New Jersey. He obtained a certificate in art from Cooper Union in 1949 and also attended the New School for Social Research, both in New York City. He has illustrated dozens of books, magazine articles, and filmstrips. His art has been exhibited widely, including at New York's Museum of Natural History in *The Children of Africa* show. His memberships include the National Conference of Artists and the Society of Illustrators.

BIBLIOGRAPHY

The Black BC's. By Lucille Clifton. Dutton, 1970.
Langston Hughes: American Poet. By Alice Walker. Crowell, 1974.
A Bicycle from Bridgetown. By Dawn C. Thomas. McGraw-Hill, 1975.
The Creoles of Color. By James Haskins. Crowell, 1975.
Jocko: A Legend of the American Revolution. By Earl Koger. Prentice-Hall, 1976.

See also Clifton, (Thelma) Lucille (Sayles); Haskins, James; Thomas, Dawn C.; Walker, Alice

Miller, Robert H(enry)

(1944-)

AUTHOR

"When I first endeavored to write about African American cowboys, I must admit, secretly as a youngster, I frequently envisioned myself as a western hero. The fantasy of rescuing damsels in distress and saving a town from evil men has always intrigued me. In some small way I'm doing that now as I write about the heroics of African American pioneers and mountain men but especially the 'cowboys.'

When I visit classrooms across the country, it's apparent my books are rescuing young African American boys and girls from the ignorance of not knowing that the American frontier was settled by people who looked like them. To see ourselves as heroes in the shaping of America is vital, in my view."

Miller was born in San Antonio, Texas. He holds a bachelor of science degree in urban studies and a master's degree in communications. He has worked as a U.S. marshal in Washington, D.C., and as an international account executive for a major hotel chain.

The Reflections of a Black Cowboy series was the American Booksellers Association's Pick of the List in 1991. The series was also reviewed in *School Library Journal* in 1991 and the *Multicultural Review* in 1994.

Miller is single and lives in Camden, New Jersey.

BIBLIOGRAPHY

Cowboys. Illustrated by Richard Leonard. Reflections of a Black Cowboy Series. Silver Burdett, 1992.

Buffalo Soldiers: The Story of Emanuel Stance. Illustrated by Michael Bryant. Reflections of a Black Cowboy Series. Silver Burdett, 1994.

Mountain Men. Illustrated by Richard Leonard. Reflections of a Black Cowboy Series. Silver Burdett, 1993.

Pioneers. Illustrated by Richard Leonard. Reflections of a Black Cowboy Series. Silver Burdett, 1993.

The Story of Nat Love. Illustrated by Michael Bryant. Stories from the Forgotten West Series. Silver Burdett, 1994.

John Baptist DuSable: Founder of Chicago. Illustrated by Richard Leonard. Stories from the Forgotten West Series. Silver Burdett, 1995.

The Story of Stagecoach Mary Fields. Illustrated by Richard Leonard. Stories from the Forgotten West Series. Silver Burdett, 1995.

A Pony for Jeremiah. Illustrated by Mneka Bennett. Silver Burdett, 1997.

See also Bryant, Michael; Hanna, Cheryl (Irene)

Mitchell, Margaree King

(1953–)

AUTHOR

"I knew it was important that children view themselves positively. I thought if I could somehow write a book that would inspire children to achieve their dreams, then maybe children would be motivated to stay in school and look to the future for a better life for themselves. Shortly after Uncle Jed's Barbershop *was published, I was invited to read the book to seven- and eight-year-olds during story hour at a public library. As I was leaving, a little girl was waiting for me by the door. She said to me, 'I liked your story about Uncle Jed. I want to be a doctor when I grow up. But my grandmama keeps telling me that I will never be one. Now I know I can be a doctor.' I knew then that I had achieved my goal in writing* Uncle Jed's Barbershop.*"*

Mitchell was born and reared in Holly Springs, Mississippi, growing up on her grandfather's farm. She received a bachelor's degree in 1975 from Brandeis University.

Uncle Jed's Barbershop was the winner of the 1995 Living the Dream Award, and the 1994 Coretta Scott King Honor Book Award for illustration by James Ransome. It was an American Library Association Notable Children's Book and an American Booksellers Association Pick of the List, and it was selected as one of Thirty-Three Favorite Reads of 1994 by librarians. The book was also featured as a *Reading Rainbow* book on the Public Broadcasting System (PBS) in 1995 and was mentioned in the 1995 movie *Losing Isaiah*.

A member of the Society of Children's Book Writers and Illustrators, Mitchell is a full-time writer.

She lives in Houston, Texas.

BIBLIOGRAPHY

Uncle Jed's Barbershop. Illustrated by James Ransome. Simon & Schuster, 1993.
Granddaddy's Gift. Illustrated by Larry Johnson. BridgeWater, 1997.

See also Ransome, James (Earl)

Mollel, Tololwa M(arti)

$(1952-)$

AUTHOR

"Writing for children for me is both challenging and rewarding. You have to find a way of writing about a big idea in simple terms. You have to be innovative in order to catch a child's attention. At the same time, the story has to appeal to you the writer, first. Simple and clear doesn't mean being frivolous. Writing for children is a good way to learn the fundamentals of fiction and story making. You have to put everything that you put in adult fiction and then some. When I first started writing, I used to write everything. I wrote short stories for adults, I wrote a novella. However, it wasn't until my first son was born that I decided to write for children. I remember reading to my son some stories that I enjoyed as a kid (like 'The Little Red Hen,' 'The Lion and the Rat,' 'The Emperor's New Clothes,' etc.) and the writer in me appreciating the brilliant simplicity of the tales. I remember saying to myself that I would like to be able to write with such conciseness and evocative clarity, and it seems to me that writing for children offers an opportunity for doing that."

Mollel is a storyteller born in Arusha, Tanzania, in East Africa, and author of several children's books who credits his upbringing, his grandfather, and growing up in an oral culture as major influences. In 1991, *The Orphan Boy* won a Parents Choice Storybook Award, was a Notable Children's Book in the Language Arts, a Notable Children's Trade Book in the Field of Social Studies, and the American Bookseller Pick of the List for that year. The book was also a 1992 American Library Association Notable Children's Book. He has done readings, storytelling, talks, and workshops in and outside of schools in Edmonton, Alberta, Canada, across Canada, and in the United States.

Mollel received his bachelor of arts degree from the University of Dar-es-Salaam in Tanzania and his master of arts from the University of Alberta, and he is working on his doctoral thesis on African drama. He was a university lecturer, an actor with Paukwa Theater, and codirector of a children's theatrical group in Tanzania from 1979 to 1986.

He is married with two sons, Lese and Emeka, and lives in Edmonton, Alberta, Canada, with his family.

BIBLIOGRAPHY

The Orphan Boy. Illustrated by Paul Morin. Oxford University Press, 1990. Houghton, 1991.

The Princess Who Lost Her Hair. Illustrated by Charles Reasoner. Troll, 1992.

A Promise to the Sun: An African Story. Illustrated by Beatriz Vidal. Joy Street, 1992.

Rhinos for Lunch and Elephants for Supper! Illustrated by Barbara Spurll. Clarion, 1992.

The King and the Tortoise. Illustrated by Kathy Blankley. Houghton, 1993.

The Flying Tortoise: An Igbo Tale. Illustrated by Barbara Spurll. Clarion, 1994.

Big Boy. Illustrated by E.B. Lewis. Clarion, 1995.

Ananse's Feast. Illustrated by Andrew Glass. Houghton Mifflin, 1997.

Kele's Secret. Illustrated by Catherine Stock. Lodestar, 1997.

Moore, Carman Leroy

(1936–)

AUTHOR

The composer was born in Lorain, Ohio, and received his bachelor's degree from Ohio State University and his master's degree from the Juilliard School of Music. He was an assistant professor of music at Yale University and Manhattanville College, a record reviewer and columnist for the Sunday *New York Times,* a music critic for the *Village Voice* and the *Saturday Review,* and a columnist for *Essence* and *Vogue* magazines.

Moore was founder and secretary-treasurer of the Society of Black Composers. The San Francisco Symphony Orchestra commissioned his composition *Gospel Fuse,* and the New York Philharmonic Orchestra commissioned *Wildfires and Field Songs.*

BIBLIOGRAPHY

Somebody's Angel Child: The Story of Bessie Smith. Crowell, 1969.

Moore, Emily R.

(1948–)

AUTHOR

Moore was born in New York City and educated in city schools. At City College of New York, she majored in Russian and earned her bachelor's degree, graduating cum laude. She earned her master's degree from Columbia University Teachers College. Her then unpublished manuscript, "Letters to a Friend on a Brown Paper Bag," was declared a winner of the Council on Interracial Books for Children's seventh annual contest.

She also received a master's degree in English from C.W. Post in 1987 and is studying for her doctorate at the City University of New York Graduate Center. Moore is an English teacher in a Queens Village high school in New York.

Her memberships include the Society of Children's Book Writers and Illustrators, the Modern Language Association, the National Council of Teachers of English, and the Authors Guild.

BIBLIOGRAPHY

Something to Count On. Dutton, 1980.
Just My Luck. Dutton, 1983.
Whose Side Are You On? Farrar, 1988. Sunburst, 1990.

Mordecai, Pamela Claire

(1 9 4 2 –)

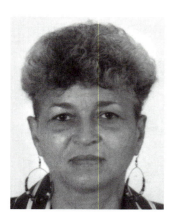

AUTHOR, ILLUSTRATOR

Mordecai was born in Kingston, Jamaica, the second of five children. She went to Convent of Mercy Alpha from 1946 to 1959, then to Newton College, a liberal-arts school in Massachusetts, where she received her bachelor of arts degree in English in 1963. She returned to Jamaica in 1963 to teach, first in high school, then at Mico, Jamaica's largest teachers college. At Mico, she was motivated to write poems for children when she discovered that the trainee teachers could find few Caribbean poems to use in their teaching-practice lessons.

In 1974, she was hired by the University of the West Indies, where she spent the next fourteen years as publications officer in the faculty of education. She now operates a Canadian branch of Sandberry Press with her husband, Martin Mordecai.

In addition to authoring and coauthoring many textbooks, Mordecai has edited and coedited five anthologies on writings by Caribbean women. She is completing a doctoral thesis on Caribbean poetry. Mordecai received the Institute of Jamaica's Tercentenary Medal in 1980 and, in 1993, the inaugural Vic Reid Award for Children's Literature for *Ezra's Goldfish and Other Storypoems*.

Mordecai has three children and lives in Toronto, Ontario, Canada.

BIBLIOGRAPHY

Storypoems: A First Collection. Ginn, 1987.
Don't Ever Wake a Snake. Sandberry, 1991.
Ezra's Goldfish and Other Storypoems. National Book Development Council, 1995.

Morninghouse, Sundaira
Carletta Wilson

(1951–)

AUTHOR

"I have had the unique opportunity to share the treasures of the literary world in a personal and professional manner. In my work as a librarian, I have been amazed at how far we've come in the development of literature for African American children and how far we've yet to go in terms of the range of themes, subjects, and artistic exploration of the African American experience, in particular, and the African diaspora as a whole."

Sundaira Morninghouse is the pseudonym used by Carletta Wilson. She has published fiction, poetry, and essays under her given name since 1984 and created the name Sundaira Morninghouse to be used for works intended for children. *Habari Gani? What's the News?* received the Midwest Book Achievement Award for Best Children's Book in 1993.

Wilson was born in Philadelphia, Pennsylvania, and received her bachelor's degree in fine arts from Cheyney University of Pennsylvania and her master's degree in library science from the University of Washington. She has worked as a museum educator, an art and creative-writing teacher, and a children's and adult services librarian.

She decided to write books for children when she became inspired by a children's-literature course while working on her master's degree in library science. Recognizing how few poetry titles were available for preschool African American children, she began writing what was to become her first children's book, *Nightfeathers*.

She is a member of the Society of Children's Book Writers and Illustrators and lives in Seattle, Washington, where she works as a librarian in the Fine and Performing Arts Department of the Seattle Public Library.

BIBLIOGRAPHY

Nightfeathers. Illustrated by Jody Kim. Open Hand, 1989.

Habari Gani? What's the News? Illustrated by Jody Kim. Open Hand, 1992.

Moses, Shelia P(atricia)

AUTHOR

Born in Rich Square, North Carolina, the ninth of ten children, Moses graduated from Shaw University and moved to Atlanta, Georgia, to attend law school, working at a local law firm as a paralegal.

After working at Coca Cola Enterprises in community relations and giving years of service as a volunteer to the Urban League and other nonprofit organizations, when she was twenty-three years old she began her own business, M-Promotions, a sports and entertainment agency that markets notable celebrities for endorsements, special appearances, lectures, and speaking engagements.

Moses was featured in *Women Looking Ahead* magazine in 1994 and also named 1994 Woman to Watch by *Dollars and Sense* magazine.

She lives in Pacific Palisades, California.

BIBLIOGRAPHY

One More River to Cross. Shelia Moses, 1994.

Musgrove, Margaret (Wynkoop)

(1943–)

AUTHOR

"Today there are more books with African American themes than ever before, but the actual percentage of these books is still low. Because Black writers' perspectives have not always been well represented, there aren't enough African American children's books that interpret and depict our history from our perspective in our own words. We need more books to help African American children understand their reality in America today."

Musgrove was born in Plainville, Connecticut, where she attended the local schools. She is a graduate of the University of Connecticut and Central Connecticut State University, from which she received her master's degree. She also has a doctorate in education from the University of Massachusetts.

The author has lived and taught in Accra, Ghana, where she studied at the University of Ghana and taught at Lincoln Community School, an American elementary school. She taught English at Hartford Public High School in Hartford, Connecticut, and at three community colleges: South Central Community College in New Haven, Connecticut; Berkshire Community College in Pittsfield, Massachusetts; and the New Community College of Baltimore in Baltimore, Maryland. She is a professor of writing at Loyola College in Maryland, where she teaches a course in writing children's literature.

She is a member of the Society of Children's Book Writers and Illustrators and the International Women's Writing Guild and is a teacher-consultant with the Maryland Writing Project.

Her book, *Ashanti to Zulu: African Traditions,* was the 1977 Caldecott Medal winner.

Musgrove is the mother of two adult children and lives in Baltimore, Maryland.

BIBLIOGRAPHY

Ashanti to Zulu: African Traditions. Illustrated by Leo and Diane Dillon. Dial, 1976.

See also Dillon, Leo

Myers, Walter Dean

(1937–)

Myers was born in Martinsburg, West Virginia. He speaks of his adoptive parents fondly; the Dean family adopted him informally after his mother's death. He attended City College in New York City and received his bachelor's degree in communications from Empire State College in 1984. In 1981, he received a fellowship from the New Jersey State Council of the Arts; in 1982, a grant from the National Endowment of the Arts.

Myers is a member of the Harlem Writers Guild, the New Renaissance Writers Guild, and P.E.N. International. He has written articles for magazines and was an editor for Bobbs-Merrill publishing house.

Although most of his books are about the Black experience or have urban settings, a few of his books have been based on travels to the East and Africa. His book *Motown and Didi: A Love Story* won the Coretta Scott King Award for fiction in 1985, as did *The Young Landlords* in 1980, *Fallen Angels* in 1989, and *Now Is Your Time! The African American Struggle for Freedom* in 1992. *Malcolm X: By Any Means Necessary* was a Coretta Scott King Honor Book in 1994, as was *Somewhere in Darkness* in 1993 and *Fast Sam, Cool Clyde, and Stuff* in 1976. *Scorpions* was a Newbery Honor Book in 1989.

His *Where Does the Day Go?*, another prize-winning book, was submitted to Parents Magazine Press in the late 1960s by the Council on Interracial Books for Children. He has published a series of books under the title of *Eighteen Pine Street*. Myers was named the 1997 recipient of the Coretta Scott King Author Award Winner for *Slam!* His book, *Harlem*, illustrated by Christopher Myers, won the 1998 Coretta Scott King Honor Book Illustrator Award and a 1998 Caldecott Honor Book Award.

Myers lives in Jersey City, New Jersey, and has three children, Karen, Michael, and Christopher.

BIBLIOGRAPHY

Where Does the Day Go? Illustrated by Leo Carty. Parents, 1969.

Fly Jimmy Fly! Illustrated by Moneta Barnett. Putnam, 1974.

Fast Sam, Cool Clyde, and Stuff. Viking, 1975.

It Ain't All for Nothin'. Viking, 1978.

The Young Landlords. Viking, 1979.

The Black Pearl and the Ghost. Illustrated by Robert Quackenbush. Viking, 1980.

The Golden Serpent. Illustrated by Alice and Martin Provensen. Viking, 1980.

Hoops. Delacorte, 1981.

The Legend of Tarik. Viking, 1981.

Won't Know Till I Get There. Viking, 1982.

Tales of a Dead King. Morrow, 1983.

Motown and Didi: A Love Story. Viking, 1984.

Mr. Monkey and the Gotcha Bird. Illustrated by Leslie Morrill. Delacorte, 1984.

Crystal. Viking, 1987.

Fallen Angels. Scholastic, 1988.

Me, Mop, and the Moondance Kid. Illustrated by Rodney Pate. Delacorte, 1988.

Scorpions. Harper, 1988.

The Mouse Rap. Harper, 1989.

Now Is Your Time! The African-American Struggle for Freedom. HarperCollins, 1991.

Me, Mop, and the Nagasaki Knights. Illustrated by Rodney Pate. Delacorte, 1992.

A Place Called Heartbreak: A Story of Vietnam. Illustrated by Frederick Porter. Steck-Vaughn, 1992.

The Righteous Revenge of Artemus Bonner. HarperCollins, 1992.

Somewhere in the Darkness. Scholastic, 1992.

Brown Angels: An Album of Picture and Verse. HarperCollins, 1993.

Dangerous Games. Bantam, 1993.

Fashion by Tasha. Bantam, 1993.

HeartBreak. Illustrated by Leonard Jenkins. Steck-Vaughn, 1993.

Malcolm X: By Any Means Necessary. Scholastic, 1993.

Young Martin's Promise. Illustrated by Higgins Bond. Steck-Vaughn, 1993.

Darnell Rock Reporting. Delacorte, 1994.

The Glory Field. Scholastic, 1994.

The Dragon Takes a Wife. Illustrated by Fiona French. Scholastic, 1995.

Glorious Angels: A Celebration of Children. HarperCollins, 1995.

One More River to Cross. Harcourt, 1995.

Shadow of the Red Moon. Illustrated by Christopher Myers. Scholastic, 1995.

The Story of the Three Kingdoms. Illustrated by Ashley Bryan. HarperCollins, 1995.

How Mr. Monkey Saw the Whole World. Illustrated by Synthia Saint James. Doubleday, 1996.

Smiffy Blue, Ace Crime Detective: The Case of the Missing Ruby and Other Stories. Illustrated by David J. Sims. Scholastic, 1996.

Slam! Scholastic, 1996.

Toussaint L'Ouverture: The Fight for Haiti's Freedom. Illustrated by Jacob Lawrence. Simon & Schuster, 1996.

Harlem. Illustrated by Christopher Myers. Scholastic, 1997.

See also Barnett, Moneta; Bond, Higgins (Barbara); Bryan, Ashley; Carty, Leo; Jenkins, Leonard; Lawrence, Jacob; Saint James, Synthia

Negatu, Tewodros

(1973–)

ILLUSTRATOR

Negatu was born in the capital city of Ethiopia, Addis Ababa. At ten years old, he won a school art competition and also won third prize in a national Red Cross art competition.

Upon leaving secondary school, he was among the top 15 percent of artists in the country to be chosen to study graphic art at the Addis Ababa School of Fine Art. Four years later, in 1991, Negatu graduated with an advanced diploma. While at college, he won first prize for his painting in a national competition held by the Italian Cultural Center.

After graduation, he worked for the Swedish International Development Agency as a cartoonist and illustrator for developmental magazines. For political reasons, after the arrest of his father, Negatu was forced to flee Ethiopia in January 1993, and he traveled alone to Kenya, where he has refugee status.

In 1994, he illustrated the cover of *Meskel: An Ethiopian Family Saga* (1926–1981), and his artwork appears in the anthology *Zamani*.

Negatu lives in Nairobi, Kenya.

BIBLIOGRAPHY

Zamani: The Mouse Who Would Be King. By Tom Nevin. Jacaranda Designs, 1995.

Nelson, Vaunda Micheaux

(1953–)

AUTHOR

"I grew up the fifth and youngest child and lived in a rural community south-east of Pittsburgh. I had a wonderful childhood. Our extended family spent Sundays together with my grandparents, went on picnics, and the cousins took turns spending the night at each other's houses during vacations. Things seemed simpler then. Being Black, we had some obstacles growing up, but my family gave me the strength to deal with whatever came my way. My parents brought books into my life on the day I was born; my mother found my name in a novel she was reading. Mommy read to us every day, and my father wrote and recited poetry. They taught me the power of language, and this helped me to become a writer. Through my work as a writer and a children's librarian, I hope to pro-vide children with some of what my parents gave me—the opportunity to grow through story. Writing helps me to understand because it forces me to really look at things closely and to think about more than one way of seeing. I write for children, but I write for myself first. It's my way of coping with the world. My best writing grows from personal experience. It's not simply a matter of telling about something that has happened to me, it's more about facing the questions I still have and allowing my characters to find answers. My books are fiction, but they carry the threads of my real experience."

Nelson holds a bachelor's degree in English from Point Park College in Pittsburgh, a master's degree from the Bread Loaf School of English at Middlebury College in Vermont, and a master's degree from the University of Pittsburgh School of Library and Information Science (now the School of Information Science), where she specialized in children's services. Prior to seeking her degree in library science, the author spent nearly three years working at the Pinocchio Bookstore for Children in Pittsburgh, immersed in children's literature.

While there, she wrote her first book, *Always Gramma*, which was selected by the Children's Book Council as a 1988 Notable Children's Trade Book in the field of social studies. Her first novel, *Mayfield Crossing*, was named one of the Best Children's Books of 1993 by the Child Study Children's Book Committee at Bank Street College in New York. *Mayfield Crossing* also won the twenty-seventh Georgia Children's Book Award in 1995.

Nelson has taught English and writing at the secondary and the university levels, including part-time positions at the University of Pittsburgh and at Chatham College. She was a member of the 1991 Newbery Award Committee and is a children's librarian at Rio Rancho Public Library in New Mexico.

She lives with her husband, Drew, author of *Wild Voices*, in Rio Rancho, New Mexico.

BIBLIOGRAPHY

Always Gramma. Putnam, 1988.
Mayfield Crossing. Illustrated by Leonard Jenkins. Putnam, 1993.
Possibles. Putnam, 1995.

See also Jenkins, Leonard

Ngoje, Samwel

(1970-)

ILLUSTRATOR

Ngoje was born in Omware village, Kamagambo location, in the Migori District of western Kenya on the shores of Lake Victoria. He is a member of the Luo tribe of Nilotic origin and excels in portraying the people and landscapes of his lakeside home.

Ngoje discovered his talent as an artist during his early school days. After leaving school, he was informally trained by the renowned Kenyan artist Joel Oswaggo, who came from the same village. He received no other formal art education, but, having worked successfully on a book illustration for Jacaranda Designs in Nairobi, Kenya, he was taken onto their full-time staff in recognition of his talent.

Ngoje is one of four illustrators in the anthology *Inkishu: Myths and Legends of the Maasai,* and chief illustrator for the book *Russelas: A Rhino in Search of His Horn.* He also illustrated *The Guilty Lion* story in the anthology *Zamani.* His storyboard illustrations for the Kenya Television Network have been shown on the children's program *Club Kiboko.* He was selected as a character designer and general illustrator for the *Adolescent Girl Child Initiative* produced by UNICEF (United Nations Children's Fund), and his work has been exhibited at the Signature Gallery and Museum Arts Festival in Nairobi.

Ngoje is married with one daughter and lives in Nairobi, Kenya.

BIBLIOGRAPHY

The Treasure of the Trees. By Valerie Cuthbert. Jacaranda Designs, 1992.

Hugo Hippo at the East African Coast. By Bridget King and Susan Salm. Jacarandu Designs, 1994.

Inkishu: The Forest of the Lost Child. By Kioi wa Mbugua. Jacaranda Designs, 1994.

Mingo the Flamingo. By Kariuki Gakuo. Jacaranda Designs, 1994.

Russelas: A Rhino in Search of His Horn. By Chryssee Perry Martin. Jacaranda Designs, 1995.

Zamani: The Guilty Lion. By Tom Nevin. Jacaranda Designs, 1995.

See also Mbugua, Kioi wa

Njambi, Kang'ara wa

(1 9 5 7 –)

ILLUSTRATOR

Njambi studied education and fine art at Kenyatta University in Nairobi, Kenya. For many years, he was a renowned lecturer in art and fashion, and he is widely published on the subject in Kenya. In 1994, Njambi's illustrations for *The Cave of Horns,* in the anthology *Beneath the Rainbow, Vol. II,* contributed toward the book being awarded first prize by the Kenyan Bureau for Children's Literature. In 1995, his artwork for the Zambian children's story *The Enchanted River Tree,* published in the anthology *Zamani,* was chosen as the front-cover illustration.

As one of Kenya's top artists, Njambi was commissioned to paint the cover artwork for a publication entitled *Protected Area Conservation Strategy* by a consortium of the World Wildlife Fund. Njambi's artwork has been exhibited widely, both in Kenya and internationally, and his paintings are held in both public centers and private collections worldwide.

He is the winner of several national art competitions and continues to work both as a lecturer and an artist.

He lives in Nairobi, Kenya, with his wife, who is also an artist, and family.

BIBLIOGRAPHY

Beneath the Rainbow: The Cave of Horns. By Kariuki Gakuo. Jacaranda Designs, 1994.
Inkishu: Nkai's Great Gift. By Kioi wa Mbugua. Jacaranda Designs, 1994.
Zamani: The Enchanted River Tree. By Tom Nevin. Jacaranda Designs, 1995.

Nolen, (Harold) Jerdine

(1953-)

AUTHOR

"I can't ever recall a time when I wasn't writing. From as early as I can remember, I have been writing something. I collected words. I simply like the sound of words and the feelings they evoke as they come out of me. I even like the sound the pencil makes as it travels across the page."

Nolen was born in Crystal Springs, Mississippi, and raised in Chicago, Illinois. The author received a bachelor's degree in special education from Northeastern Illinois University in 1981 and a master's in interdisciplinary arts education from Loyola University. She lectures on a variety of topics related to her books and other books for children, as well as on writing and the writing process.

Her professional experience includes being an elementary teacher in Evanston, Illinois, an artist in residence at the Chicago Office of Fine Arts, and a special-education teacher in the Baltimore County public schools in Maryland. She works part-time for the Baltimore County public schools as a specialist in the Language Arts Department.

In 1994, she was featured in *People* magazine and was the recipient of the Apple for the Teacher Award presented by Iota Phi Lambda sorority. Her book *Harvey Potter's Balloon Farm* was named an American Library Association Notable Book, an IRA/CTC Children's Choice and will be produced by Disney Studios as a live-action film.

Her professional affiliations include memberships in the National Education Association and the Chicago Reading Round Table, and she was a cofounder of Black Literary Umbrella.

Nolen lives in Ellicott City, Maryland.

BIBLIOGRAPHY

Harvey Potter's Balloon Farm. Illustrated by Mark Buchner. Lothrop, 1994.

Momma's Kitchen. Illustrated by Colin Bootman. Lothrop, 1998.

Raising Dragons. Illustrated by Elise Primavera. Harcourt, 1998.

O'Keragori, Abel

(1952–)

AUTHOR, ILLUSTRATOR

O'Keragori was born in the town of Kisii in the western province of Kenya. In primary school, his artistic talents emerged as he explored the world of art through painting, clay modeling, woodcarving and papier-mâché. He passed art at ordinary and advanced levels but could not find employment as an artist in Africa. Inspired by an excellent math teacher, he made the decision to study accounting.

Combining his career with painting was challenging, but his reputation grew as the quality of his work became widely appreciated. His first solo exhibition at the prestigious Signature Gallery in Nairobi, Kenya, met with enthusiastic reviews, and he has since participated in more than thirty group shows both in Kenya and internationally. In 1993, he gave up his career and became a professional artist.

During a visit to his grandmother at the family homestead in Kisii, O'Keragori collected a series of ancient stories from the oral traditions of his tribe. He felt strongly that these should be preserved for future generations and presented them to the publishers Jacaranda Designs in Nairobi. They invited him to work on a book as both author and artist, and his first publication, *Totems of the Kisii,* appeared in 1994. The book was launched at the National Arts Festival in 1995 to much acclaim.

O'Keragori has won many national prizes for his artwork and has exhibited at the National Museum, the French Cultural Center, and the National Arts Festival. His work is held in collections in the United Kingdom, the United States, Germany, and France.

He lives in Nairobi, Kenya.

BIBLIOGRAPHY

Totems of the Kisii. Jacaranda Designs, 1994.

Olaleye, Isaac

(1941–)

AUTHOR

"Nobody inspired me. At the time I started writing children's books, I didn't know any writer of children's books."

Olaleye was born and reared in a little rainforest village called Erin in western Nigeria; he has four brothers and two sisters. He attended the local school, then went to Thurrock Technical College in Essex, England, and graduated from the Institute of Transport.

Olaleye worked for Pan American Airways as a sales agent. To maintain his writing habit, he has done all kinds of odd jobs, including house painting. In 1991, he published an adult nonfiction book entitled *Did God Make Them Black?*

A member of the Society of Children's Book Writers and Illustrators, Olaleye lives in Keyser, West Virginia.

BIBLIOGRAPHY

Bitter Bananas. Illustrated by Ed Young. Boyds Mills, 1994.
The Distant Talking Drum. Illustrated by Frané Lessac. Boyds Mills, 1995.

Onyefulu, Ifeoma (Ebele)

(1959–)

AUTHOR, ILLUSTRATOR

"In my opinion, there is a void in the realm of literature for Black children, for example, the absence of "fun to read books." I think it will be fun to tell stories like in the good old days. Children like to be entertained as well as allowing them to use their imaginations when stories are told. As a child, I enjoyed listening to stories that stretched my imagination—stories that drew wonderful, colorful pictures in my mind. I also think that women are not represented enough as heroes.

My approach is to keep it simple but colorful and fun to read. Children have a huge hunger for knowledge, always asking question after question. Therefore, children's-book illustrations should meet that requirement. And I think some books are now beautifully illustrated, especially the skin tones."

Onyefulu was born in Nigeria, her father a lawyer and her mother a businesswoman. She is employed as a freelance photographer and loves to read and travel. She is married and has two children, Emeka and Ikenna, and lives in London, England.

BIBLIOGRAPHY

A Is for Africa. Cobblehill, 1993.
Emeka's Gift: An African Counting Story. Cobblehill, 1995.
Ogbo: Sharing Life in an African Village. Gulliver, 1996.
Chidi Only Likes Blue. NAL/Dutton, 1997.

Owens, Vivian (Williams)

AUTHOR

Owens grew up in Florida, the third child in a family of thirteen. She holds a bachelor's degree in chemistry from Tuskegee University and a master's degree in education from James Madison University. Having enjoyed a long career in education, as both a teacher and a program developer, Owens also had an early career as an industrial chemist and taught chemistry in both private and public schools.

In early 1980, Owens developed a local radio program organized around the theme of parenting for education. Later, she wrote a newspaper column around the same theme, and in 1989 she started Eschar Publications to publish her own works and to develop customized workshops and seminars. Today, she writes a nationally syndicated column.

She is the recipient of several awards, including the American Institute of Chemists Award in 1968, the Outstanding Young Woman of America Award in 1983, and the 1992 Who's Who Among America's Teachers Award. *Nadanda, the Wordmaker* received the Writer's Digest Award for Best Children's Book in the 1994 Writer's Digest National Self-Published Book Awards.

Owens lives in Waynesboro, Virginia, with her husband, John, one son, and two daughters.

BIBLIOGRAPHY

Create a Math Environment. Eschar, 1992.
Nadanda, the Wordmaker. Illustrated by Richard Jesse Watson. Eschar, 1994.
The Rose Bush Witch. Eschar, 1996.
I Met a Great Lady. Illustrated by Richard Jesse Watson. Eschar, 1998.
I Met a Great Man. Illustrated by Richard Jesse Watson. Eschar, 1998.
Chemistry Quickies. Eschar, 1998.

See also Watson, Richard Jesse

Palmer, C(yril) Everard

(1930–)

AUTHOR

Palmer was born in Kendal, Jamaica, and educated at Mico Training College in Jamaica and Lakehead University in Thunder Bay, Ontario. A writer and a teacher, he has contributed short stories and articles to Jamaica's leading newspaper. Among his awards is a certificate of merit from the Jamaican Reading Association for his contribution to Jamaican children's literature.

He teaches and lives in Nipigon, Ontario, Canada.

BIBLIOGRAPHY

The Cloud with the Silver Lining. Bobbs-Merrill, 1966.
Big Doc Bitteroot. Bobbs-Merrill, 1968.
The Sun Salutes You. Bobbs-Merrill, 1970.
Baba and Mr. Big. Illustrated by Lorenzo Lynch. Bobbs-Merrill, 1972.
A Cow Called Boy. Bobbs-Merrill, 1972.
Houdini, Come Home. Illustrated by Gavin Rowe. Deutsch, 1981.

See also Lynch, Lorenzo

Patrick, Denise Lewis

(1 9 5 7 –)

AUTHOR

"I come from a storytelling and talking family. My father wrote poetry, and that's what I began writing when I was eight years old. I even handwrote and bound my own books as a child. Reading was as great a passion for me as actual writing was. I went to the public library every week. Some of my early favorites included the authors Madeline L'Engle (for the Wrinkle in Time series), and poets Nikki Giovanni and Paul Laurence Dunbar. Later, I fell in love with Zora Neale Hurston, Flannery O'Connor, and Gabriel Garcia Marquez, all fantastic storytellers and masters of language. I think great writers have the incredible ability to turn ordinary words into music and song."

Patrick was born in Natchitoches, Louisiana. She attended local schools and earned a bachelor of arts degree in journalism from Northwestern State University of Louisiana in 1977.

She moved to New York City in 1977. She has worked at *Essence* magazine and the *New York Times,* has been a staff editor and writer at *Scholastic* magazines, Joshua Morris Publishing, and Macmillan, and has done freelance editing and writing for Children's Television Workshop.

She is married, has three young sons, and lives in New York City.

BIBLIOGRAPHY

Animal ABC's and How Many Animals? Illustrated by Kate Gleeson. Golden, 1990.
Happy Birthday! Illustrated by Cara Marks. Golden, 1990.
Opposites and Shapes and Colors. Illustrated by Kersten Brothers Studios. Golden, 1990.
What Does Baby Hear? Illustrated by Kathy Cruikshank. Golden, 1990.
What Does Baby See? Illustrated by Kathy Cruikshank. Golden, 1990.

Who's Coming to Visit? Illustrated by Cara Marks. Golden, 1990.

Baby's Favorite Foods. Illustrated by Kathy Wilburn. Golden, 1991.

Baby's Favorite Toys. Illustrated by Kathy Wilburn. Golden, 1991.

Ariel's Secret. Illustrated by Sue DiCicco. Golden, 1992.

The Car Washing Street. Illustrated by John Ward. Tambourine, 1993.

Goodnight, Baby. Illustrated by Barbara Lanza. Golden, 1993.

Red Dancing Shoes. Illustrated by James Ransome. Tambourine, 1993.

I Can See a Rainbow. Illustrated by Linda LaGalia. SRA/Macmillan, 1995.

Case of the Missing Cookies. Illustrated by Stacey Schuett. Alladin, 1996.

I Can Count, Illustrated by Fred Willingham. Golden, 1996.

No Diapers for Baby. Illustrated by Sylvia Walker. Golden, 1996.

Peekaboo, Baby! Illustrated by Ray Simmons. Golden, 1996.

See What I Can Do! Illustrated by Thomas Hudson. Golden, 1996.

Shaina's Garden. Illustrated by Stacey Schuett. Alladin, 1996.

The Adventures of Midnight Sun. Holt, 1997.

See also Ransome, James (Earl); Simmons, Ray; Ward, John (Clarence)

Patterson, Lillie

AUTHOR

Patterson has been a teacher as well as chairman of the Elementary Book Reviewing Committee for the Baltimore public schools and a library-services specialist. Her book *Martin Luther King, Jr.: Man of Peace* won the Coretta Scott King Award in 1970, and three other works have been named Coretta Scott King Honor Books: *Coretta Scott King* in 1978, *Benjamin Banneker* in 1979, and *Martin Luther King, Jr., and the Freedom Movement* in 1990.

BIBLIOGRAPHY

Booker T. Washington: Leader of His People. Illustrated by Anthony D'Adamo. Garrard, 1962.

Francis Scott Key: Poet and Patriot. Illustrated by Vic Dowd. Garrard, 1963.

Halloween. Illustrated by Gil Miret. Garrard, 1963.

Frederick Douglass: Freedom Fighter. Illustrated by Gray Morrow. Garrard, 1965.

Martin Luther King, Jr.: Man of Peace. Illustrated by Victor Mays. Garrard, 1969.

Sequoyah: The Cherokee Who Captured Words. Illustrated by Herman B. Vestal. Garrard, 1975.

Coretta Scott King. Garrard, 1977.

Benjamin Banneker. Abingdon, 1978.

Sure Hands, Strong Heart: The Life of Daniel Hale Williams. Illustrated by David S. Brown. Abingdon, 1981.

David: The Story of a King. Abingdon, 1985.

Martin Luther King, Jr., and the Freedom Movement. A Makers of America Book. Facts on File, 1989.

Oprah Winfrey: Talk Show Host and Actress. With Cornelia H. Wright. Contemporary Women Series. Enslow, 1990.

A. Philip Randolph: Messenger for the Masses. Facts on File, 1996.

Perkins, Charles Derrick

(1950–)

AUTHOR

"My approach to my work is very open. I get ideas and concepts for my stories from life in general."

Perkins is employed at the Water Revenue Bureau in the city of Philadelphia. His professional affiliations include membership in the National Association of Black School Educators and the National Association of Black Administrators.

He does a God-centered rap presentation at schools, and, as a result of his children's book, he is a part of the *Vicki and Friends* children's television show on Comcast Cable. The show, which was filmed in January 1995 at the Afro-American Museum in Philadelphia, Pennsylvania, has been sent to the Martin Luther King Center for Non-Violence.

Perkins lives in Philadelphia, Pennsylvania.

BIBLIOGRAPHY

Swinging on a Rainbow. Illustrated by Thomas Hamilton. African World, 1993.

Perkins, Useni Eugene

(1 9 3 2 –)

AUTHOR

Perkins was born in Chicago, Illinois. After reading Richard Wright's *Black Boy* as a twelve-year-old, he was motivated to become a writer. His early writings were poetic expressions and were frequently published in local Chicago newspapers. Later, in high school, he became the sports editor of the school newspaper, and he continued to pursue his interest in journalism at Knoxville College in 1953. He received a bachelor's and a master's degree in group work at George Williams College in 1961 and 1964, respectively.

Perkins served in the United States Air Force, and after his discharge he had his first book of poems, *An Apology to my African Brother*, published. This volume was followed by *Black Is Beautiful* in 1958 and *Silhouette* in 1961. During this period, he also founded the Free Black Press.

He worked as a social worker and continued to write, and in 1975 his seminal book on Black youth, *Home Is a Dirty Street: The Social Oppression of Black Children*, was published by Third World Press. This book was cited by historian Lerone Bennett as " . . . one of the most important books on the sociology of the streets."

Perkins began writing children's plays in 1973, and his musical *Black Fairy*, also known as *Ghetto Fairy*, has enjoyed wide success, as have his other children's plays, *Young John Henry* and *The Legend of Deadwood Dick*. These plays were anthologized in a book entitled *Black Fairy and Other Children Plays*. In 1991, his workbook for children, *Afrocentric Self-Inventory and Discovery Workbook*, was awarded second place in the Multicultural Publisher's Exchange Book Awards of Excellence competition. His poster poem, *Hey Black Child*, written in 1981, has gained national recognition.

Perkins has helped other aspiring writers; he served as cochairperson of the South Side Art Center's Writers Workshop from 1971 to 1973 and founded the Northwest African American Writers Workshop in 1988. He is also the publisher and editor of *Black Child Journal* and was president of the Urban League of Portland from 1987 to 1989. Perkins served as interim president for the DuSable Museum of African American History in Chicago, Illinois, in 1990. He is also the founder and president of the Association for the Positive Development of Black Youth and the director of the Family Life Center, Chicago State University.

Perkins is divorced and the father of two children. He lives in Chicago, Illinois.

BIBLIOGRAPHY

Home Is a Dirty Street: The Social Oppression of Black Children. Third World, 1975.

When You Grow Up: Poems for Children. Self-published, 1982.

Explosion of Chicago's Black Street Gangs. Third World, 1987.

Harvesting New Generations: Positive Development of Black Youth. Third World, 1987.

Afrocentric Self Inventory and Discovery Workbook. Third World, 1989.

The Black Fairy and Other Children's Plays. Illustrated by Patrick Hill. Third World, 1993.

Petry, Ann (Lane)

(1908–1997)

AUTHOR

Petry was born in Old Saybrook, Connecticut, and attended Connecticut College of Pharmacy, now known as the University of Connecticut School of Pharmacy. She also attended Columbia University.

Her writing career started with her work for the *Amsterdam News* in Harlem, New York, as a writer and reporter and as women's editor in the 1940s for the *People's Voice,* a New York City newspaper. During 1974 and 1975, she was a visiting professor of English at the University of Hawaii. Her awards include a grant from the National Endowment for the Arts. She was married to George D. Petry and had one daughter.

Petry died in Old Saybrook, Connecticut, in 1997.

BIBLIOGRAPHY

The Drugstore Cat. Illustrated by Susanne Suba. Crowell, 1949.

Harriet Tubman: Conductor on the Underground Railroad. Illustrated by Marshall Cavendish. Crowell, 1955.

Tituba of Salem Village. Crowell, 1964.

Legends of the Saints. Illustrated by Anne Rockwell. Crowell, 1970.

Pinkney, Andrea Davis

(1963–)

AUTHOR

Pinkney was born in Washington, D.C., the eldest of three children. Her mother was constantly reading books, and her father was, and still is, a master storyteller. She credits these influences as the "gentle hands" that helped shape her into a teller of her own stories for young readers.

Pinkney holds a bachelor's degree in journalism from Syracuse University's Newhouse School of Public Communications. She began her career as a gardening editor for a small home-decorating magazine in New York City, where she met illustrator Brian Pinkney, who worked in the Art Department at the sports-and-fishing magazine across the hall. Years later, he became her husband.

While working at the magazine, she spent nights and weekends writing short stories, essays, poems, and whatever came to mind, for fun. One weekend, she wrote an essay about her experiences as an African American girl growing up in Wilton, Connecticut, a suburb where there were only a few Black families. On a whim, she sent the piece to the *New York Times,* which published it within one week's time! Years later, she used her *New York Times* essay as the basis for her first young-adult novel, *Hold Fast to Dreams,* which was named Pick of the List by the American Booksellers Association (ABA) in 1995.

She has written articles for *American Visions, Essence, Executive Female,* and *Highlights for Children* magazines. She is also the award-winning author of several children's picture books, all illustrated by her husband, Brian Pinkney. *Alvin Ailey,* published in 1993, was a National Association for the Advancement of Colored People (NAACP) Image Award nominee and winner of the Parenting Publication Award Gold Medal. *Dear Benjamin Banneker,* published in 1994, was named an ABA Pick of the List title, a Child Study Children's Book Committee Best

Books for Children, the winner of the Carter G. Woodson Honor Award, and a *New York Times* Bookshelf Selection. *Seven Candles for Kwanzaa,* published in 1993, was also named an ABA Pick of the List book.

Formerly a senior editor at *Essence* magazine, Pinkney works as a children's book editor. She lives with her husband, Brian Pinkney, in Brooklyn, New York.

BIBLIOGRAPHY

Alvin Ailey. Illustrated by Brian Pinkney. Hyperion, 1993.
Seven Candles for Kwanzaa. Illustrated by Brian Pinkney. Dial, 1993.
Dear Benjamin Banneker. Illustrated by Brian Pinkney. Harcourt, 1994.
Hold Fast to Dreams. Morrow, 1995.
Bill Pickett: Rodeo Ridin' Cowboy. Illustrated by Brian Pinkney. Harcourt, 1996.
I Smell Honey. Illustrated by Brian Pinkney. Harcourt, 1997.
Pretty Brown Face. Illustrated by Brian Pinkney. Harcourt, 1997.
Duke Ellington. Illustrated by Brian Pinkney. Hyperion, 1997.

See also Pinkney, Brian; Woodson, Carter G(odwin)

Pinkney, Brian

(1961–)

AUTHOR, ILLUSTRATOR

Born in Boston, Massachusetts, Pinkney's family later moved to Croton-on-Hudson, New York. Pinkney grew up in an artistic family. His father, Jerry Pinkney, is an award-winning illustrator of children's books, and his mother, Gloria Jean Pinkney, is an award-winning children's-book writer. From an early age, Pinkney knew he wanted to be an illustrator like his father, and later he began to write, like his mother. He holds a bachelor of fine arts degree from the University of the Arts in Philadelphia, Pennsylvania, and a master's degree in illustration from the School of Visual Arts in New York City. His career began with assignments for publications such as the *New York Times, Woman's Day, Ebony Man, Business Tokyo,* and *Amtrak Express* magazines. His illustrations have also appeared in numerous textbooks.

Pinkney has illustrated more than twenty children's books. He received the 1996 Caldecott Honor Book Award and the 1996 Coretta Scott King Honor Book Award for *The Faithful Friend* and is a four-time winner of the Parents Choice Award for illustrations that appeared in *The Boy and the Ghost, The Ballad of Belle Dorcas, Where Does the Trail Lead?,* and *Sukey and the Mermaid. Sukey and the Mermaid* was also awarded the 1993 Coretta Scott King Honor Book Award for illustration; named an American Bookseller Pick of the List, one of *Parenting* magazine's Ten Best Books of 1992, and a *Booklist* Editors Choice for 1992; and chosen by *School Library Journal* as one of the Best Books 1992. His picturebook *The Adventures of Sparrowboy* won the 1997 Boston Globe-Horn Book Award.

Pinkney has also illustrated several picture books written by his wife, Andrea Davis Pinkney. His works have been exhibited at the Detroit Institute of Art, the Cleveland Museum of Art, the Cinque Gallery in New York City, and the Schomburg Center for Research in Black Culture, among others.

He lives with his wife, author Andrea Davis Pinkney, in Brooklyn, New York.

BIBLIOGRAPHY

The Storyteller. By Derrick Gantt. Songhai, 1981.

The Boy and the Ghost. By Robert D. San Souci. Simon & Schuster, 1989.

The Ballad of Belle Dorcas. By William H. Hooks. Knopf, 1990.

Harriet Tubman and Black History Month. By Polly Carter. Silver Burdett, 1990.

The Lost Zoo. By Christopher Cat and Countee Cullen. Silver Burdett, 1991.

A Wave in Her Pocket: Stories from Trinidad. By Lynn Joseph. Clarion, 1991.

Where Does the Trail Lead? By Burton Albert. Simon & Schuster, 1991.

The Dark-Thirty: Southern Tales of the Supernatural. By Patricia C. McKissack. Knopf, 1992.

The Elephant's Wrestling Match. By Judy Sierra. Lodestar, 1992.

Sukey and the Mermaid. By Robert D. San Souci. Four Winds, 1992.

Alvin Ailey. By Andrea Davis Pinkney. Hyperion, 1993.

Cut from the Same Cloth. By Robert D. San Souci. Philomel, 1993.

Happy Birthday, Martin Luther King. By Jean Marzollo. Scholastic, 1993.

Seven Candles for Kwanzaa. By Andrea Davis Pinkney. Dial, 1993.

Day of Delight. By Maxine Rose Schur. Dial, 1994.

Dear Benjamin Banneker. By Andrea Davis Pinkney. Harcourt, 1994.

The Dream Keeper and Other Poems. By Langston Hughes. Knopf, 1994.

Max Found Two Sticks. Simon & Schuster, 1994.

The Faithful Friend. By Robert D. San Souci. Simon & Schuster, 1995.

Jojo's Flying Side Kick. Simon & Schuster, 1995.

When I Left My Village. By Maxine Rose Schur. Dial, 1995.

Bill Pickett: Rodeo Ridin' Cowboy. By Andrea Davis Pinkney. Harcourt, 1996.

Wiley and the Hairy Man. By Judy Sierra. Lodestar, 1996.

The Adventures of Sparrowboy. Simon & Schuster, 1997.

I Smell Honey. By Andrea Davis Pinkney. Harcourt, 1997.

Pretty Brown Face. By Andrea Davis Pinkney. Harcourt, 1997.

Duke Ellington. By Andrea Davis Pinkney. Hyperion, 1997.

See also Cullen, Countee (Porter); Hughes, (James) Langston; Joseph, Lynn; McKissack, Patricia C(arwell); Pinkney, Andrea Davis; Pinkney, Gloria Jean; Pinkney, Jerry

Pinkney, Gloria Jean

(1941-)

AUTHOR

Pinkney was born in Lumberton, North Carolina, and treasures many childhood memories of family reunions. Her first picture book, *Back Home,* is based on an early experience of a trip back to her hometown. It won the 1992 American Library Association Notable Children's Book Award, was also selected as the *Booklist* Children's Editors Choice, and was listed among the New York Public Library's 100 Titles for Reading and Sharing.

Pinkney has worked as a model, a window designer, an arts and crafts instructor, a silversmith, and an artist representative. She is a member of Black Women in Publishing and the Society of Children's Book Writers and Illustrators. She is married to artist Jerry Pinkney, who illustrated *Back Home* and her second book, *The Sunday Outing.*

Pinkney and her husband have four children, Troy Bernardette, Brian, Scott, and Myles, all involved in some aspect of the creative arts. They live in Croton-on-Hudson, New York.

BIBLIOGRAPHY

Back Home. Illustrated by Jerry Pinkney. Dial, 1992.
The Sunday Outing. Illustrated by Jerry Pinkney. Dial, 1994.

See also Pinkney, Andrea Davis; Pinkney, Brian; Pinkney, Jerry

Pinkney, Jerry

(1939–)

ILLUSTRATOR

Pinkney was born in Philadelphia, Pennsylvania, and studied at the Philadelphia Museum College of Art (now the University of the Arts). In 1968, he and his family moved to Boston, Massachusetts, and he began his career as an illustrator-designer for the Rustcraft Publishing Company. He was next employed by the Barker-Black Studio, where he illustrated his first children's book, *The Adventures of Spider: West African Folk Tales*. Then, he and two other artists opened Kaleidoscope Studio and he opened his own studio in Boston in 1968. In 1971, he moved to the New York area and began to freelance out of his studio in Croton-on-Hudson.

Pinkney has illustrated more than seventy-five children's books and twelve novels for adults. He has received three Caldecott Honor Medals, four Coretta Scott King Awards, and two Coretta Scott King Honor Book Awards, two *New York Times* Best Illustrated Awards, two Christopher Awards, and the Boston Globe-Horn Book Award for illustration, among numerous other commendations. His works have been honored by the American Institute of Graphic Arts and the New York Art Directors Club, the Council on Interracial Books for Children, and the National Conference of Christians and Jews. In addition, he has been honored for his body of work with a citation for children's literature from Drexel University.

He has been a visiting critic for the Rhode Island School of Design, an associate professor at Pratt Institute, Brooklyn, New York, an associate professor of art at the University of Delaware, and a visiting professor in the Department of Art at the University at Buffalo, New York.

Best noted for his book illustrations, Pinkney has also designed twelve stamps for the United States Postal Service and served on the

United States Postal Service Citizen Stamp Advisory Committee. Pinkney won the Coretta Scott King Illustrator Award for *Minty: A Story of Young Harriet Tubman.*

He and his wife, author Gloria Jean Pinkney, have collaborated on two books. They live in Croton-on-Hudson, New York, and have four children. Their son Brian is also a children's-book illustrator and author.

BIBLIOGRAPHY

The Adventures of Spider: West African Folk Tales. By Joyce Arkhurst. Little, Brown, 1964.

More Adventures of Spider. By Joyce Arkhurst. Scholastic, 1971.

Femi and Old Grandaddie. By Adjai Robinson. Coward, 1972.

J.D. By Mari Evans. Doubleday, 1973.

Kasho and the Twin Flutes. By Adjai Robinson. Coward, 1973.

The Great Minu. By Beth P. Wilson. Follett, 1974.

Song of the Trees. By Mildred D. Taylor. Dial, 1975.

Yagua Days. By Cruz Martel. Dial, 1976.

Mary McLeod Bethune. By Eloise Greenfield. Crowell, 1977.

Childtimes: A Three-Generation Memoir. By Lessie Jones Little and Eloise Greenfield. Harper, 1979.

Count on Your Fingers, African Style. By Claudia Zaslafsky. Crowell, 1980.

Jahdu. By Virginia Hamilton. Greenwillow, 1980.

The Patchwork Quilt. By Valerie Flournoy. Dial, 1985.

Forever Friends (formerly *Breadsticks and Blessing Places*). By Candy (Marguerite) Dawson Boyd, Macmillan, 1985.

Half a Moon and One Whole Star. By Crescent Dragonwagon. Macmillan, 1986.

The Tales of Uncle Remus: The Adventures of Brer Rabbit. Volume One. By Julius Lester. Dial, 1987.

Wild Wild Sunflower Child Anna. By Nancy White Carlstrom. Macmillan, 1987.

The Green Lion of Zion Street. By Julia Fields. Macmillan, 1988.

Mirandy and Brother Wind. By Patricia C. McKissack. Knopf, 1988.

More Tales of Uncle Remus: Further Adventures of Brer Rabbit, His Friends, Enemies and Others. By Julius Lester. Dial, 1988.

Rabbit Makes a Monkey of Lion. By Verna Aardema. Dial, 1989.

The Talking Eggs. By Robert D. San Souci. Dial, 1989.

Song of the Trees. By Mildred D. Taylor. Dial, 1975.

Turtle in July. By Marilyn Singer. Macmillan, 1989.

Further Tales of Uncle Remus: The Misadventures of Brer Rabbit, Brer Fox, Brer Wolf, the Doodang and Other Creatures. By Julius Lester. Dial, 1990.

Homeplace. By Crescent Dragonwagon. Macmillan, 1990.

Pretend You're a Cat. By Jean Marzollo. Dial, 1990.

In for Winter, Out for Spring. By Arnold Adoff. Harcourt, 1991.

The Man Who Kept His Heart in a Bucket. By Sonia Levitan. Dial, 1991.

Tonweya and the Eagles, and other Lakota Tales. By Rosebud Yellow Robe. Dial, 1991.

Back Home. By Gloria Jean Pinkney. Dial, 1992.

Drylongso. By Virginia Hamilton. Harcourt, 1992.

David's Songs. By Colin Eisler. Dial, 1992.

I Want to Be. By Thylias Moss. Dial, 1993.

New Shoes for Sylvia. By Johanna Hurwitz. Morrow, 1993.

A Starlit Somersault Downhill. By Nancy Willard. Little, Brown, 1993.

The Hired Hand. By Robert D. San Souci. Dial, 1994.

John Henry. By Julius Lester. Dial, 1994.

The Last Tales of Uncle Remus. By Julius Lester. Dial, 1994.

The Sunday Outing. By Gloria Jean Pinkney. Dial, 1994.

The Jungle Book: The Mowgli Stories. By Rudyard Kipling. Morrow, 1995.

Tanya's Reunion. By Valerie Flournoy. Dial, 1995.

Minty: A Story of Young Harriet Tubman. By Alan Schroeder. Dial, 1996.

Sam and the Tigers. Retold by Julius Lester. Dial, 1996.

The Hired Hand: An African-American Folktale. By Robert D. San Souci. Dial, 1997.

See also Arkhurst, Joyce (Cooper); Boyd, Candy (Marguerite) Dawson; Evans, Mari; Flournoy, Valerie; Greenfield, Eloise (Glynn Little); Hamilton, Virginia (Esther); Lester, Julius (Bernard); Little, Lessie Jones; McKissack, Patricia C(arwell); Pinkney, Brian; Pinkney, Gloria Jean; Ransome, James (Earl); Robinson, Adjai; Taylor, Mildred D.; Wilson, Beth P(ierre)

Porter, A(nthony) P(eyton)

(1945–)

AUTHOR

"As a child, I knew Negro professionals—all my doctors were Black—but I didn't know anybody in the arts—no musicians or writers or artists. In trying to avoid admitting that what I really wanted to do was write, I've had more than forty jobs. I took proofreading and copyediting tests wherever I could until I was hired by a book publisher. When the acquisitions committee decided they wanted a biography of Greg LeMond, a bicycle racer, I was offered the project, and, in 1990, I became a published author."

Porter was born in Chicago, Illinois. For two years, he was managing editor of *Colors: Minnesota's Journal of Opinion by Writers of Color*. Now a freelance writer and editor, he also does broadcast commentary for KTCA Public Television and Minnesota Public Radio. He belongs to the Professional Editors Network and the Authors Guild and serves on the panels of the Minnesota State Arts Board and the Metropolitan Regional Arts Council in Minneapolis, Minnesota.

Jump at de Sun: The Story of Zora Neale Hurston was selected by the Young Adult Library Services Association of the American Library Association as a Recommended Book for Reluctant Young Adult Readers. He is a founding member of SASE, an organization for writers.

Porter is married to illustrator Janice Lee Porter and has three children, Joseph Lee, Adesola Peyton, and Jai Imani Henry. Porter lives in Minneapolis, Minnesota.

BIBLIOGRAPHY

Greg LeMond: Premier Cyclist. Lerner, 1990.
Kwanzaa. Illustrated by Janice Lee Porter. Carolrhoda, 1991.
Nebraska. Lerner, 1991.

Zina Garrison: Ace. Lerner, 1991.

Jump at de Sun: The Story of Zora Neale Hurston. Carolrhoda, 1992.

Minnesota. Lerner, 1992.

Prather, Ray

AUTHOR, ILLUSTRATOR

Prather grew up in Marianne, Florida. He studied art at Florida Chipola Junior College and continued his studies at Cooper Union in New York City. He has been an art assistant and designer for *Look* magazine, and his illustrations have appeared in the *Nation* and *Black Enterprise*.

He lives in Pergassona, Switzerland.

BIBLIOGRAPHY

Anthony and Sabrina. Macmillan, 1973.
Time-Ago Lost: More Tales of Jahdu. By Virgina Hamilton. Macmillan, 1973.
No Trespassing. Macmillan, 1974.
Double Dog Dare. Macmillan, 1975.
New Neighbors. McGraw, 1975.
The Ostrich Girl. Scribner, 1978.
Fish and Bones. HarperCollins, 1992.

See also Hamilton, Virginia (Esther)

Pritchett, Doris D.

(1 9 5 6 –)

ILLUSTRATOR

"My mother was a social worker, a seamstress, and very active in both community and national politics. My father worked by day hanging wallpaper and painting, and by night as a mechanic and short-haul trucker. It is from these two people that I inherited my creativity, sense of humor, and sense of independence. Though (my father's) stories, told with much humor and reflection, were never heavy with moralizing, still they always seemed to carry a lesson. This is what I grew up with and what I believe many young people (especially Black children) are missing these days—a voice that guides and teaches. Working for Black children gives me the chance to take part in an effort to present positive images and exciting ideas."

Pritchett was born in Camden, New Jersey, and has three brothers and three sisters. She graduated from Pratt Institute in Brooklyn, New York, with a bachelor of fine arts degree in fashion design and endured a brief career in the fashion industry. Finally, she committed herself to what she loves doing most—illustration—and she continues to take art and art-related courses or a sketch class whenever there is time.

All of Pritchett's published work has been in watercolors, which is her favorite medium. She also makes wood and linoleum block prints and plans to do a children's book entirely in prints.

She lives in Brooklyn, New York.

BIBLIOGRAPHY

The Birth of Christ. By Yvette Moore. Jubilee, 1993.

Quarles, Benjamin

(1905–1996)

AUTHOR

Quarles was born in Boston, Massachusetts, educated in local public schools, and in 1931 graduated from Shaw University. He earned his doctorate in 1940 and is widely recognized for his knowledge of African-American history and scholarly achievements.

Quarles was professor of history and dean of instruction at Dillard University and a professor at Morgan State College, where he received fellowships and grants-in-aid from the Social Science Research Council. He also received the President Adams Fellowship in Modern History from the University of Wisconsin and other awards from the Rosenwald and Guggenheim foundations.

His affiliation with the Association for the Study of Negro Life and History was productive. He was also president of Associated Publishers and associate editor of the *Journal of Negro History*.

Quarles received sixteen honorary doctorates from universities and colleges in the United States. He died in 1996.

BIBLIOGRAPHY

Lift Every Voice. With Dorothy Sterling. Illustrated by Ernest Crichlow. Doubleday, 1964.

See also Crichlow, Ernest

Ransome, James (Earl)

(1961–)

ILLUSTRATOR

"Like so many children today, I grew up in a household where reading was not a priority. I lived with my Grandmother, who could not go to school beyond the first grade in order to help her family sharecrop. The only book I recall being in our home was the Bible, which she would often ask me to read aloud. It was the combination of these graceful, strongly illustrated Bible stories, dramatic comic books, MAD *magazine, and Disney cartoons that both sparked, then captured, my interest.*

I read because I was interested in the images that accompanied the story. These pictures also became my introduction to art, first by copying comics and later by illustrating my own books about me and my friends. It is with this realization that I understand the importance an illustration can have on a reader. Now that I am illustrating books, I take on the responsibility of drawing the reader to a story. Colors both strong and subtle, dramatic compositions, and familiar characters are the tools I use to make my pictures interesting."

Ransome was born in Rich Square, North Carolina. He graduated from Pratt Institute in Brooklyn, New York, with a bachelor's degree in illustration. He continued to study at the Art Students League in New York City with award-winning illustrator and painter Burt Silverman. Ransome credits the eminent artist Jerry Pinkney for a large part of his development as an illustrator, noting that visiting Pinkney's home studio helped his artwork to grow.

In 1995, Ransome received both the Coretta Scott King and the IBBY (International Board on Books for Young People) awards for the book *The Creation* written by James Weldon Johnson. Ransome has also illustrated other award-winning picture books for children, including *Do Like Kyla,* his first picture book, and *Aunt Flossie's Hats (and Crab*

Cakes Later), both of which received *Parenting* magazine's Reading Magic Award. *Sweet Clara and the Freedom Quilt* was a *Reading Rainbow* selection and winner of the International Reading Association Award in 1994, and *Uncle Jed's Barbershop*, also featured on the *Reading Rainbow* and *Storytime*, was both a Coretta Scott King Honor Book and an American Library Association Notable Book in 1994.

In collaboration with other distinguished authors and illustrators, Ransome was selected to contribute to *Home*, a picture book whose proceeds are donated to benefit the homeless, and *Speak! Children's Book Illustrators Brag About Their Dogs*, which contributes to the Company of Animals Fund.

In addition to picture books, Ransome has illustrated textbooks for elementary and college students used throughout the country, as well as a number of book jackets for young adults. In 1995, he completed a mural for the Children's Museum of Indianapolis, Indiana. Original paintings from his published works have been exhibited in group and solo shows throughout the United States and Canada and also in private and public collections such as the permanent children's-book collection of North Carolina's Charlotte Library.

A Society of Illustrators member, Ransome lives in Poughkeepsie, New York, with his wife, two daughters, and a dalmation.

BIBLIOGRAPHY

Do Like Kyla. By Angela Johnson. Orchard, 1990.

All the Lights in the Night. By Arthur Levine. Tambourine, 1991.

Aunt Flossie's Hats (and Crab Cakes Later). By Elizabeth Fitzgerald Howard. Clarion, 1991.

How Many Stars in the Sky? By Lenny Hort. Morrow, 1991.

The Girl Who Wore Snakes. By Angela Johnson. Orchard, 1993.

The Hummingbird Garden. By Christine Widman. Macmillan, 1993.

Red Dancing Shoes. By Denise Lewis Patrick. Tambourine, 1993.

Sweet Clara and the Freedom Quilt. By Deborah Hopkinson. Knopf, 1993.

Uncle Jed's Barbershop. By Margaree King Mitchell. Simon & Schuster, 1993.

Bonesy and Isabel. By Michael J. Rosen. Harcourt, 1994.

The Creation. By James Weldon Johnson. Holiday House, 1994.

My Best Shoes. By Marilee Burton. Morrow, 1994.

Ziggy and the Black Dinosaurs. By Sharon M. Draper. Just Us Books, 1994.

Celie and the Harvest Fiddler. By Valerie and Vanessa Flournoy. Tambourine, 1995.

The Old Dog. By Charlotte Zolotow. Harper Collins, 1995.

Bimmi Finds a Cat. By Elizabeth Stewart. Clarion, 1996.

Dark Day, Light Night. By Jan Carr. Hyperion, 1996.

Freedom's Fruit. By William Hooks. Knopf, 1996.

The Wagon. By Tony Johnston. Tambourine, 1996.

Rum-A-Tum-Tum. By Angela Medearis. Holiday House, 1997.

Ziggy and the Black Dinosaurs: Shadows of Ceasar's Creek. By Sharon M. Draper. Just Us Books, 1997.

See also Draper, Sharon M(ills); Flournoy, Valerie; Howard, Elizabeth Fitzgerald; Johnson, Angela; Johnson, James Weldon; Medearis, Angela Shelf; Mitchell, Margaree King; Patrick, Denise Lewis; Pinkney, Jerry

Reid, Desmond

(1945–)

AUTHOR

Reid grew up in Jamaica, the third of nine children, and remembers seeking solace in books to keep away from the hectic doings in a household with so many children. From 1961 to 1965, he attended the Gleaner School of Printing in Jamaica, and in 1965 he moved to the United States and was employed in the printing trade with the Theo. Gaus Company until he joined the United States Air Force. It was service in the Air Force that enabled him to complete his secondary schooling. After Gaus closed, he and three other employees bought the company's printing operation. They later sold it in 1981.

His interest in writing children's books began after a brief visit to Jamaica, when he wrote his first children's book. Since then, he has occupied himself with the pursuit of advanced studies and community work in Brooklyn, New York.

BIBLIOGRAPHY

Dana Meets the Cow Who Lost Its Moo. Gaus, 1984.

Riley, Martin K., Jr.

(1 9 8 3 –)

ILLUSTRATOR

"The artist that inspires me the most is Bob Ross and I enjoy drawing. My mother recognized my talent and has encouraged me to keep at it. I feel that when you have a dream and have been given a gift, you should use it. I am striving to work hard on my academic skills to succeed in my goals."

Riley was born in Berkeley, California, and has been drawing since the age of two. In 1986, he and his mother moved to Akron, Ohio, where he attended elementary school and gained acknowledgment for his artistic skills. His art was displayed on Cable Channel 7 television. Riley is working to advance his artistic skills in the future. He also credits his younger brother Peter for his input and encouragement.

BIBLIOGRAPHY

Why Polly Wants a Cracker! By Debbie M. Matthews. Dibora, 1995.

See also Matthews, Debbie M.

Ringgold, Faith (Jones)

(1930–)

AUTHOR, ILLUSTRATOR

A native of Harlem, New York, Ringgold received her bachelor of science and master of arts degrees from the City College of New York and then worked as an art teacher. She has taught beadwork and mask making. She began to paint professionally in 1960. After making figurative soft sculptures, she decided in 1980 to make quilts.

She had worked earlier with her mother, a fashion designer and dressmaker, who told her stories of slave ancestors making quilts incorporating a painting. Her quilt *Echoes of Harlem* was the first and last project made in collaboration with her mother. Her quilts have a central large painted image framed with a text written on the quilt.

Ringgold's work is found in collections of several museums in New York City, including the Museum of Modern Art; the Studio Museum in Harlem; the Metropolitan Museum of Art; the Solomon R. Guggenheim Museum; the Fine Arts Museum in Long Island, Hempstead, New York; and the High Museum in Atlanta, Georgia. Her work can also be found in private and corporate collections throughout the United States and has been exhibited in Europe, Asia, South America, and Africa. A grant from the LaNapoule Foundation enabled her to work on a series of quilts during a four-month residence in France in 1990.

Her quilt *Tar Beach*, completed in 1988, is from her Woman on a Bridge series, now part of the Guggenheim collection. It served as the basis of Ringgold's first picture book, *Tar Beach*, which re-creates scenes of Harlem from a rooftop overlooking the George Washington Bridge in New York City. The book was a 1992 Caldecott Honor Book and won the 1992 Coretta Scott King Award for illustration.

Ringgold also received a National Endowment for the Arts Award for painting in 1989, and she has been awarded six honorary doctorates in fine arts, from the Massachusetts College of Art in Boston, Massachusetts; Moore College of Art in Philadelphia, Pennsylvania; and her alma mater, the City University of New York, among others.

Ringgold is writing her first book for an adult audience, with a working title of *We Flew Over the Bridge,* based on an unpublished manuscript written in 1979.

She is the mother of two daughters, Michele and Barbara Wallace.

Ringgold lives in Englewood, New Jersey.

BIBLIOGRAPHY

Tar Beach. Crown, 1991.
Aunt Harriet's Underground in the Sky. Crown, 1993.
Dinner at Aunt Connie's House. Hyperion, 1993.
Bonjour, Lonnie. Hyperion, 1996.

Roberts, Brenda C(ecelia)

(1947–)

AUTHOR

Roberts received a master's degree in English from the University of California. She was a press secretary for Tom Bradley when he was mayor of Los Angeles, California, and has also worked as an education writer for the *Santa Monica Evening Outlook* newspaper and as a writer for the *Sacramento Bee* newspaper.

Among the honors and awards she has received are the 1977/1978 Southern Christian Leadership Conference/West Media Relations Award and the 1971/1972 Gwendolyn Brooks Award for Literature.

In addition to writing children's books, Roberts is writing an adult novel. She is married with two teenage children and lives in Los Angeles, California.

BIBLIOGRAPHY

Sticks and Stones, Bobbie Bones. Scholastic, 1993.
Friend of Mine. Scholastic, 1998.

See also Brooks, Gwendolyn

Robinet, Harriette Gillem

(1 9 3 1 –)

AUTHOR

Robinet was born and reared in Washington, D.C. She spent her childhood summers across the Potomac in Arlington, Virginia, where her mother's parents had been slaves under General Robert E. Lee. Robinet received a bachelor's degree from the College of New Rochelle in New Rochelle, New York, in 1953 and graduate degrees from the Catholic University of America in Washington, D.C., in 1957 and 1962.

For thirty-five years a freelance writer, she has published many magazine articles in addition to her children's books. She completed the Famous Writers Correspondence Course and is a member of the Society of Children's Book Writers and Illustrators, the Children's Reading Roundtable, and the Black Literary Umbrella.

Her book *Ride the Red Cycle* is based on personal observations of her son, disabled by cerebral palsy, and many other disabled youngsters she met. It is in Houghton Mifflin's fifth-grade reader and Scott Foresman's fourth grade reader. *Children of the Fire* and *Mississippi Chariot* were named Notable Books in Social Studies by the Children's Book Council and the National Council of Social Studies, and *Children of the Fire* was awarded the 1991 Young People's Literature Award by Friends of American Writers. She writes historical fiction for children eight to twelve years old.

Robinet lives in Oak Park, Illinois, with her husband, McLouis Robinet, a health physicist at Argonne National Laboratory. They have six children and four grandchildren.

BIBLIOGRAPHY

Jay and the Marigold. Illustrated by Gertrude Scott. Children's Press, 1976.
Ride the Red Cycle. Illustrated by David Brown. Houghton, 1980.

Children of the Fire. Atheneum, 1991.

Mississippi Chariot. Atheneum, 1994.

If You Please, President Lincoln. Atheneum, 1995.

Washington City Is Burning. Atheneum, 1996.

The Twins, the Pirates and the Battle of New Orleans. Illustrated by Keinyo White. Atheneum, 1997.

Forty Acres and Maybe a Mule. Atheneum, 1998.

Robinson, Adjai

(1 9 3 2 –)

AUTHOR

Robinson was born in Freetown, Sierre Leone, Africa, and studied at Columbia University. He began collecting folktales from Nigeria and his native country for storytelling on radio in Sierra Leone. His folktale collection and storytelling skills helped him with his studies at Hunter College in New York City and the United States International School.

He has a bachelor's degree from Fourah Bay and a master's degree from Columbia University.

BIBLIOGRAPHY

Femi and Old Grandaddie. Illustrated by Jerry Pinkney. Coward, 1972.
Kasho and the Twin Flutes. Illustrated by Jerry Pinkney. Coward, 1973.
Singing Tales of Africa. Illustrated by Christine Price. Scribner, 1974.
Three African Tales. Illustrated by Carole Byard. Putnam, 1979.

See also Byard, Carole; Pinkney, Jerry

Robinson, Aminah Brenda Lynn

(1940–)

AUTHOR, ILLUSTRATOR

Robinson is a nationally and internationally acclaimed artist whose skills, acquired in a formal art-school setting, through family, and those she taught herself, include painting, drawing, sewing, weaving, and papermaking. She has created more than 25,000 paintings, drawings, books, sculptures, prints, quilts, and mixed-media assemblages. Her subjects derive from her research of family and friends and her own sensitive experience of the world.

Born in Columbus, Ohio, Robinson is a graduate of the Columbus College of Art and Design in Columbus, Ohio. Robinson has done postgraduate work at Ohio State University and the University of Puerto Rico. She has taught as a visiting artist at all levels in public and private schools, churches, museums, and colleges. Her work is promoted by the Printmaking Workshop in New York City, the Carl Solway Gallery in Cincinnati, Ohio, and Winning Images and the Art Exchange, both in Columbus.

Robinson has had solo and group shows throughout the United States and Europe. In Ohio, she has exhibited in, and/or has work in the permanent collections of the Columbus Museum of Art, the Wexner Center at Ohio State University, the Carl Solway Gallery, the Dunlap Gallery in Otterbein, the Concourse Gallery in Upper Arlington, the Martin Luther King Center, the Columbus Foundation, the Columbus Metropolitan Library, Capital University, the Columbus College of Art and Design, the Akron Art Museum, and others.

Beginning in 1992, she turned her talents to writing and illustrating published books in addition to her other work. Robinson authored, illustrated and published *The Teachings* and has illustrated *Elijah's Angel, Sophie, A School for Pompey Walker,* and *No Place Like Home.*

Robinson lives in Columbus, Ohio.

BIBLIOGRAPHY

Elijah's Angel. By Michael J. Rosen. Harcourt, 1992.

No Place Like Home. With Mimi Bradsky Chenfield. Harcourt, 1992.

The Teachings. Harcourt, 1992.

Sophie. By Mem Fox. Harcourt, 1994.

A School for Pompey Walker. By Michael J. Rosen. Harcourt, 1995.

A Street Called Home. Harcourt, 1997.

Robinson, Dorothy (Washington)

(1 9 2 9 –)

AUTHOR

"Every child brings into the world a very special and unique gift. Every adult must work to see to it that the children's gifts are nurtured, protected, and developed toward the creation of a peaceable community."

Robinson was born in Waycross, Georgia. She earned a bachelor of arts degree from Fisk University and a master's degree in library science from Atlanta University. Her career as a children's librarian in the Chicago Public Library and the Chicago Public Schools led her into what she calls "a gold mine about the natural learning gifts of young people" and her desire to share these discoveries with others has resulted in a multi-faceted career.

She is a former member of the American Library Association and the Association for the Study of Negro Life and History. In 1975, she received the Coretta Scott King Award for her book *The Legend of Africania*. As a consultant, she has developed a number of highly successful projects which promote reading while reducing behavorial problems. As a speaker, her lecture, "The Genie In Every Child," has been presented to audiences ranging from national professional organizations to local community groups.

Robinson lives in Chicago, Illinois.

BIBLIOGRAPHY

The Legend of Africania. Illustrated by Herbert Temple. Johnson, 1974.
Martin Luther King and the Civil Rights Movement. Jehara, 1986.

Robinson, Louie

(1926–)

AUTHOR

Robinson was born in Dallas, Texas, and attended Lincoln University in Jefferson City, Missouri. He served in the United States Army during World War II. He has contributed to *Jet, Ebony, Tan*, and *Negro Digest* magazines. He was also an editor for *Jet* and *Romance* magazines and served as *Ebony*'s West Coast bureau chief. Robinson was editorial consultant to actor Sidney Poitier for his autobiography. He also wrote a television drama, *The Invincible Weapon,* which won the Catholic Broadcasters Award in 1966 and was submitted by the producers for an Emmy consideration.

The writer has published more than 200 magazine articles and short fiction in *Ford Times, Black World, Black Enterprise* and *Pageant* magazines among others and has done extensive reporting for *Time, Life, People,* and *Cable-TV Week*.

He has also served as a special consultant to the President of Cal Poly Pomona University, and to other officers and departments at the University. In 1975, Robinson was presented a Distinguished Alumni Award for Achievement in Journalism at his alma mater, Lincoln University in Jefferson City, Missouri.

He lives in Claremont, California.

BIBLIOGRAPHY

Arthur Ashe: Tennis Champion. Doubleday, 1967.
Getting Started in Tennis. With Arthur Ashe. Illustrated by Jeanne Moutoussamy Ashe. Atheneum, 1978.

Rochelle, Belinda

(1958–)

AUTHOR

"I love to read! I especially enjoy reading the work of authors Toni Morrison, Walter Moseley, and Julia Alvarez. I also love poetry. At a fairly young age, I knew that a poet did not have to look a certain way, or fit a certain mold, but that a poet had to love the spoken word, had to have hope in moments of great despair, had to rejoice not in spite of, but because of! My daughter, Shevon, inspires me to write. Young children today are surrounded by violence and hopelessness. Nevertheless, as writers we must remember that children continue to imagine, continue to dream, and still can find beauty and promise in a simple story that begins with 'Once upon a time. . . .'"

The author was born in McKeesport, Pennsylvania. Rochelle is a senior program and policy associate at the Center for Women Policy Studies in Washington, D.C. She has served as a co-chair of the National Organizations Responding to AIDS and until 1997 was a member of the advisory panel of the National Network of Runaway and Youth Services.

The author of children's books, she also writes poetry. Her poetry has appeared in *Obsidian: Black Literature in Review, Atlantis, Catalyst, Kuumba,* and many other journals and magazines.

She has a teenage daughter, Shevon, and lives in Washington, D.C.

BIBLIOGRAPHY

Witnesses to Freedom: Young People Who Fought for Civil Rights. Dutton, 1993.
When Jo Louis Won the Title. Illustrated by Larry Johnson. Houghton, 1994.
Jewels. Illustrated by Cornelius Van Wright and Ying-Hwa Hu. Lodestar, 1995.
Words with Wings. Lodestar, 1995.

Rollins, Charlemae (Hill)

(1897–1979)

AUTHOR

Rollins was born in Yazoo City, Mississippi, and attended Western University, the University of Chicago, and Columbia University, from which she received an honorary doctorate in 1974. She moved to Chicago, Illinois, in 1927.

Her attempts to collect materials on Blacks revealed that little positive information was available for children. She began collecting material to combat existing stereotypes and was, as a result, instrumental in editing the bibliography *We Build Together*. It was published by the National Council of the Teachers of English in 1963 and revised in 1967. The bibliography defined criteria for selecting literature depicting minorities in a positive light.

Rollins was a well-known librarian, children's-literature specialist, author, and lecturer. In 1979, she was voted Young Readers Choice by children in Alaska, Idaho, Montana, Oregon, Washington, British Columbia, and Alberta in a contest sponsored by the Children's and Young Adult Divisions of the Pacific Northwest Library Association. She received the American Library Association Library Letter Award in 1953, the Grolier Society Award in 1955, the Constance Lindsay Skinner Award of the WNBA in 1970, and the Coretta Scott King Award in 1971. She was also an honorary member of Phi Delta Kappa.

After working for thirty-six years in the Chicago Public Library, Rollins retired in 1963 as head of the children's room at the George C. Hall branch. She served as president of the American Library Association's Children's Services Division in the years 1957–1958 and was a member of the Newbery-Caldecott Committee.

Rollins attributed her love for books to her grandmother, a former slave. A room of the Carter G. Woodson Regional Library in Chicago was dedicated to her in 1977.

BIBLIOGRAPHY

Christmas Gif': An Anthology of Christmas Poems, Songs and Stories. Compiled with Augusta Baker. Follett, 1963. Morrow (Illustrated by Ashley Bryan), 1993.

They Showed the Way: Forty American Negro Leaders. HarperCollins, 1964.

Famous American Negro Poets. Dodd, 1965.

Famous Negro Entertainers of Stage, Screen and TV. Dodd, 1967.

Black Troubador: Langston Hughes. Rand McNally, 1970.

See also Baker, Augusta (Braxston); Bryan, Ashley; Woodson, Carter G(odwin)

Rosales, Melodye (Benson)

(1956–)

AUTHOR, ILLUSTRATOR

"I first thought of becoming an artist when I found that my toys could not bend and move the way my imagination wanted them to. So my Mom would bring home the used photocopy paper from her office and the grocery flyers, and I would draw on the blank backsides. I would act out scenes many times before I actually drew them. I would recruit all of the neighborhood kids to partici-pate in these fantasies. After we exhausted our creative energy, we'd go home for our lunch or dinner break. That's when I'd continue the fantasies, only now I could incorporate all the things that were impossible to do in real life—like fly or look exactly like the characters I'd imagined—all through the magic of paper and pencil."

Rosales was born in Los Angeles, California, and received her educa-tion and additional studies at the University of Illinois, Urbana-Champaign; Universidad de Barcelona, Barcelona, Spain; the School of the Art Institute of Chicago and Columbia College, Chicago, Illinois, earning a bachelor of fine arts degree.

She has been an illustrator for more than seventeen years. Among her clients are Scholastic, Pleasant Company, Random House, and Little, Brown, to name a few. She was honored in 1989 and 1991 by the Children's Reading Round Table. *Meet Addy, Addy Learns a Lesson,* and *Addy's Surprise,* all by Connie Porter with illustrations by Rosales, won the Cuffy Award (*Publishers Weekly*) for Best New Series of 1993 and were featured on the *Oprah Winfrey* show. *Meet Addy,* having sold over one million hardcover copies, was listed in *Publishers Weekly* as the only African American title to make the All-Time Best-Selling Children's Hardcover Books list. Also in 1993, *Kwanzaa* was read on the Public Broadcasting System's *Storytime* show as one of its featured books. In addition, the book was read on Barbara Bush's 1991 Storytime Christmas Special. Rosales also illustrated *On the Day I Was Born*, which was listed among the Children's Book Council's Notable Books for Social Studies for 1996.

She lives in Champaign, Illinois, with her husband, three children, and St. Bernard, Thunder.

BIBLIOGRAPHY

Beans on the Roof. By Betsy Byars. Delacorte, 1988.

48 Weeks Until Summer Vacation. By Mona Kirby. Viking, 1989.

The Good Witch. By Mary L. Wang. Children's Press, 1989.

The Mystery of the Hard Luck Rodeo. By Susan Saunders. Random House, 1989.

Kwanzaa. By Debbi Chocolate. Children's Press, 1990.

Corey's Dad Drinks Too Much. By Anne Courtney. Tyndale, 1991.

Double-Dutch and the Voodoo Shoes. Children's Press, 1991.

Addy Learns a Lesson. By Connie Porter. Pleasant, 1993.

Addy's Surprise. By Connie Porter. Pleasant, 1993.

Meet Addy. By Connie Porter. Pleasant, 1993.

Elizabeth's Wish. By Debbi Chocolate. Just Us Books, 1994.

Jackson Jones and the Puddle of Thorns. By Mary Quattlebaum. Delacorte, 1994.

The Twins Strike Back. By Valerie Flournoy. Just Us Books, 1994.

On the Day I Was Born. By Debbi Chocolate. Scholastic, 1995.

Irene Jennie and the Christmas Masquerade: The Johnkankus. By Irene Smalls. Little, Brown, 1996.

'Twas the Night B'fore Christmas. Scholastic, 1996.

A Strawbeater's Thanksgiving. By Irene Smalls. Little, Brown, 1998.

See also Chocolate, Debbi (Deborah Mique Newton Chocolate); Flournoy, Valerie; Smalls, Irene

Roy, Lynette Edwina

(1942–)

AUTHOR

Roy was born in Trinidad, West Indies, and grew up with two cousins and a vivid imagination. As a young reader, she enjoyed fiction. One of her favorite characters was Jane Eyre, in the book of the same name by Charlotte Brontë. After completing high school in Trinidad, Roy studied nursing in Surrey, England, and she immigrated to Canada in 1972. She completed a bachelor of arts degree (with honors) in sociology at York University in 1987. A professor at York University encouraged her to write professionally, describing her writing as sensitive. One of her hobbies is coordinating clubs for children, so writing for children became her focus.

Her first book, *Brown Girl in the Ring,* a biography on Rosemary Brown, the first Black woman to be elected to a provincial-government post in Canada, was published in 1992. The book cover wears a gold seal of approval from the Canadian Children's Book Center, a recommendation for schools and libraries as required reading for children.

Professional memberships include the Canadian Society for Authors, Illustrators, and Performers; the Ontario Black History Society; and the Writers Union of Canada.

Roy enjoys visiting junior and senior high schools, doing book readings, lectures, and workshops to encourage students in their education.

She is single and lives in Uxbridge, Ontario, Canada.

BIBLIOGRAPHY

Brown Girl in the Ring. Sister Vision, 1992.
Cancer: Challenging the Disease. Umbrella, 1996.
Lincoln Alexander. Fitzhenry & Whiteside, 1996.
Four Courageous Black Women. Natural Heritage/Natural History, 1997.

Ruffins, Reynold

(1930–)

AUTHOR, ILLUSTRATOR

Ruffins was born in New York City and grew up in Queens, New York. He remembers drawing at a very early age. He attended the High School of Music and Art and later Cooper Union, both in New York City. While at Cooper Union, he, Milton Glaser, Seymour Chwast, John Alcorn, Paul Davis, and some others formed the Push Pin Studios on Thirteenth Street in New York City, sharing the loft space with a dancer.

He has taught at the School of Visual Arts and Parsons School of Design, both in New York City, and Syracuse University's College of Visual and Performing Arts and has been a designer and illustrator for commercial advertisements and magazines, including *Family Circle*. He began illustrating books after meeting author Jane Sarnoff at a civil-rights protest march in 1973.

Ruffins has received awards from the Art Directors Club and the American Institute of Graphic Arts, as well as the Cooper Union Professional Achievement Award. He has also received prizes from the Bologna Children's Book Fair in 1976, *California* magazine, the Society of Illustrators, and the New York Historical Society.

Running the Road to ABC was named a 1997 Coretta Scott King Honor Book for illustration.

He lives in Queens, New York.

BIBLIOGRAPHY

The Chess Book. With Jane Sarnoff. Scribner, 1973.
A Great Bicycle Book. Scribner, 1973, 1976.
My Brother Never Feeds the Cat. Scribner, 1979.
If You Were Really Superstitious. By Jane Sarnoff. Scribner, 1980.
That's Not Fair. By Jane Sarnoff. Scribner, 1980.

Words: A Book About the Origins of Everyday Words and Phrases. By Jane Sarnoff. Scribner, 1981.

Running the Road to ABC. By Denizé Lauture. Simon & Schuster, 1996.

Everywhere Faces Everywhere. By James Berry. Simon & Schuster, 1997.

See also Berry, James; Lauture, Denizé

Russell, Neil

(1970–)

ILLUSTRATOR

Russell was born in Pittsburgh, Pennsylvania, and attended the Creative and Performing Arts High School in Pittsburgh, graduating in 1989. He earned a bachelor of fine arts degree in 1993 from Cooper Union in New York City and is studying for a master of fine arts degree at Carnegie Mellon University in Pittsburgh.

He works as a photography instructor at the Manchester Craftsmen's Guild and has also done freelance graphic design and illustration.

Russell lives in Pittsburgh, Pennsylvania.

BIBLIOGRAPHY

The Putting on the Brakes Activity Book for Young People with ADHD. By Patricia O. Quinn. Magination, 1993.

Saint James, Synthia

(1949–)

ILLUSTRATOR, AUTHOR

Self-taught artist Saint James was born in Los Angeles, California. Her professional career as an artist began in 1969 in New York City, where she sold her first commissioned oil painting. Today she has an international following. Her work is not only on canvas and limited-edition prints and posters, but on more than thirty book covers, which include books by Alice Walker, Terry McMillan, Iyanla Vanzant, and Julia A. Boyd, and more than eighty greeting cards, including UNICEF's (United Nations Children's Fund) card line. She has also licensed her images on T-shirts, magnets, boxes, gift bags, deck cards, puzzles, and mugs.

She has completed numerous commissions for major organizations and corporations, including the House of Seagram; Brigitte Matteuzzi's School of Modern Jazz Ballet in Geneva, Switzerland; the Mark Taper Forum; the National Bar Association; *Essence* magazine's twenty-fifth anniversary; UNICEF; the Children's Institute International, and the first Kwanzaa stamp for the United States Postal Service. She has received several awards for her books: the 1996 Parents Choice Silver Honor for her book *Sunday* and a 1997 Coretta Scott King Honor Book Award for illustrating *Neeny Coming . . . Neeny Going*.

She lives in Los Angeles, California.

BIBLIOGRAPHY

The Gifts of Kwanzaa. Whitman, 1994.

Snow on Snow on Snow. By Cheryl Chapman. Dial, 1994.

Tukama Tootles the Flute. By Phyllis Gershator. Orchard, 1994.

How Mr. Monkey Saw the Whole World. By Walter Dean Myers. Doubleday, 1996.

Neeny Coming . . . Neeny Going. By Karen English. BridgeWater, 1996.

Sunday. Whitman, 1996.

Girls Together. By Sherley Anne Williams. Harcourt, 1998.

Greeting, Sun. By Phillis Gershator. DK, Inc., 1998.

No Mirrors in My Nana's House. By Ysaye Barnwell. Harcourt, 1999.

See also Myers, Walter Dean; Walker, Alice; Williams, Sherley Anne

Salkey, (Felix) Andrew

(1928–1995)

AUTHOR

Salkey was born in Colon, Panama, and grew up in Jamaica. He attended St. George's College in Kingston and Munro College in St. Elizabeth and earned his bachelor's degree in English from the University of London. He received the Thomas Helmore Poetry Prize in 1955 and a Guggenheim fellowship in 1960. Salkey taught English in a London comprehensive school and in 1952 became a radio interviewer and scriptwriter for BBC External Services.

He lived in London from the early 1950s until 1976.

Salkey received an honorary doctorate from Franklin Pierce College in 1981 and was a professor of creative writing at Hampshire College in Amherst, Massachusetts when he died in 1995.

BIBLIOGRAPHY

Earthquake. Illustrated by William Papas Roy. Oxford, 1968.

Jonah Simpson. Oxford, 1969.

Hurricane. Oxford, 1979.

Brother Anancy and Other Stories. Longman, 1993.

Serwadda, William Moses

(1931–)

The author was born in Kikwayi, Uganda. Serwadda, son of a Mukanja farmer from the shores of Lake Victoria, in central Africa, was on the faculty of the Department of Music and Dance at Makarerell in Kampala, Uganda. His popular biweekly television program of traditional African music for children received the highest rating. Highly regarded by the Ministry of Culture for his personal musical style, Serwadda was considered a model for his performance of traditional music. After Uganda won its independence in 1962, he traveled around the country training local clubs interested in preserving traditional music.

Serwadda has a master's degree in African studies from the University of Ghana. He has directed choirs in many festivals celebrating African music in his own country as well as Canada, the United States, and Europe. The songs and stories from his book, *Songs and Stories from Uganda,* come from his personal collection of folk material, much of which was acquired in childhood when he lived with his grandfather, an administrator appointed by the king of the Baganda.

BIBLIOGRAPHY

Songs and Stories from Uganda. Transcribed and edited by Hewitt Pantaleoni. Illustrated by Leo and Diane Dillon. Crowell, 1974.

See also Dillon, Leo

Shaik, Fatima

(1952–)

AUTHOR

"Fiction for children does not require different values than adult literature. Children face many of the same challenges as adults. But, unlike adults, children need access to a wide range of strategies for dealing with the world. Prime among them is the ability to recognize the positive in their environments."

Shaik was born in New Orleans, Louisiana, and was formally educated there until 1972. She attended Xavier University and in 1974 earned a bachelor's degree from Boston University. In 1978, she received a master's degree from New York University.

The books *Mardi Gras Day* and *The Jazz of Our Street* mark Shaik's debut as a children's writer. She had previously published an adult book called *The Mayor of New Orleans*. Her work has appeared in *Callaloo, Southern Review, Review of Contemporary Fiction* and *Double Dealer Redux*. She is included in the anthologies *Breaking Ice* and *African American Literature: The Mosaic Series*. *Melitte* was named an American Booksellers Pick of the List in the Fall of 1997.

The author is on the English Department faculty of Saint Peter's College in Jersey City, New Jersey, where she directs the Communication Program.

She lives in New York City and New Orleans, Louisiana, with her husband, painter James Little, and two children.

BIBLIOGRAPHY

Melitte. Dial, 1997.
The Jazz of Our Street. Dial, 1988.
Mardi Gras Day. Dial, 1998.

Sharp, S(aundra) Pearl

(1942-)

AUTHOR

Sharp was born in Cleveland, Ohio, into a family that celebrated the creative arts, and she has been expressing her creative talents for more than thirty years as actress, writer, publisher, producer, and filmmaker. She is the author of several nonfiction books and volumes of poetry. She performs her work on stage with other artists in *On the Sharp Side.*

As an undergraduate, Sharp began producing children's radio programs at Bowling Green State University and in Cleveland, Ohio. In New York City, she performed on the stage in *Black Girl, To Be Young, Gifted, and Black,* and the Broadway musical *Hello Dolly!* and made her film debut in Gordon Parks's classic *The Learning Tree.* She became a leading commercial spokeswoman, appearing in the first all-Black television commercial. Between acting jobs in 1974, she wrote the stage play *The Sistuhs,* which has been produced at theaters across the country.

In 1975, Sharp moved to Hollywood, where she starred in the television movies *Hollow Image* and *Minstrel Man* and played recurring roles on *St. Elsewhere, Knots Landing,* and other series. She established Poets Pay Rent, Too, which published author Robert Earl Price's *Blood Lines* and in 1989 *The Black History Film List.* As head writer for Voices, Incorporated, she has created more than 250 infomercials for Black radio, which include the series The Spirit in Us, Freedom's Journal, A Woman's Touch, and Look What They've Done to My Song. Her work has appeared in *Essence* and *Crisis* magazines and numerous anthologies. Sharp has produced, written and directed seven independent projects including *Life Is a Saxaphone* in 1985, a documentary on poet Kamau Daaood, *It's O.K. to Peek,* a women's health video, in 1995 and *Did You Lose Somebody?,* a documentary on The Middle Passage as expressed by visual artist Riva Akinshegun.

A volunteer literacy tutor and a Black women's health advocate, Sharp lives in Los Angeles, California.

BIBLIOGRAPHY

Black Women for Beginners. Illustrated by Beverly Hawkins Hall. Writers & Readers, 1993.

See also Hall, Beverly Hawkins

Shearer, John

(1947–)

AUTHOR, ILLUSTRATOR, PHOTOGRAPHER

Shearer was born in New York City and attended the Rochester Institute of Technology and the School of Visual Arts in New York City. His photography has been exhibited in numerous galleries, including IBM galleries in New York, the Metropolitan Museum of Art's exhibition *Harlem on My Mind,* and Eastman Kodak galleries. Shearer was a staff photographer for *Look* magazine in 1970 and *Life* magazine from 1971 to 1973 and taught journalism at Columbia University in 1975. He was president of Shearer Visuals in White Plains, New York, from 1980 to 1984. He produces films featuring characters Billy Jo Jive and Susie Sunset for the Public Broadcasting System's (PBS) *Sesame Street.*

Shearer has won more than twenty national awards, including a communications award in 1978 for *Super Private Eye: The Case of the Missing Ten Speed Bike,* and the Ceba Award, also in 1978, for his animated film, *Billy Jo Jive.* His *Billy Jo Jive* books, a mystery series for younger readers, are illustrated by his father, cartoonist Ted Shearer.

BIBLIOGRAPHY

I Wish I Had an Afro. Cowles, 1970.

Little Man in the Family. Delacorte, 1972.

Billy Jo Jive and the Case of the Missing Pigeons. Illustrated by Ted Shearer. Delacorte, 1978.

Billy Jo Jive and the Walkie Talkie Caper. Illustrated by Ted Shearer. Delacorte, 1981.

Billy Jo Jive and the Case of the Midnight Voices. Illustrated by Ted Shearer. Delacorte, 1982.

Sherlock, Sir Philip (Manderson)

(1902–)

AUTHOR

Sherlock was born in Jamaica and educated at the University of London as an external student, earning his bachelor's degree with first-class honors. He later received honorary Doctor of Laws degrees from the University of New Brunswick and Acadia University. He was vice chancellor of the West Indies and was named Knight Commander of the British Empire in 1968.

His memberships have included the Association of Caribbean Universities and Research Institutes, the Authors Guild, the National Liberal Club, and the West India Club.

BIBLIOGRAPHY

Anansi, the Spider Man. Illustrated by Marcia Brown. Crowell, 1954.

Three Finger Jack's Treasure. Illustrated by William Reeves. St. Martin, 1961.

West Indian Folk Tales. Illustrated by Joan Kiddell Monroe. Oxford, 1966.

The Iguana's Tail: Crick Crack Stories from the Caribbean. Illustrated by Gioia Fiammenghi. Crowell, 1969.

Ears and Tails and Common Sense: More Stories from the Caribbean. With daughter Hilary Sherlock. Illustrated by Aliki. Crowell, 1974.

Simmons, Alex(ander)

AUTHOR

Simmons was born and reared in New York City, and graduated from the New York High School of Art and Design, where he studied illustration and advertising. After several years working at CBS as a day-of-air logging coordinator, he turned to acting, appearing in Off-Off-Broadway theater productions, doing radio voice-overs and commercials, and working as a film extra. He has been an artist in residence at the Westco Children's Theater Company, the Creative Arts Team Conflict Resolution Theater Company, and the Westchester, New York, school system. He also has taught creative writing and acting.

Simmons has written and directed scripts for video and screen, including *If At First*, an educational drama on youth employment produced for national distribution by the Creative Arts Team, and scripts for radio, one of which won the Ohio State Award for Radio Drama. He has also written more than thirty songs, including "Stardust Lady," recorded by Noel Pointer for United Artists, and the song lyrics for several theater productions, as well as three adult plays: *Sherlock Holmes and the Hands of Othello, Starchild,* and *Once Upon a Miracle.* Simmons is working on an original sci-terror trilogy for Tor Books.

He is artistic director for the Bronx Creative Arts for Youth, a non-profit children's theatre arts organization, and lives in the Bronx, New York.

BIBLIOGRAPHY

The Cool Karate School. Troll, 1993.
Please Call Back. Steck-Vaughn, 1993.
Smoke. Steck-Vaughn, 1993.
Stolen Bases. Steck-Vaughn, 1993.

Terror Trail. Steck-Vaughn, 1993.

Ben Carson: Medicine Man. Steck-Vaughn, 1994.

John Lucas: The Come Back. Steck-Vaughn, 1994.

Denzel Washington. Steck-Vaughn, 1997.

Simmons, Ray

(1945–)

ILLUSTRATOR

Simmons received a diploma in advertising art from the Newark School of Fine and Advertising Art and successfully freelanced for twenty years as an illustrator and television storyboard artist. Advertising agencies he has worked with include Benton and Bowles; Cline, Davis and Mann; and J.W. Thompson.

In the latter 1980s, Simmons converted his knowledge of color, design, and composition from illustration to fine art. Among his awards are Best of Show in 1992 at the Glenridge Art Festival and a First-Place Art Award from the South Orange, New Jersey, Art League in 1991.

He lives in Cambria Heights, New York.

BIBLIOGRAPHY

Peekaboo, Baby! By Denise Lewis Patrick. Golden, 1996.

See also Patrick, Denise Lewis

Smalls, Irene

(1 9 5 0 –)

AUTHOR

"I never thought I would be a writer. I think I first became a writer in kinder-garten before I even knew it. I had a wonderful kindergarten teacher, who never read us stories with us sitting still. We sang the stories, we danced the stories, or we played games to the stories. I fell in love with the sounds of language, the music that I heard. My teacher read to us the poetry and stories of (Paul Laurence) Dunbar, James Weldon Johnson, (and others).

I always tell young children that all of my ideas come from the tip of my nose. There, right at the tip of my nose, was my young son Jonathan running and at the tip of my nose was my baby daughter, Dawn, who always woke up early in the morning. My first stories were about my children and growing up in Harlem. Writing is hard for me. I struggle. But I have found that I can write. I have become fascinated with the enslavement of African Americans."

The author was born in Harlem, New York, the oldest of four children. She was reared by her godmother, whom she credits with much of her success. That is one of the reasons she uses "I love you, Black Child" as one of the dedications in all of her books.

She attended New York public schools and graduated from Cornell University with a bachelor's degree in Black Studies and was active in the Black student movement. She also attended New York University and received a master's degree in marketing and behavioral science.

Irene and the Big, Fine Nickel, her first book, was reviewed in the *New York Times.* Her second book, *Jonathan and His Mommy,* was a Junior Literary Guild main selection and was televised on the Public Broadcasting System (PBS) reading show *Storytime. Dawn and the Round To-It* received a pointer review in *Kirkus Reviews.* The author of more than a dozen books, Smalls is also a former Miss Black New York State and Young Ambassador to Europe.

Irene Jennie and the Christmas Masquerade: The JOHNKANKUS won the Global Society Award in 1997 given by the International Reading Association. Smalls has signed a contract with WGBH Public Broadcasting Television to write four African American picture books about slavery to accompany the television series Africans in America to be broadcast in 1998. She will also have an Internet site www.melanet.com/JOHNKANKUS called "Roots of an African American Christmas" to be presented and updated each holiday season.

She lives in Boston, Massachusetts, and has three children, Dawn, Kevin Logan, and Jonathan.

BIBLIOGRAPHY

Irene and the Big, Fine Nickel. Illustrated by Tyrone Geter. Little, Brown, 1991.

Jonathan and His Mommy. Illustrated by Michael Hays. Little, Brown, 1992.

Dawn's Friends. Illustrated by Tyrone Geter. D.C. Heath, 1993.

Dawn and the Round To-It. Illustrated by Tyrone Geter. Simon & Schuster, 1994.

Alphabet Witch. Illustrated by Kevin McGovern. Longmeadow, 1995.

Ebony Sea. Illustrated by Jon O. Lockard. Longmeadow, 1995.

Father's Day Blues. Illustrated by Kevin McGovern. Longmeadow, 1995.

Beginning School. Illustrated by Toni Goffe. Silver Press, 1996.

Irene Jennie and the Christmas Masquerade: The JOHNKANKUS. Illustrated by Melodye Rosales. Little, Brown, 1996.

Jenny Reen and the Jack Muh Lantern on Halloween. Illustrated by Keinyo White. Atheneum, 1996.

Louise's Gift: Or What Did She Give Me That For? Illustrated by Colin Bootman. Little, Brown, 1996.

Jonathan and Kevin Are Lucky. Little, Brown, 1997.

Kevin and His Dad. Little, Brown, 1998.

Because You're Lucky. Illustrated by Michael Hays. Little, Brown, 1997.

A Strawbeater's Thanksgiving. Illustrated by Melodye Rosales. Little, Brown, 1998.

See also Dunbar, Paul Laurence; Geter, Tyrone; Johnson, James Weldon: Rosales, Melodye

Steptoe, John (Lewis)

(1950–1989)

AUTHOR, ILLUSTRATOR

Steptoe was born in Brooklyn, New York, attended the New York High School of Art and Design, and studied with painter Norman Lewis. Recognition of his talents began with his first published book, *Stevie,* written and illustrated when he was sixteen years old.

Among his awards are the Society of Illustrators Gold Medal in 1970, the Coretta Scott King Award in 1982 and 1988, the Irma Simonton Black Award from Bank Street College in New York City in 1975, Caldecott Honor Book Awards in 1985 and 1988, and the Boston Globe-Horn Book Award in 1987.

BIBLIOGRAPHY

Stevie. Harper, 1969.

Uptown. Harper, 1970.

Train Ride. Harper, 1971.

All Us Come Cross the Water. By Lucille Clifton. Holt, 1973.

My Special Best Words. Viking, 1974.

She Come Bringing Me That Little Baby Girl. By Eloise Greenfield. Lippincott, 1974.

Marcia. Viking, 1976.

Daddy Is a Monster . . . Sometimes. Lothrop, 1980.

Mother Crocodile = Maman–Caiman. By Birago Diop. Translated and adapted by Rosa Guy. Delacorte, 1981.

OUTside/INside: Poems. By Arnold Adoff. Lothrop, 1981.

All the Colors of the Race: Poems. By Arnold Adoff. Lothrop, 1982.

Jeffrey Bear Cleans Up His Act. Lothrop, 1983.

The Story of Jumping Mouse: A Native American Legend. Lothrop, 1984.

Mufaro's Beautiful Daughters: An African Tale. Lothrop, 1987.

Baby Says. Lothrop, 1988.

Birthday. Holt, 1991.

Creativity. Illustrated by E.B. Lewis. Clarion, 1997.

See also Clifton, (Thelma) Lucille (Sayles); Diop, Birago (Ismael); Greenfield, Eloise (Glynn Little); Guy, Rosa (Cuthbert)

Stewart, Ruth Ann

(1942–)

AUTHOR

"In writing Portia, *it was my intention to tell the story, in an interesting and lively manner, of a talented, courageous woman whose life also provided a previously unknown perspective on an important chapter in African American history. I wanted the results to be enjoyable to both young adult and adult readers and to stimulate their interest in delving further into Black history, especially Black women's history. It is my belief that far too little has been written about the Black middle-class woman and the important role she has played as both a mainstay of Black family life and an accomplished member of a variety of professions.*

Even though Portia was the daughter of a famous man, her career aspirations and personal struggles are common to the stories yet to be written of many Black women. Through further scholarship into the rich mine of human lore posed by African American life, and with the encouragement of an alert and interested reading public, it is my hope that this literary shortcoming will be vigorously addressed and there will be many Portias (including a few more of mine) taking their place on the shelves of libraries and bookstores in the near future."

Stewart was born in Chicago, Illinois, where she attended the University of Chicago in 1961–1962. She completed her undergraduate studies at Wheaton College in Massachusetts with a bachelor of arts degree in 1963. She earned a master's degree from Columbia University and took courses at Harvard University in 1974 and at the Kennedy School of Government in 1987.

Her book, *Portia: The Life of Portia Washington Pittman, the Daughter of Booker T. Washington,* was cited as a Coretta Scott King Honor Book in 1978. She also received an International Council of Museums fellowship.

She has been a member of Library Visiting Committees at Harvard University and the Massachusetts Institute of Technology (MIT), the board of visitors at the University of Pittsburgh School of Library and Information Science, the board of trustees at Wheaton College and the Council on Foreign Relations, and the District of Columbia Historical Records Advisory Board.

She lives in Washington, D.C.

BIBLIOGRAPHY

Portia: The Life of Portia Washington Pittman, the Daughter of Booker T. Washington. Doubleday, 1977.

Strickland, Dorothy S(alley)

(1933–)

AUTHOR

Strickland was born in Newark, New Jersey. She received a bachelor's degree from Newark State College (now Kean College of New Jersey) and master's and doctoral degrees from New York University. She has served on the faculties of Kean College and Jersey City State College and has worked in the New Jersey public schools as a classroom teacher and as a reading consultant and learning-disabilities specialist.

She has published more than 100 items, including books and articles in major educational journals, and was a member of the commission from 1983 to 1985 that prepared the report for educators and the general public, *Becoming a Nation of Readers*.

She has held elective office in both the National Council of Teachers of English and the International Reading Association, of which she is a past president, and serves on numerous state and national advisory boards.

The recipient of a National Council of Teachers of English award for research and an International Reading Association's Outstanding Teacher Educator of Reading, she has also received a Distinguished Alumnus Award from New York University, an Outstanding Alumnus Award from Kean College, and an honorary doctorate of humane letters from Bank Street College. Elected into the Reading Hall of Fame, Strickland is a member of five honorary societies and included in various listings of *Who's Who*.

Strickland, the mother of author Michael R. Strickland, lives in Orange, New Jersey, and is a Professor of Reading, Rutgers University Graduate School of Education.

BIBLIOGRAPHY

Listen Children: An Anthology of Black Literature. Illustrated by Leo and Diane Dillon. Bantam, 1982.

Families: Poems Celebrating the African American Experience. Edited with Michael R. Strickland. Illustrated by John Ward. Boyds Mills, 1994.

See also Dillon, Leo; Strickland, Michael R.; Ward, John (Clarence)

Strickland, Michael R(aymond)

(1965–)

AUTHOR

"I've wanted to be a writer since I was old enough to understand what writing was. I remember teaching myself to write in my parents' basement. Our house was full of these wonderful things called books. My mother and father and older brothers were always very excited about books. I was literally tripping over them. I wanted to be able to do this myself—this thing called reading and writing. As a preschooler, I would run my fingers across pages of books. I would draw letters, words, and figures on a green chalkboard. Today, as a scholar of English education, I know that when I scribbled and when I turned pages, I was reading and writing. I was literate. It was the start of a process that has developed me into the writer I am now. I don't believe there is enough literature for African American children that is written by males, young and old. I hope I can be an inspiration to other men to break into the field. Women are well represented, and there are many great, Black male illustrators. But we have a huge dearth of male writers."

The author was born in Newark, New Jersey. His first book, the critically acclaimed *Poems That Sing to You,* is an anthology of fifty-five poems. Michael collaborated with his mother, Dorothy S. Strickland of Rutgers University, on another anthology, *Families: Poems Celebrating the African American Experience.*

Strickland was a Paul Robeson Fellow of the Institute for Arts and Humanities Education in 1993–1994. He is a poetry consultant to Literacy Place, the first core reading program of Scholastic, and he is a trustee of the Maurice R. Robinson Fund, a foundation that provides grants to grass-roots projects that directly affect the lives of children. Strickland holds a bachelor's degree in communications from Cornell University and earned a master of arts degree in corporate and public communication from Seton Hall University. He works closely with Bernice Cullinan of New York University, a widely influential scholar in children's literature, and he teaches writing at Jersey City State College.

Strickland lives in West Orange, New Jersey.

BIBLIOGRAPHY

Poems That Sing to You. Illustrated by Alan Leiner. Edited by Michael R. Strickland. Boyds Mills, 1993.

Families: Poems Celebrating the African American Experience. Edited with Dorothy Strickland. Illustrated by John Ward. Boyds Mills, 1994.

African American Poets: Guardians of a Culture. Enslow, 1996.

Encylopedia of African American Literature. ABC-CLIO, 1996.

My Own Song: And Other Poems to Groove To. Illustrated by Eric Sabee. Selected by Michael Strickland. Boyds Mills, 1997.

Another Haircut at Sleepy Sam's. Illustrated by Keaf Holliday. Boyds Mills, 1998.

See also Strickland, Dorothy S.; Ward, John (Clarence)

Stroud, Bettye M(oore)

AUTHOR, PHOTOGRAPHER

Stroud is a native of Athens, Georgia. She attended public schools in Athens and developed a love of books and reading at an early age. She graduated from Fort Valley State College with a degree in English and a minor in library science. Opting to become a library media specialist, Stroud studied at the University of Georgia, receiving both master's and education-specialist degrees.

Her work in elementary schools provided Stroud with a rewarding career, bringing children and good books together. She received grants from the Southeastern Advocates of Literature for Children and the Georgia Council for the Arts to further her work.

Stroud has been appointed to, and serves on, several education and library committees and boards and has helped shape the future of school media centers in her state. She reviews children's books for *Multicultural Review* and contributes articles to regional and national magazines and newspapers. Her work received an award at the Sandhills Writers Conference in 1993. She is a retired elementary school library media specialist.

A full-time writer, Stroud lives in Athens, Georgia.

BIBLIOGRAPHY

Down Home at Miss Dessa's. Illustrated by Felicia Marshall. Lee & Low, 1996.
Dance Y'All. Illustrated by Cornelius Van Wright and Ying-Hwa Hu. Cavendish, 1998.

Sutherland, Efua
(Theodora Morgue)

(1924–1996)

AUTHOR

"What we cannot buy is the spirit of originality and endeavor which makes a people dynamic and creative."

Born in Cape Coast, Ghana, Sutherland, whose middle and maiden names were Theodora Morgue, was a native of Ghana, a founder of the Ghana Society of Writers, the Ghana Drama Studio, Ghana Experimental Theater, and a community project called the Kodzidan (the story house). She studied at St. Monica's College, Cambridge, England, and the School of Oriental and African Studies at the University of London. She was a research fellow in literature and drama at the Institute of African Studies, University of Ghana, and was a cofounder of *Okyeame* magazine.

Sutherland published widely in her native land, and her work has been included in short-story anthologies in the United States. She taught school from 1951 to 1954 and in 1954 married African American William Sutherland. They had three children and lived in Ghana. Sutherland, best known for her work as a cultural visionary, was living in Ghana when she died in 1996.

BIBLIOGRAPHY

Playtime in Africa. Photographs by Willis E. Bell. Atheneum, 1962.

Tadjo, Veronique

(1 9 5 5 –)

AUTHOR, ILLUSTRATOR

"I write children's books because it is important for children to get plenty of the right reading material, which is going to help them shape their personality. Black children in this respect are not sufficiently provided for. It is my belief that Black writers should write more books of quality for the young readership. There is a need for positive images of Black people from the past and present. I am also interested in promoting African culture and introducing it to children with different experiences. It is a way of preparing them for a more sophisticated view of the world."

The author is from the Côte d'Ivoire (Ivory Coast) in West Africa, but was born in Paris, France. Tadjo received her bachelor's degree from the University of Abidjan in 1980, a master's degree in 1981 and a doctorate in 1983 from the Sorbonne in Paris. Her father is the auditor general in the Côte d'Ivoire and her mother, a painter and sculptor.

Tadjo's book *Lord of the Dance: An African Retelling* appeared at the Twenty-Fourth Exhibition of Original Pictures of Children's Books in Japan in the summer of 1988. *Mammy Water and the Monster* won the UNICEF (United Nations Children's Fund) Prize in 1993 at the Biennale des Arts et des Lettres du Sénégal. It was also singled out for honorable mention for the 1994 Noma Award for publishing in Africa.

Tadjo became enamored with the culture of the Senufo people of the northern part of the Côte d'Ivoire after teaching there for three years. At a wedding in England, she first heard the hymn "Lord of the Dance," which reminded her of the masks the Senufo people carve for special celebrations. It inspired her to write her book of the same title.

Tadjo is a member of the Ecological Movement of the Ivory Coast and lives in Nairobi, Kenya.

BIBLIOGRAPHY

Lord of the Dance: An African Retelling. Lippincott, 1989.

The Song of Life (La Chanson de la Vie). Hatier-Ceda (France), 1989.

The Magic Grain of Corn (Le Grain de Mais Magique). N.E.I. (Ivory Coast), 1993.

Mammy Water and the Monster (Mamy Wata et le Monstre). N.E.I. (Ivory Coast), 1993.

Tarry, Ellen

(1906–)

AUTHOR

Tarry was born in Birmingham, Alabama. After her arrival in New York City, she joined the Writers Workshop at Bank Street College. The Writers Workshop was the brainchild of Lucy Sprague Mitchell, the progressive educator and founder of Bank Street College. Tarry's book *My Dog Rinty*, which grew out of a collaboration with children's author Marie Hall Ets, was popular because of its portrayal of Harlem, New York, in the 1940s. She worked in New York City as an intergroup relations specialist with the Department of Housing and Urban Development.

Tarry lives in New York City.

BIBLIOGRAPHY

Janie Bell. Illustrated by Myrtle Sheldon. Garden City, 1940.

Katharine Drexel, Friend of the Neglected. Illustrated by Donald Bolognese. Farrar, Straus & Cudahy, 1958.

Martin dePorres, Saint of the New World. Illustrated by James Fox. Farrar Straus, 1963.

My Dog Rinty. With Marie Hall Ets. Illustrated by Alexander and Alexandra Alland. Viking, 1946, (1965).

The Runaway Elephant. Illustrated by Oliver Herrington. Viking, 1950.

Young Jim: The Early Years of James Weldon Johnson. Dodd, 1967.

Tate, Eleanora E(laine)

(1948–)

AUTHOR

Tate was born in Canton, Missouri, and raised by her grandmother. She graduated from Roosevelt High School in Des Moines, Iowa, and received a bachelor's degree in journalism with a news-editorial specialty from Drake University in 1973.

Her first poem was published when she was sixteen years old. She started her career as a news reporter and news editor in Des Moines and Jackson, Tennessee. In 1981, Tate received a fellowship in children's literature for the Bread Loaf Writers Conference in Middlebury, Vermont, and in 1982 she completed five weeks' travel and research in selected ethnic folk and fairy tales in West Germany, France, and Florence and Collodi, Italy.

The Secret of Gumbo Grove, the first of her Carolina trilogy of books set in the Carolinas, was named a Parent's Choice Gold Seal Award winner. The second book, *Thank You Dr. Martin Luther King, Jr.!,* was named a National Council for the Social Studies-Children's Book of the Year and *A Blessing in Disguise,* the third book, was named an American Bookseller "Pick of the List." Her book *Just an Overnight Guest* became the basis for a film of the same name produced by Phoenix Films of New York, starring Richard Roundtree and Rosalind Cash. It was named to the Selected Films for Young Adults 1985 List by the Youth Services Committee of the American Library Association. It also aired on PBS's Wonderworks Series and on the Nickelodeon Children's Television Network.

Tate is also a journalist and publicist. With her husband, noted photographer Zack E. Hamlet, III, she was co-owner for ten years of Positive Images, a small award-winning public relations company in Myrtle Beach, South Carolina.

She is a former national president of the National Association of Black Storytellers, and a former president of the Horry County South Carolina Arts Council. She helped to design and implement its Arts in Education Program.

Tate has spoken widely on children's literature and has been a frequent speaker in elementary schools, libraries, and conferences around the country over the years of her long career, including the International Black Writers Conference, Chicago Illinois, the Broadside Press Festival of Poets in Detroit, Michigan, the National Council of Teachers of English National Conference, and was the keynote speaker at the Fifth Regional Caribbean Conference of the International Reading Association (IRA) in Hamilton Bermuda.

Memberships include the Twin Rivers Reading Council of the International Reading Association (IRA), the National Council of Teachers of English; and the North Carolina Writers Network.

Tate and her husband live in Morehead City, North Carolina. They have one daughter, Gretchen.

BIBLIOGRAPHY

The Secret of Gumbo Grove. Watts, 1987.
Thank You, Dr. Martin Luther King, Jr.! Watts, 1990.
Front Porch Stories at the One-Room School. Bantam, 1992.
Retold African Myths. Perfection Learning Corporation, 1993.
A Blessing in Disguise. Delacorte, 1995.
Don't Split the Pole. Delacorte, 1997.
Just an Overnight Guest. Just Us Books, 1997.

Taylor, Mildred D.

(1 9 4 3 –)

AUTHOR

Taylor's first book, *Song of the Trees,* won the Council on Interracial Books for Children competition, was voted an outstanding book of 1975 by the *New York Times,* and in 1976 was named a Children's Book Showcase book. *Roll of Thunder, Hear My Cry* won the Newbery Medal in 1977 and a nomination for the National Book Award; it also was a 1977 Coretta Scott King Honor Book.

Taylor's Logan-family trilogy ended with *Let the Circle Be Unbroken* in 1981. This title was a 1982 American Book Award nominee and a Coretta Scott King Award winner. It was also listed among the American Library Association's Best Books for Young Adults in 1981. Taylor has also won Coretta Scott King Awards for *The Road to Memphis* in 1991 and *The Friendship* in 1988. The latter book received a Boston Globe-Horn Book Award that same year.

Taylor lives in Boulder, Colorado.

BIBLIOGRAPHY

Song of the Trees. Illustrated by Jerry Pinkney. Dial, 1975.
Roll of Thunder, Hear My Cry. Dial, 1976.
Let the Circle Be Unbroken. Dial, 1981.
The Gold Cadillac. Illustrated by Michael Hays. Dial, 1987.
The Friendship. Illustrated by Max Ginsburg. Dial, 1987.
The Road to Memphis. Dial, 1989.
Mississippi Bridge. Illustrated by Max Ginsburg. Dial, 1990.
The Well: David's Story. Dial, 1995.

See also Pinkney, Jerry

Thomas, Anika D(awn)

(1976–)

AUTHOR

"Inspired by my Mom, I wrote Life in the Ghetto *when I was thirteen years old for a contest of writers and illustrators. I entered it and won the grand prize out of over 7,500 entries. I wrote down things about my life that I wanted everyone to read. I was so lonely and desperately wanted a friend. Outside of my family, I had no friends, only enemies. I am a different person now. I enjoy traveling to different cities and states, talking to school and college students about my life as in my book. I graduated high school in June 1995 and started college in Pittsburgh, Pennsylvania. My life has had a turn-about over the years . . . one I am very pleased with."*

Thomas was born in Pittsburgh, Pennsylvania. Her first children's book received national attention, including public appearances on a television talk show hosted by Julian Bond, a former member of the House of Representatives in the United States Congress, and ABC's *Good Morning, America,* as well as profiles on local television stations. She has been featured in numerous magazines, among them *Mega-New York, National Geography World, Faith 'N Stuff, Jet, Boomerrang,* and *Teaching Tolerance.*

Special recognitions and proclamations have been presented by Mayor Cathy Chanler in Kent, Ohio, and by the City of Pittsburgh. A certificate of achievement was presented in 1990 by the Pittsburgh Public School Board of Education, and in 1991 she received a letter of recognition from then President George Bush and his wife, Barbara. In 1992, Pennsylvania State University and the Catholic library assistant, Bishop M. Vincent, honored Thomas with a certificate of outstanding achievement.

Her book is required reading in the third and fourth grades in Pennsylvania schools.

She lives in Pittsburgh, Pennsylvania.

BIBLIOGRAPHY

Life in the Ghetto. Landmark, 1990.

Thomas, Dawn C.

AUTHOR

Thomas is a teacher who was actively involved in the social issues of her New Jersey community. Some of her childhood experiences in Barbados, Harlem, New York, and Brooklyn, New York, can be found in her books. She lives in Brooklyn, New York.

BIBLIOGRAPHY

A Tree for Tompkins Park. Illustrated by Leo Carty. McGraw-Hill, 1971.
A Bicycle from Bridgetown. Illustrated by Don Miller. McGraw-Hill, 1975.
Kai: A Mission for Her Village (Girlhood Journey Series). Illustrated by Vanessa D. Holley. Simon & Schuster, 1996.

See also Carty, Leo; Holley, Vanessa D.; Miller, Don

Thomas, Ianthe

$(1951-)$

AUTHOR

Thomas was a nursery school teacher, worked in children's theater, and developed educational curricula. She studied sculpture at the Universidad de Coimbra in Portugal and has exhibited her wrought-iron and milled-steel pieces in one-woman shows. Her books are noted for their use of Black speech patterns and focus on personal relationships.

She lives in New York City.

BIBLIOGRAPHY

Lordy Aunt Hattie. Illustrated by Thomas Di Grazia. Harper, 1973.
Walk Home Tired, Billy Jenkins. Harper, 1974.
Eliza's Daddy. Illustrated by Moneta Barnett. Harcourt, 1976.
My Street's a Morning Cool Street. Illustrated by Emily A. McCully. Harper, 1976.
Hi, Mrs. Mallory! Illustrated by Ann Toulmin-Rothe. Harper, 1979.
Willie Blows a Mean Horn. Illustrated by Ann Toulmin-Rothe. Harper, 1981.

See also Barnett, Moneta

Thomas, Joyce Carol

(1938–)

AUTHOR

Thomas was born in Ponca City, Oklahoma, one of nine children. She recalls picking cotton as a child. As an adult, she worked as a telephone operator by day while attending night classes and raising her children. She earned her bachelor's degree in Spanish at San Jose State University and her master's degree in education from Stanford University.

She has received many awards for her books, including the 1982 and 1983 Djerassi Fellowship for Creative Artists at Stanford University, the 1983 National Book Award, and the 1983 Before Columbus American Book Award for her first novel, *Marked by Fire*. In addition, *Marked by Fire* was named a 1982 Best Book by the Young Adult Services Division of the American Library Association and cited as one of the Outstanding Books of the Year in 1982 by the *New York Times*.

Thomas subsequently published additional novels, including *Bright Shadow*, which won a Coretta Scott King Honor Book Award in 1984, *Water Girl*, *The Golden Pasture*, and *Journey*. The multicultural anthology *A Gathering of Flowers: Stories About Being Young in America*, which she edited, received a Best Book for Young Adults Award from *Voya* in 1990 and was honored as the Millionth Acquisition of the University of California at Santa Cruz Library Special Collections in 1991.

Her sixth novel, *When the Nightingale Sings*, won the Kentucky Blue Grass Award in 1994. Her picture-book collection of poems, *Brown Honey in Broomwheat Tea*, won a Coretta Scott King Honor Book Award, a Kentucky Blue Grass Award, a Notable Children's Book Award by the National Trade Council for Social Studies, and a listing by the National Conference of Christians and Jews, all in 1994.

Thomas taught at San Jose State University, the University of California at Santa Cruz, and Purdue University. She retired as a full professor of English at the University of Tennessee, Knoxville, where she taught creative writing. Thomas is a member of the Dramatists Guild and the Authors Guild.

She lives and writes full time in Berkeley, California, near her children and grandchildren, to whom she often dedicates her books.

BIBLIOGRAPHY

Marked by Fire. Avon, 1982.

Bright Shadow. Avon, 1983.

The Golden Pasture. Scholastic, 1986.

Water Girl. Avon, 1986.

Journey. Scholastic, 1989.

A Gathering of Flowers: Stories About Being Young in America. Harper, 1990.

When the Nightingale Sings. Trophy, 1994.

Gingerbread Days. Illustrated by Floyd Cooper. HarperCollins, 1995.

Brown Honey in Broomwheat Tea. Illustrated by Floyd Cooper. HarperCollins, 1993, 1996.

The Blacker the Berry: Poems. Illustrated by Brenda Joysmith. HarperCollins, 1997.

Crowning Glory. Illustrated by Brenda Joysmith. HarperCollins, 1998.

I Have Heard of a Land. Illustrated by Floyd Cooper. HarperCollins, 1998.

See also Cooper, Floyd (Donald)

Turner, Glennette Tilley

(1933–)

AUTHOR

Turner was born in Raleigh, North Carolina. Growing up, she loved to read and listen to stories—especially family stories and stories about people who overcame obstacles. She majored in English at Lake Forest College in Illinois. While there, she entered a nationwide college competition, and her poem was selected for publication in an anthology. Later, she earned a master's degree in history and juvenile literature from Goddard College in Vermont.

An elementary school teacher in the Chicago area for almost twenty-five years, she has written for such publications as *Ebony Jr., Scholastic Scope,* and *Black Child Journal.* She served as consulting and contributing editor for an issue of *Cobblestone* magazine, She has stories or articles in *Open Court, Scott Foresman, Encyclopedia Britannica,* Simon & Schuster, and *Scholastic* educational materials, among others.

Turner has had a longtime fascination with the Underground Railroad in U.S. history, which helped Black slaves escape to freedom, and is a recognized authority on its operation in the Midwest. She was an adviser to the National Park Service on the subject and discussed it during an interview on the Lincoln-Douglas Debates on the C-SPAN cable network. She also served as a consultant to NBC News on a special that featured Harriet Tubman, an escaped Black slave who was one of the major "conductors" on the Underground Railroad.

Turner's work has been reviewed in numerous publications, including the *New York Times Book Review,* the *Christian Science Monitor, Publishers Weekly, Booklist,* and *School Library Journal.* She is a Road Scholar for the Illinois Humanities Council and often speaks on the Underground Railroad and the people she has profiled in her writing.

Retired from public school teaching in 1988, she is on the editorial board of *Black Child Journal* and presents discussions and workshops for students of all ages, teachers, and members of historical societies and other organizations. Her honors in this field include being named Outstanding Woman Educator in DuPage County, Illinois, and being cited by the Illinois General Assembly for excellence in teaching. She is a past president of Children's Reading Roundtable of Chicago and the Black Literary Umbrella.

Turner contributed an essay "Nana" to *In Praise of Our Fathers and Mothers* and a biographical sketch of Bessie Coleman to be included in the forthcoming *Encyclopedia of Chicago Area Women*.

She has been recognized as a writer by Illinois Reading Association, International Black Writers Conference, Illinois Young Authors Conference and is the recipient of the Margaret Landon Award.

Turner lives in Wheaton, Illinois.

BIBLIOGRAPHY

Surprise for Mrs. Burns. Illustrated by Dan Siculan. Whitman, 1971.
The Underground Railroad in DuPage County, Illinois. Newman, 1981, 1984.
Take a Walk in Their Shoes. Illustrated by Elton C. Fax. Cobblehill, 1989.
Lewis Howard Latimer. Silver Burdett, 1990.
Make and Keep Family Memories. Newman, 1990.
Running for Our Lives. Illustrated by Samuel Byrd. Holiday House, 1994.
Follow in Their Footsteps. Cobblehill, 1997.
The Underground Railroad in Illinois. Newman, 1998.

See also Fax, Elton C.

Vertreace, Martha M(odena)

(1945–)

AUTHOR

"I consider myself to primarily be a poet, although I have published short stories and articles as well. My influences have come mostly from contemporary poets. The lack which I perceive in the realm of literature for Black children is that there seem to be few books which are Black but without an Afrocentric perspective. The lives which children lead are simply not African, primarily. I do not believe that ignoring other ways of being in the world is beneficial for children."

Vertreace was born in Washington, D.C., and has earned four Illinois Arts Council Literary Awards and an Illinois Arts Council fellowship, as well as the 1987 award for Excellence in Professional Writing from the Illinois Association for Teachers of English and a Creative Writing Fellowship from the National Endowment for the Arts. Vertreace is the *Glendora Review* Poet in Lagos, Nigeria and has earned five Pushcart nominations. Gwendolyn Brooks presented her with the Significant Illinois Poet Award, which Brooks established.

Vertreace was a fellow at the Hawthornden International Writers' Retreat in Lasswade, Midlothian, Scotland, for four weeks. Eastern Washington University, Cheney, chose her as poetry fellow when she was in residence at the Writers Center in Dublin, Ireland in 1993.

Her poem "Song of God's People" was set to music by Tom Weisflog and performed in 1994 at St. Thomas the Apostle Catholic Church's quasquicentennial celebration in Chicago, Illinois, with choir and organ.

She is the distinguished professor of English and poet-in-residence at Kennedy-King College in Chicago, Illinois, where she lives.

BIBLIOGRAPHY

Kelly in the Mirror. Illustrated by Sandra Speidel. Whitman, 1993.

See also Brooks, Gwendolyn

Walker, Alice

(1 9 4 4 –)

AUTHOR

Walker was born in Eatonton, Georgia. She attended Spelman College in Atlanta, Georgia, and graduated in 1965 from Sarah Lawrence College in Bronxville, New York.

Walker was a social-service caseworker for the New York City Welfare Department, a teacher of Black literature at Jackson State College in Mississippi from 1968 to 1969, and writer in residence at Tougaloo College in Mississippi from 1969 to 1970. She also designed a course on Black women writers, first taught at Wellesley College and later at the University of Massachusetts.

Among her awards are the Charles Merrill Writing Fellowship in 1967–1968, the National Foundation for the Arts Award in Fiction in 1969–1970, and the Rosenthal Award of the National Institute of Arts and Letters in 1973. In 1983, she won the American Book Award and the Pulitzer Prize for Fiction for *The Color Purple,* a novel for adults. She also won the O. Henry Award in 1986 for her short story "Kindred Spirits."

Walker has been a contributing editor to *Southern Voices, Freedomways,* and *Ms.* magazine and is cofounder, in 1984, of Wild Trees Press in Navarro, California.

Walker was married for ten years to Civil Rights lawyer Mel Leventhal. She has a daughter, Rebecca Grant, and lives on a ranch in Navarro, California.

BIBLIOGRAPHY

Langston Hughes: American Poet. Illustrated by Don Miller. Crowell, 1974.
To Hell with Dying. Illustrated by Catherine Deeter. Harcourt, 1988.
Finding the Green Stone. Illustrated by Catherine Deeter. Harcourt, 1991.

See also Miller, Don

Walter, Mildred Pitts

(1 9 2 2 -)

AUTHOR

"My greatest joy is when I see a Black child light up when finally there is comprehension that I am the writer, a part of the creation of a book. My having done it, seems to say to him/her, 'She did it, I can, too.'"

Walter was born in DeRidder, Louisiana. She is the widow of Earl Lloyd Walter, a social worker and civil-rights activist, and the mother of two sons, Earl Lloyd, Jr., and Craig Allen Walter. She received her bachelor's degree in English from Southern University. Further studies took her to California and the Antioch Extension in Denver, Colorado, where she received her master's degree in education.

She has been a teacher in the Los Angeles Unified School District, a consultant at Western Interstate Commission of Higher Education in Boulder, Colorado, and a consultant, teacher, and lecturer at Metro State College. Since 1969, she has devoted most of her time to writing.

Walter has traveled throughout the United States and to China and Africa, where in 1977 she was a delegate to the Second World Black and African Festival of the Arts and Culture at Lagos, Nigeria. Out of her experiences and interviews with people during the civil rights crisis in Little Rock, Arkansas, in the 1950s grew the ideas for one of her books, *The Girl on the Outside*.

Her book *Mississippi Challenge* won a 1993 Coretta Scott King Honor Book Award, as did *Trouble's Child* in 1986 and *Because We Are* in 1984. In 1987, she was presented the Coretta Scott King Award for *Justin and the Best Biscuits in the World*.

Walter lives in Denver, Colorado.

BIBLIOGRAPHY

Ty's One Man Band. Illustrated by Margot Tomes. Four Winds, 1980.
The Girl on the Outside. Lothrop, 1982.
Because We Are. Lothrop, 1983.
My Mama Needs Me. Illustrated by Pat Cummings. Lothrop, 1983.
Brother to the Wind. Illustrated by Leo and Diane Dillon. Lothrop, 1985.
Trouble's Child. Lothrop, 1985.
Justin and the Best Biscuits in the World. Lothrop, 1986.
Mariah Loves Rock. Illustrated by Pat Cummings. Bradbury, 1988.
Have a Happy. . . . Illustrated by Carole Byard. Lothrop, 1989.
Mariah Keeps Cool. Illustrated by Pat Cummings. Bradbury, 1990.
Two and Too Much. Illustrated by Pat Cummings. Bradbury, 1990.
Mississippi Challenge. Bradbury, 1992.
Darkness. Illustrated by Marcia Jameson. Simon & Schuster, 1995.
Kwanzaa: A Family Affair. Illustrated by Cheryl Carrington. Lothrop, 1995.
Second Daughter: The Story of a Slave Girl. Scholastic, 1996.

See also Byard, Carole; Cummings, Pat; Dillon, Leo

Walton, Darwin McBeth

(1 9 2 6 –)

AUTHOR

"My writing is based on my belief that children must be aided in establishing confidence in themselves and what they can become, provided they understand the laws of the consequences of their behavior. Too many children think they can't; consequently, they don't try to succeed in school. I want to help change that kind of thinking, to help them realize that nothing worth having comes or stays without effort—love or clean air—that we are what we think, say, and do."

Walton was born in Charlotte, North Carolina, just before the Great Depression. Having learned to defend herself in school at an early age, Walton generally writes about reconciliation and tolerance, demonstrating that being different is not bad. Her book *What Color Are You?* was first published in 1973 at a time when few books contained pictures or stories about minority children.

Walton has a bachelor of science degree from the Chicago Conservatory College of Music and a master's degree from National Louis University in Evanston, Illinois. She has taught both in elementary and junior high schools in Chicago and Elmhurst, Illinois, and at the National Louis University Graduate School of Education.

She is a founding member of Phi Delta Kappa, National College Chapter; a life member of Sigma Alpha Iota international music fraternity; president of the Black Literacy Umbrella; a board member of the Children's Reading Round Table; a past president of the Du Page City NAACP (National Association for the Advancement of Colored People) Women's Auxiliary; and clerk on the executive board of the York Center Church of Brethren.

BIBLIOGRAPHY

What Color Are You? Illustrated by Hal A. Franklin. Revised Edition. Johnson, 1985.

Bookworms Are Made, Not Born. Jadar Jr., 1987.

The Mayor Who Conquered Chicago. Path, 1990.

Dance Kayla. Whitman, 1997.

Ward, John (Clarence)

(1 9 6 3 –)

ILLUSTRATOR

Ward was born in Brooklyn, New York, and received a bachelor of fine arts degree from the School of Visual Arts in New York City.

He has received the Rhodes Family Award for Outstanding Achievement in Media Arts from the School of Visual Arts and the Parents Choice Award in 1995 for his children's book *Poppa's New Pants*. His work has been exhibited by the Society of Illustrators in New York City and appeared in *Communication Arts Illustration Annual* in 1987, *Print Magazine's Regional Design Annual* in 1989, and the *Society of Illustrators Thirty-Second Annual* in 1990. The book *Poppa's New Pants* received the 1995 Parent's Choice Award.

He is married and lives in Freeport, New York.

BIBLIOGRAPHY

The Adventures of High John, the Conqueror. By Steve Sanfield. Orchard, 1989.
We Keep a Store. By Anne Shelby. Orchard, 1990.
The Car Washing Street. By Denise Lewis Patrick. Tambourine, 1993.
Families: Poems Celebrating the African American Experience. Edited by Dorothy S. Strickland and Michael R. Strickland. Boyds Mills, 1994.
Fire Flies for Nathan. By Shulamith Levey Oppenheim. Tambourine, 1994.
The Freedom Riddle. By Angela Shelf Medearis. Lodestar, 1995.
Poppa's New Pants. By Angela Shelf Medearis. Holiday House, 1995.
Kente Colors! By Debbi Chocolate. Walker, 1996.
The Seven Days of Kwanzaa: A Holiday Step Book. By Ella Grier. Viking, 1997.
Poppa's Itchy Christmas. By Angela Shelf Medearis. Holiday House, 1998.

See also Chocolate, Debbi [Deborah Mique Newton]; Medearis, Angela Shelf; Patrick, Denise Lewis; Strickland, Dorothy S.; Strickland, Michael R.

Watson, Richard J(esse)

(1946–)

ILLUSTRATOR

Watson was born in Badin, North Carolina. Spending his early years in a rural setting, he developed an active imagination, often occupying himself with fantasies of flying and soaring like the eagles. The younger of two boys, he learned to draw from his older brother.

During his teen years, he moved to Philadelphia, Pennsylvania, and attended art classes at a community settlement house. As he was introduced to oil painting and other mediums of expression, his commitment became solidified and after graduation from Benjamin Franklin High School in Philadelphia, he entered the Pennsylvania Academy of the Fine Arts, receiving a degree in painting in 1968.

Since then, Watson has exhibited work in major museums and galleries throughout the United States. An African American artist, muralist, and portrait painter, he gives lectures on African American art, poetry, and musical renditions to audiences of all ages and also has illustrated books, covers, and articles.

Watson lives in Philadelphia, Pennsylvania, where he has served as director of exhibitions for the Afro-American Historical and Cultural Museum since 1990. He is married and the father of two sons and one daughter.

BIBLIOGRAPHY

The High Rise Glorious Skittle Skat Roarious Sky Pie Angel Food Cake. By Nancy Willard. Harcourt, 1990.

Nadanda, the Wordmaker. By Vivian W. Owens. Eschar, 1994.

The Rose Bush Witch. By Vivian W. Owens. Eschar, 1996.

I Met a Great Lady. By Vivian W. Owens. Eschar, 1996.

I Met a Great Man. By Vivian W. Owens. Eschar, 1996.

See also Owens, Vivian W(illiams)

Weatherford, Carole Boston

(1 9 5 6 –)

AUTHOR

Weatherford was born in Baltimore, Maryland, the first of two children. As a first grader, she dictated her first poem to her mother. She continues to write poetry for both children and adults. Weatherford holds a master of fine arts degree in creative writing from the University of North Carolina and a master of arts in publication design from the University of Baltimore.

She received a 1995 North Carolina Arts Council Writers Fellowship and the inaugural Furious Flower Poetry Prize, awarded to promising new poets. Her manuscript of adult poetry, *The Tan Chanteuse,* won publication through the North Carolina Writers Network's 1995 Harperprints Chapbook competition. Weatherford was also a winner of the network's 1991 Black Writers Speak competition.

Beyond the printed page, her work has appeared on radio, on stage, and in museums. Her poem "Basketweavers" was included in a Chicago Children's Museum exhibit honoring grandparents. Weatherford is an arts-education consultant and business writer. Her essays, editorials, and articles have appeared in publications such as the *Washington Post* and the *Christian Science Monitor* newspapers and *Essence* magazine.

The mother of a daughter and a son, she lives in High Point, North Carolina.

BIBLIOGRAPHY

Juneteenth Jamboree. Illustrated by Yvonne Buchanan. Lee & Low, 1995.
Grandma and Me. Illustrated by Michelle Mills. Black Butterfly, 1996.
Me & My Family Tree. Illustrated by Michelle Mills. Black Butterfly, 1996.
Mighty Menfolk. Illustrated by Michelle Mills. Black Butterfly, 1996.
My Favorite Toy. Black Butterfly, 1996.

See also Buchanan (Elizabeth), Yvonne

White, Edgar

(1947–)

AUTHOR

White was born in the British West Indies and came to the United States when he was five years old. He received his bachelor's degree at New York University and completed graduate study at Yale University. His *Underground: Four Plays* and *Crucificardo: Plays* were published by William Morrow and have been performed at theaters including the New York Shakespeare Festival Public Theater and the Eugene O'Neill Foundation. He has written for magazines and the *Yardbird Reader.*

BIBLIOGRAPHY

Omar at Christmas. Illustrated by Dindga McCannon. Lothrop, 1973.
Sati the Rastifarian. Illustrated by Dindga McCannon. Lothrop, 1973.
Children of Night. Illustrated by Dindga McCannon. Lothrop, 1974.

See also McCannon, Dindga

Wilkinson, Brenda (Scott)

(1 9 4 6 –)

AUTHOR

Wilkinson was born in Moultrie, Georgia, and grew up in Waycross, Georgia, the daughter of Malcolm and Ethel (Anderson) Scott and the second of their eight children. She attended Hunter College of the City University of New York.

Ludell, her first book, was a National Book Award nominee in 1976. It was also noted as Best of the Best in *School Library Journal's* listing for 1976–1978. In 1977, *Ludell and Willie* was voted an Outstanding Children's Book of the Year by the *New York Times* and listed among the Best Books for Young Adults by the American Library Association.

Wilkinson is a novelist, a short-story writer, and a poet. She is a member of the Authors Guild, the Authors League of America, P.E.N. International, and the Harlem Writers Guild. Her short story "Rosa Lee Loves Bennie" was included in Sonia Sanchez's anthology, *We Be Word Sorcerers*.

She has two children, Kim and Lori, and lives in New York City.

BIBLIOGRAPHY

Ludell. Harper, 1975.
Ludell and Willie. Harper, 1977.
Ludell's New York Time. Harper, 1980.
Not Separate, Not Equal. Harper, 1987.
Jesse Jackson: Still Fighting For the Dream. Silver Burdett, 1990.
Definitely Cool. Scholastic, 1993.

Williams, Donald

(1968-)

ILLUSTRATOR

Williams was born in East Orange, New Jersey, the third in a family of four children. At an early age, he developed an interest in drawing cartoon characters. They gave him the first idea that this hobby could develop into a possible career choice. He was influenced by several family members, especially his mother and grandmother.

During his four years in high school, Donald was enrolled in the Gifted and Talented Program for Art. He entered numerous art contests and was awarded various prizes, one of which was a summer scholarship to Montclair State College, where he received the Governor's Award, the highest achievement of the program.

He enrolled in the Ducret School of Arts and developed his fine-arts talent. Williams was introduced to commercial art, specifically children's literature, by his close friend artist Michael Bryant. In 1995, he completed his first illustrative work on a book, *The Conspiracy of the Secret Nine.*

Along with continuing his career as an illustrator, Williams also aspires to become an author.

BIBLIOGRAPHY

The Conspiracy of the Secret Nine. By Celia Bland. Silver Moon, 1995.
Night Raiders Along Cape Cod. By John Waters. Silver Moon, 1996.

See also Bryant, Michael

Williams, Nancy B.

AUTHOR

Williams was born in Brooklyn, New York, the seventh of nine children. Her love for reading was the only hint during an otherwise typical upbringing that writing might figure somewhere in her future. She attended Pratt Institute, where she studied graphic design before embarking on a circuitous route that led to a career in children's-book publishing.

Williams worked as a fabric painter, a package designer, and a freelance graphic designer for several national publications, including *Cosmopolitan* and *Spin*, before becoming a designer for Atheneum in 1989. Two years later, she became the art director for Margaret K. McElderry Books, a position she held until 1995. In March of that year, she returned to freelance design, which allowed her the opportunity to enjoy the success of her first children's book and continue working on her second book.

She lives in Brooklyn, New York.

BIBLIOGRAPHY

A Kwanzaa Celebration. Illustrated by Robert Sabuda. Simon & Schuster, 1995.

Williams, Sherley Anne

(1944–)

AUTHOR

Williams was born in Bakersfield, California. She received a bachelor's degree in English from California State University, Fresno, in 1966 and a master's degree in English from Brown University in 1972. She has taught both undergraduate and graduate courses in fiction and poetry writing, African American literature, and American women's literature.

Williams was a 1976 National Book Award nominee for *The Peacock Poems*, her first book of poetry, and an Emmy Award winner in 1978 for a television performance of poems from *SomeOne Sweet Angel Chile*, her second book of poetry. Williams is also the author of *Give Birth to Brightness* and the full-length one-woman drama *Letters from a New England Negro*, a featured play at the National Black Theater Festival in 1991 and the Chicago International Theater Festival in 1992.

Working Cotton, her first work for children, was a 1993 Caldecott and Coretta Scott King Honor Book, was listed among *Parents* magazine's Best Books of 1992, and was one of the American Library Association's Notable Books of 1992. She is a featured reader at jazz and poetry festivals around the country and a popular participant in college and community reading series from coast to coast.

Williams is profiled in *Contemporary Authors New Series* and the *Dictionary of Literary Biography Afro-American Writers Since 1955* and is listed in *A Directory of American Poets and Fiction Writers*.

Williams has a son, John Malcolm, and two grandchildren, Malcolm Jr. and Jayvon. She teaches literature and fiction writing in the Department of Literature at the University of California, San Diego and lives in San Diego, California.

BIBLIOGRAPHY

Working Cotton. Illustrated by Carole Byard. Harcourt, 1992.
Girls Together. Illustrated by Synthia Saint James. Harcourt, 1999.

See also Byard, Carole; Saint James, Synthia

Wilson, Beth (Pierre)

AUTHOR

"Family and friends will remember Beth Pierre Wilson as an unusually deter-mined, considerate and spiritually guided person. They are among many other adults and children in the nation who will continue to admire her love of heri-tage and her gift as a writer." (Diane Thomas, daughter)

Wilson was born in Tacoma, Washington. She graduated from the University of Puget Sound and, when discrimination placed a barrier between her and a teaching career in her home state, she migrated to Southern California. She enrolled at the University of California at Los Angeles and embraced Christian Science, a faith that would be a cornerstone of her life forever. She married William Douglas Wilson, a dentist, and they became the parents of two children, Diane and Deal. Wilson taught for twenty years as an elementary teacher and reading resource teacher and left education to pursue music and writing avocations.

Wilson was successful in writing an African folktale, *The Great Minu*, which has been included in a number of children's anthologies. A second story, *Jenny*, was published in 1990. While best known for her authorship and knowledge of children's literature, her verse has appeared in the *Christian Science Monitor* and in the collection *If a Bridge is to Cross*, which she set to music, was recorded by Rance Allen for Fantasy Records in 1978, and was cited in the Congressional Record by Congressman Ronald Dellums.

Over the years, Wilson was active in several community organizations including Alpha Kappa Alpha Sorority, the National Association for the Advancement of Colored People, the Oakland-Bay Area Links, the California Writer's Club, and the National Council of Negro Women.

BIBLIOGRAPHY

Martin Luther King, Jr. Illustrated by Floyd Sowell. Putnam, 1971.

The Great Minu. Illustrated by Jerry Pinkney. Follett, 1974.

Muhammad Ali. Illustrated by Floyd Sowell. Putnam, 1974.

Giants for Justice. Harcourt, 1978.

Stevie Wonder. Illustrated by James Calvin. Putnam, 1979.

Jenny. Illustrated by Dolores Johnson. Macmillan, 1990.

See also Johnson, Dolores; Pinkney, Jerry

Wilson, Johnniece Marshall

(1944–)

AUTHOR

"If I had to say anyone inspired me, I would have to give credit to James Baldwin. He was one of the earliest Black writers I read. This made me think I, too, could write something. I liked the rhythms of his prose, and the very real situations his characters moved about in. The children's book writers I read most are Mildred Taylor and Robert Newton Peck. Creating well-rounded people and good story situations is often frustrating, but always wonderful when it all comes together."

Wilson was born in Montgomery, Alabama, and graduated in 1962 from Polytechnic High School in San Francisco, California. She completed college coursework in institutional cooking and bacteriology, and, among other interesting work she has done, she was a stack veneer in a lumberyard, served food, and proofread copy. *Oh, Brother,* her first children's book, won a Childrens Choice Award in 1989.

A member of the National Writers Club and the Authors Guild, Wilson lives in Pittsburgh, Pennsylvania, and has three daughters.

BIBLIOGRAPHY

Oh, Brother. Scholastic, 1988.
Robin on His Own. Scholastic, 1990.
Poor Girl, Rich Girl. Scholastic, 1992.

See also Taylor, Mildred D.

Woodson, Carter G(odwin)

(1875–1950)

AUTHOR

Woodson was born in Canton, Virginia. He completed high school when he was twenty-two years old and went on to study at Berea College in Kentucky and the University of Chicago, where he earned both bachelor's and master's degrees. He earned his doctorate at Harvard University in 1912 and then enrolled at the Sorbonne in Paris. He taught elementary and high school and was a dean of the College of Liberal Arts at Howard University and West Virginia State College.

In 1915, Woodson, described as "the father of modern Negro historiography," organized the Association for the Study of Negro Life and History so that culture and history would be recognized and established the *Journal of Negro History*. In 1930, he started the *Negro History Bulletin* to give schoolchildren historical information about their heritage.

Woodson's interest in African American history led him to collect documents, write, and compile data on African American roots and heritage.

BIBLIOGRAPHY

African Heroes and Heroines. Associated, 1938, 1944.
African Myths. Revised Edition. Associated, 1948.
Negro Makers of History. Revised Edition. Associated, 1948.
Story of the Negro Retold. Revised Edition. Associated, 1959.

Woodson, Jacqueline

(1 9 6 3 –)

AUTHOR

"I have chosen to write for young adults with an emphasis on children-of-color to enlighten them to the different issues we as people of color continually struggle with. Issues such as nurturing the gifted Black child, racism, classism, and homophobia play major roles in my writing and were absent in the literature I read growing up; issues I want my own children to grow up enlightened to. My objective is to show the children that there really isn't a 'generation gap' between writers and readers. As a writer, I write remembering the child I was, am still, will always be. That is what, through literature, I hope to bring to the children."

Woodson was born in Columbus, Ohio. Her book *From the Notebooks of Melanin Sun* won a Coretta Scott King Honor Book Award in 1996, and *I Hadn't Meant to Tell You This* did the same in 1995. She lives in Brooklyn, New York.

BIBLIOGRAPHY

Last Summer with Maizon. Delacorte, 1990.
Martin Luther King, Jr., and His Birthday. Illustrated by Floyd Cooper. Silver Burdett, 1990.
The Dear One. Delacorte, 1991.
Maizon at Blue Hill. Delacorte, 1992.
Between Madison and Palmetto. Delacorte, 1993.
The Book Chase. Bantam, 1994.
I Hadn't Meant to Tell You This. Delacorte, 1994.
From the Notebooks of Melanin Sun. Blue Sky, 1995.
A Way Out of No Way. Holt, 1996.
The House You Pass Along the Way. Bantam, 1997.

See also Cooper, Floyd (Donald)

Wright, Courtni C(rump)

(1950-)

AUTHOR

"New technology is on the horizon as a means of replacing paper, causing publishers to become more selective in an already conservative environment. As is probably true of most Black writers, I see that history books have done little to enhance the perception of the value of African American people. As a teacher, I have seen the faces of Black children who see only slavery, George Washington Carver, and the civil-rights movement as their contributions to the history of this country. I write works of historical fiction to provide a truthful picture of the history of the race and an honest view of the people."

Wright was born in Washington, D.C., and graduated in 1972 from Trinity College with an undergraduate degree in English from Johns Hopkins University in Baltimore, Maryland. In 1980 she earned a master's degree in Education. Wright teaches English at the National Cathedral School in Washington, D.C. She is a member of the African American Writers Guild. She was a Council for Basic Education National Endowment for the Humanities fellow in 1990. Wright serves as a consultant to National Geographic magazine for instructional video.

She lives in Silver Spring, Maryland, with her husband and their son, Ashley.

BIBLIOGRAPHY

Women of Shakespeare's Plays. University Press of America, 1992.
Journey to Freedom: A Story of the Underground Railroad. Illustrated by Gershom Griffith. Holiday House, 1994.
Jumping the Broom. Illustrated by Gershom Griffith. Holiday House, 1994.
Wagon Train: A Family Goes West in 1865. Illustrated by Gershom Griffith. Holiday House, 1995.

See also Griffith, Gershom

Wyeth, Sharon Dennis

AUTHOR

"*I learned to write my first word in kindergarten. The word was 'beautiful.' I remember running home, waving the paper with my word on it in the air. To make a word, by myself, to make it come out of the end of my pencil—what a joyous sensation! At five years old, I already was a big sister with three little brothers at home, but my mother, very articulate and a wonderful writer herself, made time to read that word 'beautiful' over and over again, expressing her pride in me. Thus began my love of written language.*

I keep writing every day, wondering if I will continue to be published. If it doesn't happen, deep down I know it'll be okay. I have some books I can touch, that have touched lots of young people. I was in a classroom in the Bronx where I volunteer a few times a year to acquaint children with the writing process and to inspire them to read more. I shared a work in progress, my book 'Something Beautiful.' After I'd finished reading, the children were very quiet. The story is about a child living in a dense urban environment—like I did, like those children in the classroom do. 'What do you think?' I asked the children. One little voice piped up: 'I am in that book! I am in that book!' That's enough for me. In my ear, I have the memory of that child's little voice, saying 'I am in that book!'"

Wyeth was born in Washington, D.C. She is a graduate of Anacostia High School in Washington, D.C., and received her bachelor of arts degree (cum laude) from Radcliffe College, Harvard University. A formidable and entertaining public speaker and storyteller, she has been an actress, a voice coach, a teacher of public speaking, a writer for daytime television, and a family counselor. *Always My Dad* was selected as a *Reading Rainbow* feature book for 1996 and named by the New York Public Library as one of the Best 100 Children's Books of 1995.

Wyeth lives in Montclair, New Jersey, with her husband and daughter.

BIBLIOGRAPHY

The World of Daughter McGuire. Delacorte, 1994.

Always My Dad. Illustrated by Raoul Colon. Knopf, 1995.

Ginger Brown: Too Many Houses. Illustrated by Cornelius VanWright and Ying-Hwa. Random House, 1996.

Vampire Bugs: Stories Conjured from the Past. Illustrated by Curtis E. James. Delacorte, 1995.

Once On This River. Knopf, 1998.

Yarbrough, Camille

(1 9 3 4 –)

AUTHOR

Yarbrough was born in Chicago, Illinois. An actress, composer, and singer, she has appeared on television and in the theater in a number of roles. She was a member of the New York and touring companies of *To Be Young, Gifted, and Black*. *The Iron Pot Cooker,* her first album of original recorded songs and dialogues, was favorably reviewed in 1975. Yarbrough has served as a guest hostess of *Night Talk* on radio station WWRL in New York and is a popular talk show hostess on station WLIB in New York City.

Yarbrough was a member of the Katherine Dunham Dance Company for five years and taught Dunham Technique at Southern Illinois University.

Among her awards are a Jazzy Folk Ethnic Performance Fellowship from the National Endowment for the Arts, the Unity Award in Media from Lincoln University in 1982, and a Woman of the Month citation by *Essence* magazine in 1979. In 1975, she was named Griot of the Year by the Griot Society of New York. ("Griot" is a West African word for storyteller.)

Yarbrough is professor of African dance in the Black Studies Department of City College of New York. She also teaches at the African Poetry Theatre, a writing workshop in Queens, New York. In 1994 Yarbrough was enstooled by ABLADEI (Ghana) as NAA KUOKOR I, founder of the Stool House of Harriet Tubman.

Yarbrough lives in Harlem, New York.

BIBLIOGRAPHY

Cornrows. Illustrated by Carole Byard. Coward, 1979.
The Shimmershine Queens. Illustrated by Anna Rich. Putnam, 1989.

Tamika and the Wisdom Rings. Illustrated by Anna Rich. Random House, 1994.
The Little Tree Growin in the Shade. Coward, 1985. Putnam (Illustrated by Tyrone Geter), 1996.

See also Byard, Carole; Geter, Tyrone

Young, A(ndrew) S(turgeon-Nash) "Doc"

$(1924-)$

AUTHOR

The author was born in Virginia. Young obtained a bachelor's degree at Hampton Institute. He was a sports editor at the *Los Angeles Sentinel* and at *Ebony, Jet,* and *Hue* magazines. He was also managing editor of *Copper, Tan,* and *Jet* magazines and has been a radio commentator.

His memberships include the National Newspaper Publishers Association, the Greater Los Angeles Press Club, the Black Economic Union, the Publicist Guild, the Los Angeles Urban League, and the National Association for the Advancement of Colored People (NAACP).

Among his awards are the Los Angeles Ghetto Award, the President's Anniversary Sports Award, and the American Library Association Award for Negro Firsts in Sports.

BIBLIOGRAPHY

Black Champions of the Gridiron: O.J. Simpson and Leroy Keys. Harcourt, 1969.

The Mets from Mobile: Tommie Agee, Cleon Jones. Harcourt, 1970.

Young, Bernice Elizabeth

(1931–)

AUTHOR

Young was born in Cleveland, Ohio. She was one of the first of six Blacks to be accepted by Vassar College (1949–1951). Young has enjoyed writing since childhood and used her writing skills for the very popular music group, the Beatles, when she worked in advertising. Her other interests include music, ballet, and sports.

BIBLIOGRAPHY

Harlem: The Story of a Changing Community. Messner, 1972.
The Picture Story of Hank Aaron. Messner, 1974.
The Picture Story of Frank Robinson. Messner, 1975.

Young, Margaret B(uckner)

(1922–)

AUTHOR

The author was born in Campbellsville, Kentucky. Young majored in English at Kentucky State College and obtained a master's degree in educational psychology from the University of Minnesota. She is the widow of Whitney M. Young, Jr., former executive director of the National Urban League. An educator, Young taught with Christine King Farris, the sister of Martin Luther King, Jr., at Spelman College in Atlanta, Georgia.

She lives in Denver, Colorado.

BIBLIOGRAPHY

First Book of American Negroes. Watts, 1966.
The Picture Life of Martin Luther King, Jr. Watts, 1968.
The Picture Life of Ralph Bunche. Watts, 1968.
Black American Leaders. Watts, 1969.
The Picture Life of Thurgood Marshall. Watts, 1970.

Appendix I
Bookcovers and Jackets

Not a Copper Penny in Me House: Poems from the Caribbean,
by Monica Gunning, illustrated by Frané Lessac.
Jacket illustration ©1993 Frané Lessac.
Reprinted by permission of Boyds Mills Press.

Bitter Bananas, by Isaac Olaleye, illustrated by Ed Young.
Jacket illustration ©1994 Ed Young.
Reprinted by permission of Boyds Mills Press.

The Distant Talking Drum: Poems from Nigeria, by Isaac Olaleye, illustrated by Frané Lessac. Jacket illustration ©1995 Frané Lessac. Reprinted by permission of Boyds Mills Press.

FAMILIES
POEMS CELEBRATING THE
AFRICAN AMERICAN EXPERIENCE

Selected by Dorothy S. Strickland
and Michael R. Strickland

Illustrations by John Ward

Families: Poems Celebrating the African American Experience
edited by Dorothy S. Strickland and Michael R. Strickland,
illustrated by John Ward. Jacket illustration ©1994 John Ward.
Reprinted by permission of Boyds Mills Press.

Up in the Air: The Story of Bessie Coleman, by Philip S. Hart.
Reprinted by permission of Carolrhoda Books, Inc.

POEMS THAT SING TO YOU

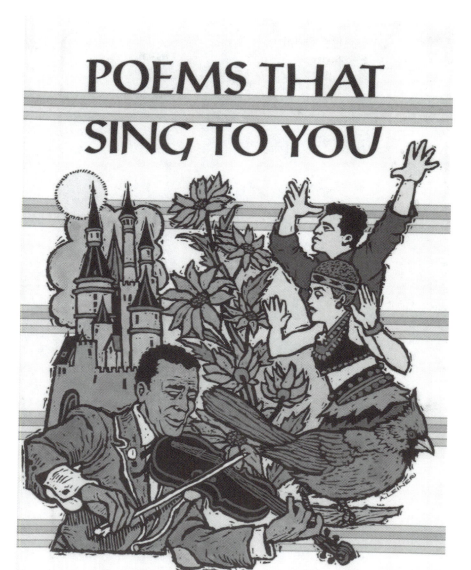

Selected by Michael R. Strickland
Illustrated by Alan Leiner

Poems That Sing to You, edited by Michael R. Strickland,
illustrated by Alan Leiner. ©1993 Boyds Mills Press.
Reprinted by permission.

Count Your Way through

Brazil

by Jim Haskins and Kathleen Benson • illustrations by Liz Brenner Dodson

Count Your Way through Brazil, by Jim Haskins and Kathleen Benson,
illustrated by Liz Brenner Dodson.
Reprinted by permission of Carolrhoda Books, Inc.

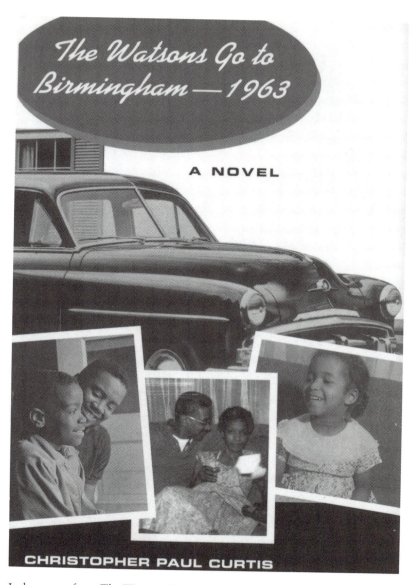

Jacket cover from *The Watsons Go to Birmingham—1963*,
by Christopher Paul Curtis. Used by permission of Delacorte Press,
a division of Bantam Doubleday Dell Publishing Group, Inc.

Jacket cover from *A Blessing in Disguise*, by Eleanora E. Tate.
Jacket illustration ©1995 Gershom Griffith. Used by permission of Delacorte
Press, a division of Bantam Doubleday Dell Publishing Group, Inc.

Jacket cover from *Darnell Rock Reporting*, by Walter Dean Myers.
Jacket illustration ©1994 Mark Smolin.
Used by permission of Delacorte Press, a division of Bantam Doubleday
Dell Publishing Group, Inc.

Jacket cover from *Can't Scare Me!*, by Melissa Milich,
illustrated by Tyrone Geter. Used by permission of Delacorte Press,
a division of Bantam Doubleday Dell Publishing Group, Inc.

Jacket cover from *How Mr. Monkey Saw the Whole World*,
by Walter Dean Myers, illustrated by Synthia Saint James.
Used by permission of Delacorte Press, a division of Bantam Doubleday
Dell Publishing Group, Inc.

Jacket cover from *Vampire Bugs: Stories Conjured from the Past*,
by Sharon D. Wyeth, illustrated by Curtis E. James.
Used by permission of Delacorte Press, a division of Bantam Doubleday
Dell Publishing Group, Inc.

Jacket cover from *Mississippi Bridge*, by Mildred D. Taylor,
illustrated by Max Ginsberg. Used by permission of Delacorte Press,
a division of Bantam Doubleday Dell Publishing Group, Inc.

Jacket cover from *The Ups and Downs of Carl Davis III*, by Rosa Guy.
Used by permission of Delacorte Press, a division of Bantam
Doubleday Dell Publishing Group, Inc.

Jacket cover from *Last Summer with Maizon*, by Jacqueline Woodson.
© 1990 Jacqueline Woodson.
Used by permission of Bantam Doubleday Dell Books for Young Readers.

Nadanda, the Wordmaker, by Vivian Owens.
Jacket illustration ©1994 Richard J. Watson.
Used by permission of Eschar Publications.

The Royal Kingdoms of Ghana, Mali, and Songhay: Life in Medieval Africa, by Patricia and Fredrick McKissack.
Jacket illustration ©1994 Vigui Maggio.
Reprinted by permission of Henry Holt and Company, Inc.

THE SINGING MAN

Adapted from a West African Folktale

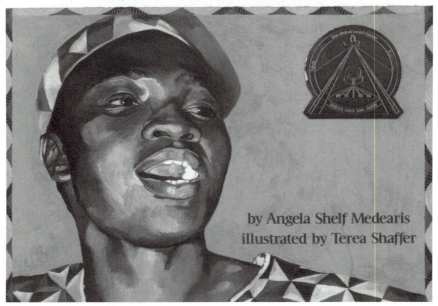

by Angela Shelf Medearis
illustrated by Terea Shaffer

The Singing Man: Adapted from a West African Folktale,
by Angela Shelf Medearis, illustrated by Terea Shaffer.
Reprinted by permission of Holiday House, Inc.

WAGON TRAIN
A Family Goes West in 1865

by Courtni C. Wright

illustrated by Gershom Griffith

Wagon Train: A Family Goes West in 1865, by Courtni C. Wright,
illustrated by Gershom Griffith.
Reprinted by permission of Holiday House, Inc.

The Tangerine Tree

By Regina Hanson ✿ Illustrated by Harvey Stevenson

The Tangerine Tree, by Regina Hanson,
illustrated by Harvey Stevenson. Illustration ©1995 Harvey Stevenson.
Reprinted by permission of Clarion Books/Houghton Mifflin Company.

Yellow Bird and Me, by Joyce Hansen.
Jacket art ©1986 Beth Peck.
Reprinted by permission of Clarion Books/ Houghton Mifflin Company.

Aunt Flossie's Hats (and Crab Cakes Later), by Elizabeth Fitzgerald Howard, paintings by James Ransome. Illustration ©1991 James Ransome. Reprinted by permission of Clarion Books/Houghton Mifflin Company.

What's in Aunt Mary's Room? by Elizabeth Fitzgerald Howard,
illustrated by Cedric Lucas. Illustration ©1996 Cedric Lucas.
Reprinted by permission of Clarion Books/Houghton Mifflin Company.

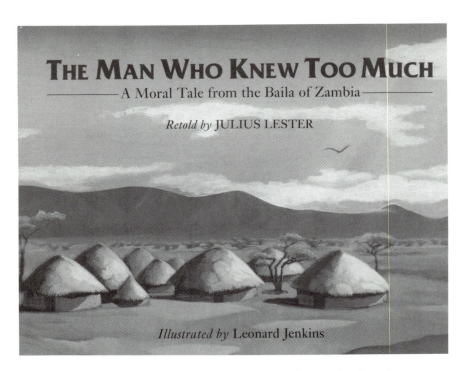

THE MAN WHO KNEW TOO MUCH
A Moral Tale from the Baila of Zambia

Retold by JULIUS LESTER

Illustrated by Leonard Jenkins

The Man Who Knew Too Much: A Moral Tale from Baila of Zambia,
retold by Julius Lester, illustrated by Leonard Jenkins.
Illustration ©1994 Leonard Jenkins.
Reprinted by permission of Clarion Books/Houghton Mifflin Company.

Big Boy, by Tololwa M. Mollel, illustrated by E.B. Lewis.
Jacket illustration ©1995 by E.B. Lewis.
Reprinted by permission of Clarion Books/Houghton Mifflin Company.

The Kids' Book of Wisdom: Quotes from the African American Tradition,
compiled by Cheryl and Wade Hudson. Jacket illustration ©1996 Anna Rich.
Reprinted by permission of Just Us Books.

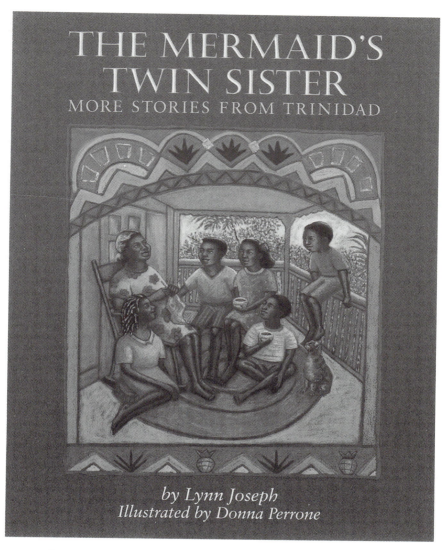

THE MERMAID'S TWIN SISTER
MORE STORIES FROM TRINIDAD

by Lynn Joseph
Illustrated by Donna Perrone

The Mermaid's Twin Sister: More Stories from Trinidad,
by Lynn Joseph, illustrated by Donna Perrone.
Jacket illustration copyright ©1994 by Donna Perrone.
Reprinted by permission of Clarion Books/Houghton Mifflin Company.

Land of the Four Winds, by Veronica Freeman Ellis,
illustrated by Sylvia Walker.
Reprinted by permission of Just Us Books.

IN PRAISE OF

OUR FATHERS AND
OUR MOTHERS

A Black Family Treasury
by Outstanding Authors and Artists

Compiled by Wade and Cheryl Hudson

In Praise of Our Fathers and Our Mothers: A Black Family Treasury by Outstanding Authors and Artists, compiled by Wade and Cheryl Hudson. Front jacket illustration © Leo and Diane Dillon. Reprinted by permission of Just Us Books.

BRIGHT EYES, BROWN SKIN

by Cheryl Willis Hudson & Bernette G. Ford
Illustrated by George Ford

Bright Eyes, Brown Skin, by Cheryl Willis Hudson and Bernette G. Ford, illustrated by George Ford. Cover illustration © George Ford. Reproduced by permission of Just Us Books.

Kid Caramel, Private Investigator: Case of the Missing Ankh,
by Dwayne J. Ferguson. Cover illustration ©1997 Don Tate.
Reprinted by permission of Just Us Books.

Kids, I'm Gonna Be! by Wade Hudson,
illustrated by Culverson Blair. Cover illustration ©1992 Culverson Blair.
Reprinted by permission of Just Us Books.

Just an Overnight Guest, by Eleanora E. Tate.
Cover illustration ©1997 Thomas Hudson.
Reprinted by permission of Just Us Books.

Elizabeth's Wish Is To Be a Star!, by Debbi Chocolate.
Cover illustration ©1994 Higgins Bond.
Reprinted by permission of Just Us Books.

0-940975-42-4
$3.95 USA
$4.95 CAN

NEATE™

To the Rescue!

CITY HALL

GORDON FOR CITY COUNCIL

Together Forever!

by Debbi Chocolate

Neate™ *To the Rescue*, by Debbi Chocolate.
Cover illustration ©1992 Melodye Rosales.
Reprinted by permission of Just Us Books.

Frederick Douglass: The Last Day of Slavery, by William Miller,
illustrated by Cedric Lucas. Jacket art ©1995 Cedric Lucas.
Reprinted by permission of Lee & Low Books Inc.

FROM A CHILD'S HEART

poems by Nikki Grimes ◆ pictures by Brenda Joysmith

Juneteenth Jamboree, by Carole Boston Weatherford,
illustrated by Yvonne Buchanan. Jacket art ©1995 Yvonne Buchanan.
Reprinted with permission of Lee & Low Books Inc.

SEPTIMA CLARK · JESTER HAIRSTON
JOSEPHINE BAKER · GWENDOLYN BROOKS
THURGOOD MARSHALL · JAMES FORMAN
ANDREW YOUNG · BARBARA JORDAN

PATHBLAZERS

EIGHT PEOPLE WHO MADE A DIFFERENCE

M. K. FULLEN · Illustrated by SELMA WALDMAN

Pathblazers: Eight People Who Made a Difference, by M.K. Fullen,
illustrated by Selma Waldman.
Reprinted by permission of Open Hand Publishing Inc.

Habari Gani? What's the News? A Kwanzaa Story,
by Sundaira Morninghouse, paintings by Jody Kim.
Reprinted by permission of Open Hand Publishing Inc.

Nightfeathers, by Sundaira Morninghouse, illustrations by Jody Kim. Cover illustration ©1989 Jody Kim.
Reprinted by permission of Open Hand Publishing Inc.

D.J. and the Zulu Parade, by Denise Walter McConduit,
illustrated by Emile F. Henriquez and Lucien C. Barbarin, Jr.
©1995 Pelican Publishing Company, Inc. Used by permission.

Olympic Black Women, by Martha Ward Plowden,
illustrated by Ronald Jones. ©1996 Pelican Publishing Company, Inc.
Used by permission.

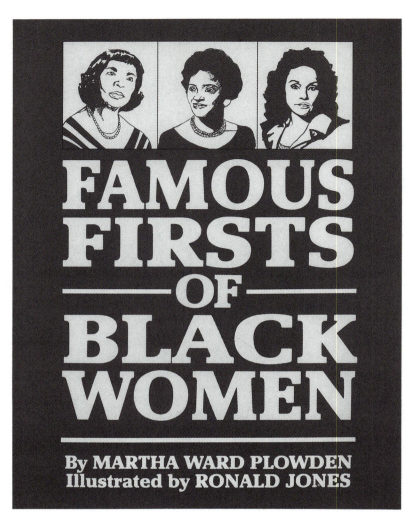

Famous Firsts of Black Women, by Martha Ward Plowden,
illustrated by Ronald Jones. ©1993 Pelican Publishing Company, Inc.
Used by permission.

Come Sunday, by Nikki Grimes,
illustrated by Michael Bryant.
Used by permission of Wm. B. Eerdmans Publishing Co.

Appendix 2
Awards and Honor Books

CORETTA SCOTT KING AWARDS

The award is presented annually by the Coretta Scott King Task Force of the American Library Association's Social Responsibilities Round Table to a Black author and/or illustrator whose books promote an understanding and appreciation of the cultures of all people and the contributions we all make to the realization of the "American dream." [Note that an asterisk (*) indicates a title not included in the bibliographies.]

AUTHORS

1998 WINNER
Sharon M. Draper, *Forged by Fire* (Atheneum)

HONOR BOOKS
James Haskins, *Bayard Rustin: Behind the Scenes of the Civil Rights Movement* (Hyperion)
Joyce Hansen, *I Thought My Soul Would Rise and Fly: The Diary of Patsy, A Freed Girl* (Scholastic)

1997 WINNER
Walter Dean Myers, *Slam!* (Scholastic)

HONOR BOOKS
Patricia C. and Fredrick McKissack, *Rebels Against Slavery: American Slave Revolts* (Scholastic)

1996 WINNER
Virginia Hamilton, *Her Stories: African American Folktales, Fairy Tales and True Tales* (Scholastic)

Christoper Paul Curtis, *The Watsons Go to Birmingham–1963* (Delacorte)

*Rita Williams-Garcia, *Like Sisters on the Homefront* (Lodestar)

Jacqueline Woodson, *From the Notebooks of Melanin Sun* (Blue Sky)

1995 WINNER

Patricia C. and Fredrick McKissack, *Christmas in the Big House, Christmas in
the Quarters* (Scholastic)

HONOR BOOKS

Patricia C. and Fredrick McKissack, *Black Diamond: The Story of the Negro
Baseball League* (Scholastic)

Jacqueline Woodson, *I Hadn't Meant To Tell You This* (Delacorte)

Joyce Hansen, *The Captive* (Scholastic)

1994 WINNER

Angela Johnson, *Toning the Sweep* (Orchard)

HONOR BOOKS

Joyce Carol Thomas, *Brown Honey in Broomwheat Tea* (HarperCollins)

Walter Dean Myers, *Malcolm X: By Any Means Necessary* (Scholastic)

1993 WINNER

Patricia C. McKissack, *The Dark-Thirty: Southern Tales of the Supernatural*
(Knopf)

HONOR BOOKS

Mildred Pitts Walter, *Mississippi Challenge* (Bradbury)

Patricia C. and Fredrick McKissack, *Sojourner Truth: Ain't I a Woman?* (Scholastic)

Walter Dean Myers, *Somewhere in the Darkness* (Scholastic)

1992 WINNER

Walter Dean Myers, *Now Is Your Time! The African-American Struggle for Freedom* (HarperCollins)

HONOR BOOK

Eloise Greenfield, *Night on Neighborhood Street* (Dial)

1991 WINNER

Mildred D. Taylor, *The Road to Memphis* (Dial)

HONOR BOOKS

James Haskins, *Black Dance in America: A History Through Its People*
(HarperCollins)

Angela Johnson, *When I Am Old with You* (Orchard)

1990 WINNER

Patricia C. and Fredrick McKissack, *A Long Hard Journey: The Story of the Pullman Porter* (Walker)

HONOR BOOKS

Eloise Greenfield, *Nathaniel Talking* (Black Butterfly)

Virginia Hamilton, *The Bells of Christmas* (Harcourt)

Lillie Patterson, *Martin Luther King, Jr., and the Freedom Movement* (Facts on File)

1989 WINNER

Walter Dean Myers, *Fallen Angels* (Scholastic)

HONOR BOOKS

James Berry, *A Thief in the Village and Other Stories of Jamaica* (Orchard)

Virginia Hamilton, *Anthony Burns: The Defeat and Triumph of a Fugitive Slave* (Knopf)

1988 WINNER

Mildred D. Taylor, *The Friendship* (Dial)

HONOR BOOKS

Alexis De Veaux, *An Enchanted Hair Tale* (Harper)

Julius Lester, *The Tales of Uncle Remus: The Adventures of Brer Rabbit* (Dial)

1987 WINNER

Mildred Pitts Walter, *Justin and the Best Biscuits in the World* (Lothrop)

HONOR BOOKS

Ashley Bryan, *Lion and the Ostrich Chicks and Other African Folk Tales* (Atheneum)

Joyce Hansen, *Which Way Freedom?* (Walker)

1986 WINNER

Virginia Hamilton, *The People Could Fly: American Black Folktales* (Knopf)

HONOR BOOKS

Virginia Hamilton, *Junius Over Far* (Harper)

Mildred Pitts Walter, *Trouble's Child* (Lothrop)

1985 WINNER

Walter Dean Myers, *Motown and Didi: A Love Story* (Viking)

James Haskins, *James Van DerZee: The Picture Takin' Man* (Dodd)

*Ellease Southerland, *Let the Lion Eat Straw* (Scribner)

Ossie Davis, *Escape to Freedom: A Play About Young Frederick Douglass* (Viking)

*Carol Fenner, *Skates of Uncle Richard* (Random)

Virginia Hamilton, *Justice and Her Brothers* (Greenwillow)

Lillie Patterson, *Benjamin Banneker* (Abingdon)

*Jeanne W. Peterson, *I Have a Sister, My Sister Is Deaf* (Harper)

Eloise Greenfield, *Africa Dream*. HarperCollins.

*William J. Faulkner, *The Days When the Animals Talked: Black Folk Tales and How They Came To Be* (Follett)

*Frankcina Glass, *Marvin and Tige* (St. Martin's)

Eloise Greenfield, *Mary McCleod Bethune* (Crowell)

James Haskins, *Barbara Jordan* (Dial)

Lillie Patterson, *Coretta Scott King* (Garrard)

Ruth Ann Stewart, *Portia: The Life of Portia Washington Pittman, the Daughter of Booker T. Washington* (Doubleday)

James Haskins, *The Story of Stevie Wonder* (Lothrop)

Lucille Clifton, *Everett Andereson's Friend* (Holt)

Mildred D. Taylor, *Roll of Thunder, Hear My Cry* (Dial)

*Clarence N. Blake and Donald F. Martin, *Quiz Book on Black America* (Houghton)

*Pearl Bailey, *Duey's Tale* (Harcourt)

Shirley Graham, *Julius K. Nyerere: Teacher of Africa* (Messner)

Eloise Greenfield, *Paul Robeson* (Crowell)

Walter Dean Myers, *Fast Sam, Cool Clyde and Stuff* (Viking)

Mildred D. Taylor, *Song of the Trees* (Dial)

Dorothy Robinson, *The Legend of Africania* (Johnson)

1974 WINNER
Sharon Bell Mathis, *Ray Charles* (Crowell)

HONOR BOOKS
Alice Childress, *A Hero Ain't Nothin' but a Sandwich* (Coward)
Lucille Clifton, *Don't You Remember?* (Holt)
*Louise Crane, *Ms. Africa: Profiles of Modern African Women* (Lippincott)
Kristin Hunter, *Guests in the Promised Land* (Scribner)
John Nagenda, *Mukasa* (Macmillan)

1973 WINNER
*Alfred Duckett, *I Never Had It Made: The Autobiography of Jackie Robinson* (Putnam)

1972 WINNER
Elton C. Fax, *Seventeen Black Artists* (Dodd)

1971 WINNER
Charlemae Rollins, *Black Troubadour: Langston Hughes* (Rand McNally)

HONOR BOOKS
*Maya Angelou, *I Know Why the Caged Bird Sings* (Random)
*Shirley Chisholm, *Unbought and Unbossed* (Houghton)
*Mari Evans, *I Am a Black Woman* (Morrow)
Lorenz Graham, *Every Man Heart Lay Down* (Crowell)
June Jordan and Terri Bush, *The Voice of the Children* (Holt)
Barney Grossman and Gladys Groom, *Black Means . . .* (Hill & Wang)
*Margaret W. Peters, *Ebony Book of Black Achievement* (Johnson)
*Janice May Udry, *Mary Jo's Grandmother* (Whitman)

1970 WINNER
Lillie Patterson, *Martin Luther King, Jr.: Man of Peace* (Garrard)

ILLUSTRATORS

1998 WINNER
Javaka Steptoe, *In Daddy's Arms I Am Tall,* by Alan Schroeder (Lee & Low)

HONOR BOOKS
Baba Wagué Diakité, *The Hunterman and the Crocodile,* by Baba Wagué Diakité (Scholastic)

Ashley Bryan, *Ashley Bryan's ABC of African American Poetry,* by Ashley Bryan
Christopher Myers, *Harlem,* by Walter Dean Myers (Scholastic)

Jerry Pinkney, *Minty: A Story of Young Harriet Tubman,* by Alan Schroeder (Dial)

HONOR BOOKS

Gregory Christie, *The Palm of My Heart: Poetry by African American Children,* edited by Davida Adedjouma (Lee & Low)

Reynold Ruffins, *Running the Road to ABC,* by Denizé Lauture (Simon & Schuster)

Synthia Saint James, *Neeny Coming, Neeny Going,* by Karen English (Bridge Water)

1996 WINNER

Tom Feelings, *The Middle Passage: White Ships, Black Cargo* (Dial)

HONOR BOOKS

Leo and Diane Dillon, *Her Stories: African American Folktales, Fairy Tales and True Tales,* by Virginia Hamilton (Scholastic)

Brian Pinkney, *The Faithful Friend,* by Robert D. San Souci (Simon & Schuster)

1995 WINNER

James Ransome, *The Creation,* by James Weldon Johnson (Holiday House)

HONOR BOOKS

Floyd Cooper, *Meet Danitra Brown,* by Nikki Grimes (Lothrop)

*Terea Shaffer, *The Singing Man,* by Angela Shelf Medearis (Holiday House)

1994 WINNER

Tom Feelings, *Soul Looks Back in Wonder,* edited by Phyllis Fogelman (Dial)

HONOR BOOKS

Floyd Cooper, *Brown Honey in Broomwheat Tea,* by Joyce Carol Thomas (HarperCollins)

James Ransome, *Uncle Jed's Barbershop,* by Margaree King Mitchell (Simon & Schuster)

1993 WINNER

*Kathleen Atkins Wilson, *The Origin of Life on Earth: An African Creation Myth,* retold by David A. Anderson. SANKOFA (Sights)

Wil Clay, *Little Eight John,* by Jan Wahl (Lodestar)

Brian Pinkney, *Sukey and the Mermaid,* by Robert D. San Souci (Four Winds)

Carole Byard, *Working Cotton,* by Sherley Anne Williams (Harcourt)

1992 WINNER

Faith Ringgold, *Tar Beach* (Crown)

HONOR BOOKS

Ashley Bryan, *All Night, All Day: A Child's First Book of African-American Spirituals* (Atheneum)

Jan Spivey Gilchrist, *Night on Neighborhood Street,* by Eloise Greenfield (Dial)

1991 WINNER

Leo and Diane Dillon, *Aida,* by Leontyne Price (Harcourt)

1990 WINNER

Jan Spivey Gilchrist, *Nathaniel Talking,* by Eloise Greenfield (Black Butterfly)

HONOR BOOKS

Jerry Pinkney, *The Talking Eggs,* by Robert D. San Souci (Dial)

1989 WINNER

Jerry Pinkney, *Mirandy and Brother Wind,* by Patricia C. McKissack (Knopf)

HONOR BOOKS

Amos Ferguson, *Under the Sunday Tree,* by Eloise Greenfield (Harper)

Pat Cummings, *Storm in the Night,* by Mary Stolz (Harper)

1988 WINNER

John Steptoe, *Mufaro's Beautiful Daughters: An African Tale* (Lothrop)

HONOR BOOKS

Ashley Bryan, *What a Morning! The Christmas Story in Black Spirituals,* selected and edited by John Langstaff (McElderry)

*Joe Sam, *The Invisible Hunters: A Legend from the Miskito Indians of Nicaragua,* compiled by Harriet Rohmer et al. (Children's Press)

1987 WINNER

Jerry Pinkney, *Half a Moon and One Whole Star,* by Crescent Dragonwagon (Macmillan)

HONOR BOOKS

Ashley Bryan, *Lion and the Ostrich Chicks and Other African Folk Tales* (Atheneum)

Pat Cummings, *C.L.O.U.D.S.* (Lothrop)

Jerry Pinkney, *The Patchwork Quilt,* by Valerie Flournoy (Dial)

Leo and Diane Dillon, *The People Could Fly: American Black Folktales,* by Virginia Hamilton (Knopf)

Pat Cummings, *My Mama Needs Me,* by Mildred Pitts Walter (Lothrop)

Peter Magubane, *Black Child* (Knopf)

John Steptoe, *All the Colors of the Race: Poems,* by Arnold Adoff (Lothrop)
Ashley Bryan, *I'm Going to Sing: Black American Spirituals* (Atheneum)
Pat Cummings, *Just Us Women,* by Jeannette Caines (Harper)

John Steptoe, *Mother Crocodile=Maman–Caiman,* by Birago Diop, Translated and adapted by Rosa Guy (Delacorte)

Tom Feelings, *Daydreamers,* by Eloise Greenfield (Dial)

Ashley Bryan, *Beat the Story-Drum, Pum-Pum* (Atheneum)

Carole Byard, *Grandmama's Joy,* by Eloise Greenfield (Philomel)
Jerry Pinkney, *Count on Your Fingers, African Style,* by Claudia Zaslavsky (Crowell)

Carole Byard, *Cornrows,* by Camille Yarbrough (Coward)

Tom Feelings, *Something on My Mind,* by Nikki Grimes (Dial)

George Ford, *Ray Charles,* by Sharon Bell Mathis (Crowell)

NEWBERY MEDAL AWARDS AND HONOR BOOKS

The John Newbery Medal is awarded annually by the Association for Library Service to Children, a division of the American Library Association, to the author of the most distinguished contribution to American literature for children. (The listing below is limited to African American winners.)

1996 HONOR BOOK

Christopher Paul Curtis, *The Watsons Go to Birmingham–1963* (Delacorte)

1993 HONOR BOOK

Patricia C. McKissack, *The Dark-Thirty: Southern Tales of the Supernatural* (Knopf)

Walter Dean Myers, *Somewhere in the Darkness* (Scholastic)

1989 HONOR BOOKS

Virginia Hamilton, *In the Beginning: Creation Stories from Around the World* (Harcourt)

Walter Dean Myers, *Scorpions* (Harper)

1983 HONOR BOOK

Virginia Hamilton, *Sweet Whispers, Brother Rush* (Philomel)

1977 WINNER

Mildred D. Taylor, *Roll of Thunder, Hear My Cry* (Dial)

1976 HONOR BOOK

Sharon Bell Mathis, *The Hundred Penny Box* (Viking)

1975 WINNER

Virginia Hamilton, *M.C. Higgins, the Great* (Macmillan)

1972 HONOR BOOK

Virginia Hamilton, *The Planet of Junior Brown* (Macmillan)

1969 HONOR BOOK

Julius Lester, *To Be a Slave* (Dial)

The Randolph Caldecott Medal is awarded annually by the Association for Library Service to Children, a division of the American Library Association, to the artist of the most distinguished American picture book for children. (The listing below is limited to African American winners.)

1998 HONOR BOOK
Christopher Myers, *Harlem,* by Walter Dean Myers (Scholastic)

1996 HONOR BOOK
Brian Pinkney, *The Faithful Friend,* by Robert D. San Souci (Simon & Schuster)

1995 HONOR BOOK
Jerry Pinkney, *John Henry,* by Julius Lester (Dial)

1993 HONOR BOOK
Carole Byard, *Working Cotton,* by Sherley Anne Williams (Harcourt)

1992 HONOR BOOK
Faith Ringgold, *Tar Beach* (Crown)

1990 HONOR BOOK
Jerry Pinkney, *The Talking Eggs,* by Robert D. San Souci (Dial)

1989 HONOR BOOK
Jerry Pinkney, *Mirandy and Brother Wind,* by Patricia C. McKissack (Knopf)

1988 HONOR BOOK
John Steptoe, *Mufaro's Beautiful Daughters: An African Tale,* by John Steptoe (Lothrop)

1985 HONOR BOOK
John Steptoe, *The Story of Jumping Mouse: A Native American Legend,* by John Steptoe (Lothrop)

1981 HONOR BOOK
Donald Crews, *Truck* (Greenwillow)

1979 HONOR BOOK
Donald Crews, *Freight Train* (Greenwillow)

1977 WINNER

Leo and Diane Dillon, *Ashanti to Zulu: African Traditions,* by Margaret Musgrove (Dial)

1976 WINNER

Leo and Diane Dillon, *Why Mosquitoes Buzz in People's Ears,* by Verna Aardema (Dial)

1975 HONOR BOOK

Tom Feelings, *Jambo Means Hello: Swahili Alphabet Book,* by Muriel Feelings (Dial)

1972 HONOR BOOK

Tom Feelings, *Moja Means One: Swahili Counting Book,* by Muriel Feelings (Dial)

BOSTON GLOBE-HORN BOOK AWARD

This award is presented annually by the *Horn Book* magazine and the *Boston Globe* newspaper for excellence in literature for children and young adults to select winners in three categories: Picture Book, Fiction, and Nonfiction. (The listing below is limited to African American winners.)

1997 FICTION HONOR BOOK

Harlem, by Walter Dean Myers. Illustrated by Christopher Myers (Scholastic)

1997 PICTURE BOOK

The Adventures of Sparrowboy, by Brian Pinkney (Simon & Schuster)

1995 PICTURE BOOK

John Henry, by Julius Lester. Illustrated by Jerry Pinkney (Dial)

1993 FICTION

Ajeemah and His Son, by James Berry (HarperCollins)

1993 NONFICTION

Sojourner Truth: Ain't I a Woman? by Patricia C. and Fredrick McKissack (Scholastic)

1974 FICTION

M.C. Higgins, the Great, by Virginia Hamilton (Macmillan)

1974 PICTURE BOOK

Jambo Means Hello: Swahili Alphabet Book, by Muriel Feelings. Illustrated by
    Tom Feelings (Dial)

Appendix 3
Bookstores and Distributors

ALABAMA

Ophelia's Art Gallery
1905 Bessemer Road
Birmingham, AL 35208

Timbuktu Books and Gifts
805G N. Lena Street
Dothan, AL 36303

ARIZONA

F.E. Distributors
P.O. Box 2467
Tucson, AZ 85702

ARKANSAS

Pyramid Gallery & Books
1308 South Main Street
Little Rock, AR 72202

CALIFORNIA

Black and Latino Bookstore
23 N. Mentor Avenue
Pasadena, CA 91106

Bright Lights
8461 S. Van Ness Avenue
Inglewood, CA 90305

Carol Books and Things
5679 Freeport Boulevard
Sacramento, CA 95822

Culture Plus Book Distributors
808 N. LaBrea Avenue
Inglewood, CA 90302

It Is Written Bookstore
6934 Federal Boulevard
Lemon Grove, CA 91945

Jahi's Books & Things
2589 Sugarplum Drive
San Jose, CA 95148

Kongo Square Gallery
4334 Degnan Boulevard
Los Angeles, CA 90008

Lushena Books, Inc.
3732 West Century Boulevard
Bldg. 1 - Unit 4 & 5
Inglewood, CA 90303

Marcus Books
3900 Martin Luther King Jr. Way
Oakland, CA 94609

Marcus Books
1712 Fillmore Street
San Francisco, CA 94115

Papyrus Book Distributors
1114 Fourth Avenue
Los Angeles, CA 90019

Torchlight Books
353 Grand Avenue
Oakland, CA 94610

COLORADO
The Hue-Man Experience
911 Park Avenue W
Denver, CO 80205

CONNECTICUT
Assegai Books
1229 Albany Avenue
Hartford, CT 06112

Tokunbo Books &
Cultural Collections
205 Orange Avenue
West Haven, CT 06516

DISTRICT OF COLUMBIA
Attitude Exact
738 8th Street SE
Washington, DC 20003

The Reprint Book Shop
455 L'Enfant Plaza SW
Washington, DC 20024

Renaissance Books
and Collectibles
644 Mass Avenue NE
Washington, DC 20002

Sisterspace and Books
1354 U Street NW
Washington, DC 20009

Ujamaa Bookstore
1554 8th Street NW
Washington, DC 20001

Vertigo Books
1337 Connecticut Avenue NW
Washington, DC 20036

Yawa Books & Gifts
2206 18th Street NW
Washington, DC 20009

FLORIDA
Afro-In-Books & Things
5575 NW 7th Avenue
Miami, FL 33127

Amen-Ra's Bookshop
1326 S Adams Street
Tallahassee, FL 32301

Pyramid Books
544-2 Gateway Boulevard
Boynton Beach, FL 33435

Tenaj Ethnic Books
1502 N 25th Street
Ft. Pierce, FL 32301

GEORGIA
Brendon Book Distributors
56 Marietta Street NW
Atlanta, GA 30303

First World Books
2801 Candler Road
Decatur, GA 30034

Oxford Books
360 Pharr Road NE
Atlanta, GA 30305

Shrine of the Black Madonna
946 Abernathy Boulevard SW
Atlanta, GA 30310

Two Friends Bookstore
593 Cascade Road
Atlanta, GA 30310

Truth Bookstore
56 Marietta Street NW
Atlanta, GA 30310

ILLINOIS
A Book For All Seasons, Inc.
105 South 3rd Steet
Bloomingdale, IL 60108

African American Images
1909 West 95th Street
Chicago, Il 60643

Afrocentric Bookstore
234 S Wabash Avenue
Chicago, Il 60643

African Institution
306 East White, Apt. 301
Champagne, IL 61820

Black Titles
25 LaSalle Street
Aurora, IL 60605

DuSable Museum Gift Shop/
Bookstore
740 East 56th Place
Chicago, IL 60637

The Reading Room
African Centered Books & Gifts
112 South State Street
Chicago, IL 60603

INDIANA
X-Pression
5912 North College Avenue
Indianapolis, IN 46220

LOUISIANA
Authentic Book Distributors
P.O. Box 52916
Baton Rouge, LA 70892

Reflections Books & Gifts
3929 Florida Boulevard
Baton Rouge, LA 70806

MARYLAND
African World Books
1356 W. North Avenue
Baltimore, MD 21217

Afrikan World Books Distributor
2217-19 Pennsylvania Avenue
Baltimore, MD 21217

Asabi International Bookstore
4610 York Road
Baltimore, MD 21212

Everyone's Place
1356 W. North Avenue
Baltimore, MD 21217

Norstar Bookstore
Woodmoor Shopping Center
7025 Liberty Road
Baltimore, MD 21207

Pyramid Bookstore Coop Corp.
3062 Mondawmin Concourse
Baltimore, MD 21215

Upper Nile Books
7006 Carroll Avenue
Takoma Park, MD 20912

MASSACHUSETTS
Cultural Collections
754 Crescent Street
Brockton, MA 02402

Rose of Sharon
1601 Blue Hill Avenue
Mattapan Square, MA 02126

Treasured Legacy
100 Huntington Avenue
Boston, MA 02116

Savanna Books
1132 Massachusetts Avenue
Cambridge, MA 02138

MICHIGAN
The Book Corner
19621 West McNichols Road
Detroit, MI 48219

Crescent Imports and Publications
P.O. Box 7827
Ann Arbor, MI 48107

Kuumba Korners
9980 Gratiot Avenue
Detroit, MI 48213

Revealers of the Hidden Truth
426 S. Washington Square
Lansing, MI 48933

Shrine of the Black Madonna
13535 Livernois Avenue
Detroit, MI 48238

MINNESOTA
Bookslinger
2402 University Avenue, #507
St. Paul, MN 55114

MISSOURI
Akbar's Books and Things
8816 Manchester, Suite 117
St. Louis, MO 63144

Culturally Speaking
1601 E 18th Street, Suite 120
Kansas City, MO 64108

Left Bank Books, Inc.
399 N. Euclid Street
St. Louis, MO 63108

Ujamma Maktaba
4267 Manchester Avenue
St. Louis, MO 63110

NEW JERSEY
BCA Books @ Crossroads Theatre
7 Livingston Avenue
New Brunswick, NJ 08901

Bridging the Gap Books
1089 Rose Street
Plainfield, NJ 07060

Harambee Market
Hudson Mall
Route 440 S.
Jersey City, NJ 07304

Mart 247
247 George Street
New Brunswick, NJ 08901

New Jersey Books
59 Market Street
Newark, NJ 07102

Princess Cultural Effects
494 Main Street
East Orange, NJ 07018

Shabazz Books & Things
393 Monroe Street
Passaic, NJ 07055

Tomi Art Gallery
31 Woodland Avenue
Fords, NJ 08863

Tunde Dada House of Africa
356 Main Street
Orange, NJ 07050-2703

NEW YORK
Bestseller Bookstore
43A Main Street
Hempstead, NY 11550

Black Books Plus
702 Amsterdam Avenue
(W 94th Street)
New York, NY 10025

Bob Law Children's Books
225 DeKalb Avenue
Brooklyn, NY 11205

Briscoe Brown Books
3907 Dyre Avenue
Bronx, NY 10466

D.A. Reid Enterprises
D.A.R.E. Books
33 Lafayette Avenue
Brooklyn, NY 11217

D&J Book Distributors, Inc.
229-21B Merrick Boulevard
Laurelton, NY 11413

Elimu Bookstore
475 Main Street
New Rochelle, NY 10801

Harambee Books & Crafts
31 St. Paul Mall
Buffalo, NY 14209

Isis & Associates
Mart 125
210 W. 125th Street
New York, NY 10026

Liberation Bookstore
421 Lenox Avenue
New York, NY 10037

Nkiru Books
76 Saint Marks Avenue
Brooklyn, NY 11217

That Old Black Magic
163 Mamaroneck Avenue
White Plains, NY 10601

NORTH CAROLINA
BCA Books @ Sunshine, Inc.
1900 Edwin Drive
Raleigh, NC 27610

Headlines Bookstore
410 Evans Street Mall
Greenville, NC 27834

Special Occasions
112 Martin Luther King Jr. Drive
Winston Salem, NC 27101

OHIO

A Cultural Exchange
12621 Larchmer Boulevard
Cleveland, OH 44120

African Bookshelf & Gift Shop
13240 Euclid Avenue
E Cleveland, OH 44112

Buckeye Books and News
51 N. Pearl Alley
Columbus, OH 43201

Lady Grace Bookshop & Gifts
214 E. Perkins Avenue
Perkins Plaza
Sandusky OH 44870

Timbuktu Bookstore
5508 Superior Avenue
Cleveland, OH 44103

OKLAHOMA

Paperback Connection
5120 North Classon Boulevard
Oklahoma City, OK 73118

SJ Book Shoppe
116 North Greenwood
Tulsa, OK 74120

OREGON

Jackson's Books
32 Liberty Street SE
Salem, OR 97301

PENNSYLVANIA

Afro-Mission
104 S 13th Street
Philadelphia, PA 19107

BCA Books @ Freedom Theatre
1346 N. Broad Street
Philadelphia, PA 19121

Mind Excursion
12 Kline Plaza
Harrisburg, PA 17104

New World Books
1519 Forbes Avenue
Pittsburgh, PA 15219

Robin's Book Store
108 South 13th Street
Philadelphia, PA 19107

Themes & Books
South 13th Street
Philadelphia, PA 19107

Third World Trading Post
623 N Homewood Avenue
Pittsburgh, PA 15208

Tyler Gift Gallery & Children's
Bookstore
6516 Frankstown Avenue
Pittsburgh, PA 15208

Wood Street Emporium
1019 Wood Street
Wilkinsburg, PA 15221

RHODE ISLAND
Cornerstore Books
P.O. Box 2591
Providence, RI 02906

SOUTH CAROLINA
Mirror Images Books & Toys
946 Orleans Road, Suite 3B
Charleston, SC 29407

TENNESSEE
Book World
499 Merrit Avenue
Nashville, TN 37203

Elbow Room Bookshop
(TRIBE ONE Headquarters)
1507 University Avenue
Knoxville, TN 37921

Winston Derek Distributors
6747 Pennywell Drive
Nashville, TN 37205

TEXAS
Ashanti Inspirations
11054 Lafferty Oaks
Houston, TX 77013

Folktales
1806 Nueces Street
Austin, TX 78701

Ivory Coast Books
303 W Rancier Avenue
Killeen, TX 76541

Main Street Books
401 Main Street
Houston, TX 77002

Nia Gallery & Bookshop
7725 W. Belfort Street
Houston, TX 77071

Sankofa Books
4905 San Jacinto Street
Houston, TX 77004

The Black Bookworm
605 E. Berry, Suite 114
Ft. Worth, TX 76110

VIRGINIA
Cultural Expressions
1814D Todds Lane
Hampton, VA 23666

Cultural Expressions
12 Walnut Grove
Newport News, VA 23606

First Impression Gallery
1310 Braddock Place
Alexandria, VA 22314

Heritage Books and Art
9700 Snowhill Road
Richmond, VA 23230

Kente's II
309 Aragona Boulevard #108
Virginia Beach, VA 23462

One Force Books
217 East Clay Street
Richmond, VA 23219

Self-Improvement
Educational Center
600 West 35th Street
Norfolk, VA 23508

WASHINGTON
Blackbird Books
3130 E Madison Avenue
Seattle, WA 98112

Brothers Books
11443 Rainier Avenue South
Seattle, WA 98178

WISCONSIN
Roots and Vision Bookstore
4758 N. 76th Street
Milwaukee, WI 53218

The Readers Choice
3805 N 20th Street
Milwaukee, WI 53206

Index
Children's and Young Adult Book Titles

"i" indicates cover illustration

Index
Authors and Illustrators

"i" indicates cover illustration

Dr. Barbara Thrash Murphy

ABOUT THE AUTHOR

A graduate of the University of Pittsburgh, Dr. Barbara Thrash Murphy has a bachelor's and a master's degree in elementary education and a doctorate in curriculum and supervision. She holds professional certification from the Commonwealth of Pennsylvania in the areas of early childhood supervision in elementary education, and early childhood education.

She began her professional career as a faculty member in the School of Education at the University of Pittsburgh at the laboratory school, where she trained undergraduate and graduate students while coordinating the Early Childhood Program. She has taught child development in the Pittsburgh public schools.

Presently retired, she devotes her time to volunteer work, reading to children in Head Start programs, participating in programs in the Carnegie Library of Pittsburgh, and writing children's stories.

Dr. Murphy is continuing to compile biographies of Black authors and illustrators of books for children and young adults and information of related interest in the genre of children's books.